MAN ON THE THRESHOLD

. . . Spiritual paths lead across a threshold, beyond which the distinction between inner and outer experience no longer holds. A human being crosses such a threshold as a whole, and takes with him what he is. What in his normal waking consciousness has seemed to exist 'within', will become equally discernable as his surroundings. Nor will it continue to have the shadowy character of our private thoughts, feelings, and intentions, which enables us to believe that what goes on inside us doesn't much matter as long as our behaviour is outwardly acceptable. The realities of the inner life begin to be experienced in full force as part of the universe.

It is no accident that a kind of threshold crossing is visible in many spheres of life today.

John Davy

Bernard Lievegoed

Man on the Threshold

The challenge of inner development

Translated by Jakob M. Cornelis

Translated from the Dutch, Mens Op De Drempel *by Bernard Lievegoed, M.D.*

ISBN 0 950 7062 64. (Psychology).
Typeset in Caslon by Artmark *Nailsworth. Glos.*
Printed by Robert Hartnoll Ltd., Bodmin.

Grateful acknowledgements for editorial assistance are made to Steve Briault, Elizabeth Lebret and Judith Large; for the kind permission of Beppe Assenza to reproduce Trapasso*; for the kind permission of Benedict Wood to reproduce his translation of the* Dream Song of Olav Åsteson*; and for the assistance of Russell Evans, John Preston, Park Attwood Therapy Centre, George and Gelda Perry, Transform, and the Mercury Provident Society with this publication.*

Contents

CONTENTS

A Personal Foreword

Time: Winter 1928-29. Place: the old 'Binnengasthuis' hospital in Amsterdam, Department of Internal Medicine, headed by Prof. Piet Ruitenga. More exact location: the 'closet', formerly a bathroom, adjacent to the women's ward. The closet was the domain of the youngest co-assistant, who carried out daily routine tests and noted the results on the patients' charts. The closet was also where in the morning the entire staff had coffee, standing room only, and where the latest news was exchanged.

On one particular morning: Prof. Ruitenga and all assistants and co-assistants are crowded together, coffee cups in hand. One of the assistants relates: "Visited my aunt this weekend. Chronic rheumatism . . . poor thing . . . all bent over she is. Tried everything – salicyl, gold – nothing worked. Now they have taken her to the new Rudolf-Steiner Clinic, and you know what they do with her there? They *talk* to her every day for half an hour! Ha, ha, ha!" Loud laughter all round. Such folly!

Then the voice of the youngest 'co': "I happened to meet some of the doctors who work there. They seemed quite reasonable people..." Abruptly Prof. Ruitenga turns round: "What do *you* know about this anthroposophical medicine?"

Youngest 'co': "Well, Professor, not much yet, but I am interested in it, and I hope eventually to find out more about it."

Prof. Ruitenga: "Strange . . . the other day I had a visit from one of those doctors, a former student of mine. He gave me a book to read. I tried, but, honestly, can you figure out what 'ether body' means?"

Youngest 'co': "I haven't got that far yet, professor."

Ruitenga: "Several of my former students went that way. Can't understand it. They were my best students . . . "

He detaches himself from the tight crowd and walks away, his cup still half full, mumbling: "They were my best students . . . "

General silence and accusing glances to the youngest 'co', who spoiled the atmosphere.

That was the first experience of the youngest 'co'. At 24, he became a doctor, and discovered that the biographic conversation is part of every therapy. Thus he became interested in psychiatry, discovered curative education, and decided to start a curative home for mentally handicapped children on the basis of anthroposophy.

In Prof. Carp in Leiden he found a teacher who was prepared to let him carry out an investigation based on the work at the institute. This led in 1939 to a doctoral thesis.[1]

In the Thirties discussions took place in the Jelgersma Clinic, in Holland, about the question whether in the future there would have to be a sub-specialization for child psychiatry, and what would have to be included in the training. I had the privilege to take part in these deliberations, with my experience of the 'Zonnehuis' (curative home). After the Second World War, this specialization did, in fact, come about.

Meanwhile, because of questions from the outside, my work took the direction of general psychotherapy. In the Thirties, psychotherapy was virtually analogous with psychoanalysis. I went my own way on the basis of anthroposophy, and was encouraged in this by regular contacts with people at the Jelgersma Clinic.

I called this form of psychotherapy 'biographic therapy' because its aim was to place the problems of the patient in the context of the biographical development of life as a whole, and not to look for the causes only in shocks and frustrations experienced in the patient's earliest past.

The concept 'development' became a central issue, and it became more and more clear to me that development occurs as a result of meeting and overcoming resistance – not only in one's own constitution, upbringing, and life experience, but also in the inability to accept the situation 'now' and in a lack of prospects for one's individual future.

It also became evident that resistance (this 'helper of development') resulted from frightening inner experiences that are not understood.

In order to find a way of dealing with these life problems, an attempt was made to provide the client in the first place with an insight into the normal laws operative in the course of human life. This also became the topic for my book *Phases – Crisis and Development in the*

Individual, which appeared in 1976.[2]

Many problems appear in a different light when they are recognized as parts of normal stages of development.

Resistance at a deeper level is the subject of this new book. This has made it necessary to refer to the totality of the anthroposophical image of man. Consequently, this book is 'more anthroposophical' than my previous one.

The book has two parts. The first part is general. It describes different aspects of human development against the background of the image of man and the world conception of anthroposophy.

The second part provides a picture of the fundamentals of biographic therapy. It is directed to more professionally oriented readers. It offers them a starting point for further individual study and practical experience. In addition, however, many aspects of what Part II is concerned with will be of benefit to those who seek therapy.

This book is the result of 50 years of personal experience, and has, therefore, a personal bias. Undoubtedly, other, or additional, points of view are possible in this area.

A detailed introduction and foundation of the concepts derived from anthroposophy has been omitted; this book would have been disproportionally voluminous. Still, the most important terminology has been briefly commented on in the notes at the back of the book, with references to the relevant literature, so that plenty of opportunity for orientation and study in this subject area is provided.

One further preliminary remark: The author initially wanted to write 'he/she' and 'him/her' respectively throughout the book. Because this would have been to the detriment of the book's readability, it was decided in consultation with the publisher to use only the masculine form in the general context, with the explicit understanding that whatever has been described for 'him' is in every way equally valid for 'her'.

October 1983 B.C.J. Lievegoed

Biography of the Author

Bernard Lievegoed was born 2 September 1905 at Medan, Sumatra, Indonesia, son of the managing editor of a local newpaper. He grew up here, and attended school, surrounded by some of the most magnificent natural beauty to be found anywhere in the world. Having moved to the Netherlands at age 17, where he completed his secondary education, Lievegoed decided to study medicine because, he reasoned rather unconventionally, that would leave his future open.

He completed his medical studies in six years. Meanwhile, Lievegoed had become interested in psychiatry, and coincidentally, became acquainted with anthroposophy through the Dutch psychiatrist Willem Zeylmans van Emmichoven. On a trip to Sweden, Lievegoed visited an anthroposophical institute for mentally disturbed children, and was so impressed with what he saw there that he decided to found a similar institution in Holland. In 1931, he opened the "Zonnehuis", during the first seven years he partly financed it by running a medium-sized general medical practice on the side. In 1939, Lievegoed completed a doctoral thesis based on the work at the institute, dealing with the therapeutic application of music, and published under the title *Maat, Ritme, Melodie* (Measure, Rhythm, Melody).

After the war years of 1940-45, the "Zonnehuis" quickly grew to more than 200 children. Lievegoed, however, was at the same time being drawn into ventures of a quite different nature as well. Having written a book on child development and its relation to education,* and being a frequent lecturer on education and pedagogy from an anthroposophical viewpoint, he was asked in 1948 to deliver a major address to a prestigious group of industrialists on the question of how education could support the post-war industrial expansion in Holland. This soon led to individual requests for advice in matters related to occupational training. Lievegoed's workload as an industrial consultant soon increased to such an extent that he decided to withdraw as the director of "Zonnehuis" and to become a full-time adviser on human problems in industry.

* *De Ontwikkelingsfasen van het kind* (Developmental phases of childhood).

In 1954, Lievegoed was invited to join the faculty of the Netherlands Economic College (later Erasmus University) at Rotterdam as a professor of 'social pedagogy'. Lievegoed acceded, and also founded the Netherlands Paedagogical Institute as a means to carry out fieldwork. NPI, as it soon became known, rapidly established a position of leadership in the approach to social questions related to business and industry. With Lievegoed as the director and taking an active part in the work, NPI broke new ground in 'social-therapeutic organization development', human relations, and occupational training.

In 1963, Lievegoed was asked for his co-operation in establishing a social sciences department at the *Technische Hogeschool* (Technical College), Twente, where eventually he was instrumental in starting a new course of study, which can be described as 'industrial-therapeutic engineering'. He also completed his book *The Developing Organization*, which was published in Holland in 1969, and became internationally known.

Meanwhile, however, other questions, too, were occupying him. Besides his professorial duties at the Economic College at Rotterdam, Lievegoed had also agreed to become the 'student psychiatrist'. He discovered that 85 per cent of all the problems the students brought to him were related to study difficulties, loneliness, and choosing the wrong subjects. In 1971, Lievegoed resigned as director of the NPI and founded the Vrije Hogeschool (Free High School, or College) to provide young people who had finished their secondary education, but were unsure about their future, with an opportunity to do a year of general orientation and personal development. In a round-about way, the 65-year-old physician, educator, industrial consultant, and professor had returned to his old love – psychiatry. This now took the form of 'individualization encouragement' for young people. It was during his years as Rector of the "VH" (he retired from this position in 1982) that Lievegoed wrote *Phases* (published in English in 1979) about human life development, which later became a best-seller in Holland.

Besides his numerous activities, which included many official functions in government and industry, Lievegoed produced no less than twenty-one books and pamphlets, not counting numerous articles, lecture reports etc., on a wide diversity of subjects, such as developmental psychology, curative pedagogy, social pedagogy, organization development, education, architecture, community development, and medicine. In December 1983, he received the "Gouden Ganzeveer" (Golden Quill), a literary award of the Royal Netherlands Publishers' Association honouring authors who are deemed to have made a significant contribution to cultural life in The Netherlands. It was on this occasion that he was described as "a true contemporary, a man who takes note of the issues of his time and of the needs of a turbulent world". Lievegoed, moreover, had always been actively occupied with some of the most pressing social and cultural questions. "Today," he says, "each question is a moral question."

Part One

Chapter One
MAN ON THE THRESHOLD

The basic premise of this book is a statement by Rudolf Steiner: "Humanity has crossed the threshold". Those safe boundaries that surrounded our consciousness during the past few centuries are no longer safe. Especially the inward boundary, towards the inner processes of body and soul, has become unreliable. Unfamiliar and compulsive forces gain entrance to our consciousness and push fears, compulsions, alienation, and depression to the surface.

The first sign of this came around the turn of the century, some 80 years ago, in psychoanalysis. At first reviled and ridiculed by those for whom the boundary was still rock-solid, psychoanalysis soon penetrated cultural life. Today, it is hard to imagine a novel or a motion picture without psychoanalytic overtones.

The sense of anxiety increases year by year. But this can't be! One is supposed to be healthy, and psychologically well adjusted, by which is meant having a 'sensible' consciousness, oriented to the tangible and visible material world.

In this century the use of tranquillizers and alcohol has increased year by year. Over the past 15 years, consumption has approximately quadrupled, and still goes up month by month. What is going on?

This book's intention is to create a deeper understanding of these phenomena from the viewpoint of anthroposophy and its image of the human being. Anthroposophy provides insights in areas that are obscure to our ordinary understanding. Real insight forms the basis for overcoming anxiety and fear. Understanding banishes fear.

When in the evening dusk one goes for a walk through the fields, and suddenly in the mist one discerns the figure of a man standing on the path ahead, one is struck by fright and fear. Then comes the discovery it is only a bush. Relieved, one breathes easily again, one's heart stops pounding. As soon as one has recognized the phenomenon for what it is, as soon as fear of the unknown has been eliminated, one can assert one's ego and face the situation with composure.

In the following chapters we will try to bring about this process of eliminating the fear of the unknown. We shall do this by making it intelligible that we are dealing here with developmental processes that are entirely justified and necessary for western mankind – processes that are just as natural as the change of teeth and puberty, and as natural, too, as the changes humanity underwent in the transition from the Middle Ages to the Renaissance, and to the New Age that brought the urge for new discoveries.

What happened then was the emergence of an irresistible urge to shift attention from philosophical speculation to the world itself, seen as an unknown planet yet to be explored, and to nature, now seen as a source of abundant wealth to be exploited. And now attention is directed to our own inner world by a force that is equally irresistible. Instead of voyages of discovery to unknown continents, exploration of unknown territories in one's own human psyche is taking place. Terrifying frontiers are being crossed. Once it was a westward voyage that was taboo; you were supposed to come to the edge of the world there, and ships would get caught in an immense waterfall and plunge into the unfathomable depths of nothingness. Now, it is taboo to cross the boundaries of the familiar day-time consciousness because on the other side one would be dragged down into the insanity of nothingness.

However, just as the ships that sailed westward did actually discover a new continent with new wonders and new treasures, so can they who complete the inward voyage in full consciousness discover that there, too, new wonders and new treasures are to be found.

Where scientific thinking goes astray is where it imagines that in essence humanity has always related to the world in the same way as it has for the past 150 years – that we have merely become more clever than our dim-witted, superstitious ancestors. Now, finally, we have become sensible and scientific, and that is how it will be forevermore.

But it is not working out that way! Just as once scholasticism was abandoned as the highest form of knowledge, to be replaced by science, so do we now experience an age in which, as an alternative to natural-scientific, naturalistic thought, there is a way of thinking that attempts to investigate both matter *and* spirit to an equal degree.

To put it differently: All ancient cultures were based on a spiritualistic world view in which the divine world was seen as the creator. The only reality was a spiritual one. Matter was the big Maya, an illusionary world. The ancient Greeks, in a way, still lived with this divine world, but developed the then still new world view of idealism, in which behind each external phenomenon the *idea* was experienced as cause and creator. Our New Age has relegated both the divine world and the ideal world to the realm of childish wishfulness, and knows only about matter. In materialism, natural laws and chance are cause and creator of everything, and spirit is the big Maya, the illusionary world.

But in this Century, classic materialism has passed its zenith. We are about to take the next step: to 'spiritual realism', in which matter and spirit both are realities and in continuous interaction. "No spirit without matter, no matter without spirit". Thus a statement by Rudolf Steiner, which shows him to be a true *realist*.[1]

This book has been written with this realistic world view in mind, as it is developed in anthroposophy

Modern man lives between two boundaries. One is an observational boundary. We view the outside of the phenomenal world. Everywhere we see only outer surfaces. If we want to know what lies behind the surface, and cut the object we are observing in two, two new surfaces are created. Even with the greatest imaginable magnification of the electron microscope we only see the surfaces of the smallest particles, until the particles dissolve into non-material, hypothetical forces, which we can infer only through their activity.

Man's view outward impinges on surfaces, made visible by illumination. Man's view inward, into his own soul (psyche), hits a dark wall, on which only memories are depicted. What goes on behind this mirror of memories in the way of organic processes and unconscious soul processes escapes our direct observation to the same extent as the forces working in nature escape our observation. On the way outward we call instruments to our aid that magnify or reduce in order to penetrate into the essence of things. On the way inward we attempt to get to know the essence of the world behind the mirror of memory by means of techniques such as dream analysis, hypnosis, and investigation of psychological phenomena.

But here, too, one gets no further than describing processes of an unconscious world in terms of the conscious. Thus, the human being lives between two boundaries he can not cross with his day consciousness.

Rudolf Steiner described these two boundaries in a lecture in 1918. He made a drawing, which is reproduced overleaf in somewhat simplified form.[2]

There are forces working out of the universe that only just touch the boundaries of our sense-perceptible world, without manifesting themselves.

Active forces bubbling up out of the metabolic system of man strain against the memory boundary.

Cosmos outside and metabolism inside are the two unknown worlds. Science has established firmly that it is powerless to penetrate into the essence of reality. The dogma, 'ontological questions may not be asked' means: no questions about the *being* of things. We are permitted only to ask *how* the forces of the universe work, not *what they are.* Thus we know well enough how a positive or a negative charge *works,* but not what a charge *is.* And when we call this 'energy', this is no more than an explanatory word. This is how materialism shows its fundamentally agnostic character, but, at any rate, it is honest about it (at least in the case of true scholars – not in the case of those who popularize science and make it appear as if naming something is the same as explaining it).

Materialism has two boundaries. The step to realism requires that the spirit, too, be investigated, in its interaction with matter. That means the outward and inward boundaries have to be breached, and spiritual 'being' has to be subjected to exact investigation in the same way we have learned to do in science. Realism in this sense does not mean a step backwards to old spiritualistic world views, but a step forward, which in fact has only been made possible by materialism, with its exact observation and strict procedural methods, preceding it.

By way of introduction, a summary is given below, which is meant to give the reader an impression of what he or she can or cannot expect in this book.

'Humanity has crossed the threshold': Unknown forces gain entry to consciousness from the 'unconscious' realm; they create confusion, which manifests itself in fears, depression, and the like. The world of the psyche, which in this book we shall refer to as the 'soul world', must be consciously put in order and strengthened so as to keep its balance. This can be brought about only through the ego of the human being, by his individuality, which finds itself somewhere along the way on a long path of development. On this path it has a past, a self-imposed task for the present, and a future in which the fruits of the present life form in turn the basis for a subsequent task.

With each incarnation, with each step in this process of development, a soul structure is built up in conjunction with the bodily nature given by heredity. In the bodily nature a number of qualities are given: firstly a physical body, made up of matter; secondly a system of life forces penetrating the physical body, continuously building it up and breaking it down, called the vegetative or ether body; and, thirdly, a system of animalistic psychical phenomena and mechanisms, called the astral body according to an old terminology, or, according to Aristotle, the animal soul.

Man is born with a physical body, vegetative forces, and animalistic soul forces. The ego must then still penetrate these 'instruments' and humanize them.

This humanizing process is the task for the first half of life; subsequently the humanized forces can be used for further development. This development always takes place in interaction with other human beings. In receiving and giving we follow our individual life's path, and augment the 'talents' with which we started this life. This we are taught by the parable of the talents.[3]

Man has the animalistic soul functions in common with the animal. Out of the life sphere, drives rise up dedicated to perpetuating life: eating, procreating, building a nest, and defending a territory – all drives that man has in common with the animal.

The stimulus-response mechanism forms the basis for the psychology of behaviourism. A materialistic psychology sees these mechanisms as the 'only real' soul life, and views all 'so-called higher' drives and desires as a flight from reality. Man, it is said, should certainly not imagine himself to be more than an intelligent animal. And the cause for all psychological disturbances would be, in fact, that man, under the influence of cultural taboos, suppresses these animalistic mechanisms. The cure, therefore, can only be the removal of these cultural obstacles, and the creation of situations in which the animalistic mechanisms can be given free reign. Most modern group therapy is based on this. It is all derived, more or less, from psychoanalysis, and acknowledges only a conscious and an unconscious psychical world. Only the logotherapy of Frankl and the psychosynthesis of Assagioli recognize a psychical world related to a higher consciousness. In the higher consciousness, man comes in contact with his 'higher ego' and with that which he has gained in cultural attributes due to this higher consciousness.

An anthroposophical therapy consists of enhancing the ego functions, which raise the animalistic soul life to the human level in a quieted-down middle sphere of the soul. This means that immediate reactions have to be held back and internalized in the central area of the human soul, where they are confronted with moral, aesthetic and intellectual qualities.

This will be elaborated in the chapters about the development of what is called the 'sentient soul', the 'intellectual and mind soul' and the 'consciousness soul'. The central point in this is that man only becomes man in the middle region, between the polar forces of sympathy and antipathy, and so on. In this middle region, man can momentarily be free, and experience the spirit. The animal is tossed between comfort and discomfort, challenge and withdrawal, and hunger and satiation, etc. Man can internalize such stimuli and reactions between two poles and live in an intimate encounter with the world. Then a new quality arises, which, besides impressions, also calls forth meaning, beauty and moral judgement.

Man is a being of the middle, and all human culture derives from the middle.

The child grows into this human culture by imitation and reverence; in a later phase, this tentative humanity is still to be tested with reference to the individual ego. This takes place in the middle phase of life. This means that after the early forties the individual character has been shaped, and then forms the basis for the ability to take one's place in cultural life – creatively, and giving of oneself.

The young person seeks to effect renewal by means of protest, and cannot do otherwise. In the third major life phase, after forty, the individual seeks renewal in drawing the consequences out of what Neumann has called the 'inner voice'.[4]

The mature, creative human being is the 'heretic' of the inner voice in relation to his environment. This inner voice had already announced itself (earlier in life) in the protest against that which came not from the self, but had been contributed by the cultural environment. Only much later can this inner voice – the voice of the higher ego – manifest itself creatively, with quiet assurance.

The common thread running through this book is the process of ego development out of the middle.

Out of a strengthened middle sphere, which has become conscious, modern man can proceed across the outward threshold, and learn to experience more and more clearly the qualities that lie within the sense perceptions, until ultimately he encounters spiritual reality – spiritual beings that in days of old were self-evident. Once they manifested themselves to a dreamy consciousness. Now, they must be sought in a clear day-consciousness that has passed through a training of the thinking, the feeling, and the will.

Out of a strengthened, conscious middle sphere, man can cross the inward boundary, and meet those forces that at the present break through the mirror of memory more and more to disrupt the day-consciousness.

This conscious path inward is the only true therapy against the increasing threat of invasion out of the unconscious soul life, just as the conscious path outward is the therapy against the urge to escape in excarnation by means of addiction to drugs, alcohol, and other intoxicants.

In order to make the experiences that can possibly occur on these two paths understandable for the present time, the approach chosen in this book is first to describe how these paths were experienced in antiquity, in what is called the 'mysteries'. In these mysteries of ancient cultures, these paths can, indeed, also be recognized. The northern, Germanic mysteries knew the outward path of initiation, into the elemental world. The southern mysteries, particularly the Egyptian ones, went the inward path, into the unconscious soul life.

The ancient Greeks placed their gods on Olympus, in the wide, etheric world of elementals. Zeus-Jupiter controlled thunder and lightening. In art and philosophy, Apollo led man into the sun-illumined world of higher consciousness via the arts of the Musae. The Greeks were terrified of the 'underworld', where Dionysus let passion run wild as a result of intoxication, to overpower man. Only once a year, the bacchants and satyrs were set free and allowed to gain the upper hand for a short time in an orgy controlled by the mysteries.

The hangover from these Dionysian festivities reinforced the loathing of the underworld for a considerable while afterwards; this was an important step in the development of the function of conscience.

Modern man faces the necessity of being able to cope with *both* worlds. The anthroposophical path of development is therefore always a matter of balance between a step outwards and a step inwards. Only then can man hold on to the middle.

The first part of this book, after a description of the old mysteries, deals with *capita selecta* from anthroposophy as a foundation for insight in psychical events for the benefit of all interested readers. Also, this lays a foundation for Part II, in which modern syndromes and psychotherapy are discussed on a more professionally oriented level.

This Part II is no textbook on neuroses, but rather an exemplifying treatise of a few syndromes, in order to enable those who wish to gain further expertise in this area to see how spiritual insight can lead to rational action. Anthroposophical psychotherapy does not have fixed techniques that can be learned, but is based on an encounter of two human beings, with one seeking help and the other offering to search with him for his further path of development.

For besides general syndromes, mostly arising as a sign of the times, there exists only the highly individual path of development for every person. Only out of the greatest degree of respect for that path, however difficult, can the other be helped to find and develop his own middle. The helper allows himself no judgements, but only wonder and a sense of personal responsibility for awakening an individual moral sense in the other.

The reinforcement of the middle sphere is not only the first step in psychotherapy, but also on each individual path of development. This path begins with the creation of a rich inner life, with the experience of nature, of culture, and of the arts. It continues with the development of inner peace and finding moments of quiet contemplation, a preliminary to meditation, in which a content selected by ourselves fills us for a short time (which, therefore, is something different from repeating words while eliminating all thoughts).

Thus, a warm, sunny middle sphere will be gradually created, with positivity and openness for the world, and rich in content deriving from human culture.

Only a middle that offers warmth and light can be the starting point for a conscious crossing of the boundaries; otherwise the crossing is forced on us as a necessity of this age while we are unprepared.

A conscious path of inner development chosen by ourselves for ourselves, and a cultural therapy and psycho-therapy are in line with each other.

The following chapters are attempts to describe how we can consciously undergo the experiences on these paths of development without falling prey to neuroses, escapism, or addiction.

Chapter Two
THE PATH INWARD: THE EGYPTIAN MYSTERIES

To begin with, we shall discuss the 'path inward', which Rudolf Steiner also called the 'mystical path' because of the form this took during the Middle Ages. It is the path of a 'deeper awakening'. It appears most clearly in the Egyptian mysteries. This will be discussed here briefly with reference to the lectures *Macrocosm and Microcosm by Rudolf Steiner*[1].

The pupil of the Isis and Osiris mysteries first had to undergo a preparation of many years, in which everything that had to do with egoistic experiences of the self had to be overcome. The path inward, across the threshold of one's own organism, means that an *ego condensation* takes place, a deeper awakening than the ordinary awakening in the morning, when our ego is immediately distracted by the sense world.

If one were to submerge consciously in the formative (astral) world of organic, unconscious drives and desires with an unprepared, still egoistic ego, one would be overpowered by these forces, and meet with hallucinatory experiences. For that reason, everything that still lives in the ego as egoism has to be overcome through moral training. The Christian mystical path sought this preliminary schooling in a long meditative immersion in the images of the Way to the Cross, beginning with the Washing of the Feet (more about this in Chapter 6). In ancient Egyptian times, in which the human ego had not yet become quite as individualized, and man lived more in the communal ego of family and tribe, this purification had a strongly ritual character.

When after the preparatory period of purification the priest-hierophant judged the pupil ready for the actual initiation, the pupil was placed in an excavation in the floor in the temple, similar to a grave. The hierophant brought the pupil into a somnambulous sleep, much deeper than ordinary sleep.

Around the initiation grave, or in an adjoining room, stood twelve helpers who had been trained to intercept the demonic forces that we know as the lower egoistic drives, and to assimilate these inwardly and thereby divert them from the pupil. In spite of his preparation the pupil would otherwise have been inwardly torn apart by these demonic forces (beings). That is a process that corresponds to what we see happening in schizophrenia.

The disciple had given over his ego entirely to the priest-teacher. He viewed himself through the priest's eyes, and thus he indirectly experienced how the forces of the astral body, the ether body, and the physical body became conscious. As will be described in later chapters, he was observing the activity of the Venus, Mercury and Moon forces in man (see Chapter 9).

The pupil now entered the world of his own *astral body*, the carrier of the animalistic soul life. First of all he now experienced everything he had *not* done, but could have and should have done; all sins of omission started to weigh on him as a heavy burden, and this burden of sin grew to a feeling of devastation so powerful that in ordinary life, if arising without preparation, it would lead to suicide.

But the Egyptian pupil was prepared for this. Already during his pre-schooling he had again and again had to look back on his own life and learn to endure the weight of his sins of omission. In the initiation, the total of the onerous aspects of life till then condensed into a figure that came into view as a 'guardian of the threshold'. This was a spiritual figure, formed out of the personal experiences of the disciple, objectified, as it were, and experienced as a hindrance to further descent. In the Egyptian cultural period this guardian took the appearance of the *sphinx*, which the pupil had already come to know outwardly on his way to the temple in the statues flanking the road. Now, he got to know his own individual sphinx. (Later on, a similar experience brought the mystics to the inner mystical vow to work, as much as humanly possible, on their own soul.)

It is appropriate to point out here that the path inward means a path *backward in time*. Just as the path outward leads to ego dilution and a dissolving in space, so the inward path signifies a merging into the stream of time. Our bodily constitution, our organs, are formed by forces out of the past. They are the fruit of previous incarnations that have, as it were, congealed in the formation and functions of our body. During initiation, this process of development was now experienced in reverse.

If the preparation had been as it should, the Egyptian pupil could during his initiation pass the guardian of the threshold fairly quickly, and face his own astral body (and specifically the area below the solar plexus – the unconscious soul life, in other words). He had developed the necessary courage and fearlessness for this. But without the leadership of the hierophant, through whose eyes he observed all this, and who interceded when the pupil threatened to become lost, the pupil would not have progressed.

The next step then was that the disciple was led into his own *ether body*, and here the forces are no longer noncommittal but *compulsive.* The ether body is the dynamic force in all life processes. It builds up the organs, breaking down food, reconstituting from it the organism's own proteins. In the ether body, unimaginably destructive as well as constructive forces are at work in the biochemical processes. These 'forces' are real etheric beings called 'elemental beings' by Rudolf Steiner.[2] They serve us, but if they work in the wrong place, they have a destructive effect. We then call this illness.

The etheric body is a *time body*, a summary of all rhythmic *processes* in the life sphere working in the formation of the individual ether body in the period before birth. This individual formation is determined by the karma one brings along from one's previous life, and it is understandable that this means that the ideal cosmic rhythms are changed as a result. To that extent the serving 'elemental beings' then take on a negative character; they haunt us in the form of pathological tendencies and constitutional one-sidedness.

This constitutional tendency to certain illnesses, which is hidden deep within us and may become active only late in life, would overpower the ego of the disciple. The twelve helpers, who prevent this, could therefore also be called the twelve healers!

The pupil, because he was protected against this danger, could concentrate on those forces that had individualized his ether body before his birth. That is to say: he could submerge in his own time stream. The first experience was how in the phase before birth man himself builds up the hereditary forces for the coming life. For that purpose, the soul has to 'accompany' the ancestry (of the coming incarnation) out of the realm of existence before birth for many centuries. This ancestry gives the ether body its characteristics through heredity. During the experience of initiation, one went back in one's own hereditary stream. A memory of these kinds of initiation can still be found among those people who practice ancestor worship.

The first experience, the astral experience of one's own sins, was like holding up a mirror. But now the pupil breaks through this mirror and encounters the forces that work in the mirror images. In order to endure this experience, the soul has to have been educated in unselfishness, love and compassion. This education of the soul was in the Egyptian period the development of the 'sentient soul'.[3]

The ether body is the bearer of the hereditary forces; accordingly, it became evident to the initiation pupil that out of his karma he had had to help in the formation of a particular heredity that fit his own karmic etheric structure. Through the characteristics of his *individual* ether body it was revealed to him that his ether body was formed out of the great span between the latest death and the recent birth. Then it became clear to him that that which worked as a disturbance in his ether body was connected with the forces that were laid down during the previous life in the ether body he had then. This previous ether body had left its mark in the ether spheres. The previous life was experienced in its effects. In order to experience the previous life, the pupil had had to discard all that which tied him to the present life. For the initiate-to-be, reincarnation was no longer a teaching – it had become an experience.

Within himself, the pupil now experienced another person, the bearer of the old karma. This other 'man', this 'double', he had to accept and heal. He experienced himself as *two persons*: an old and a new person.

And again the disciple had to submerge in his own constitution, and experience that the previous life, in turn, was 'coloured' by a life preceding it, etc., time and again, until he had reached the moment when ether bodies were first individualized in human history. That was at the beginning of the so-called Lemurian epoch (comp. *Occult Science – An Outline* by Rudolf Steiner[4]). In the preceding Hyperborian epoch ether bodies were still plant-like, not individualized. Only in Lemuria they acquired individual form through the formative activity of the astral body. Thus the Egyptian mysteries only went back to the beginning of Lemuria.

Moses, too, who had received an Egyptian initiation, reckoned the beginning of humanity to be in Lemuria. Paradise is a memory in Lemuria of the preceding Hyperborean development.

But the Egyptian pupil had to descend deeper still. He had to get to know the forces of his *physical body* as well. He had to learn how to see this physical body from within, and experience how the tribal and racial characteristics were imprinted in it. He learned to go back to the time when the races came into being; then he knew which contribution his race had to make to the development of humanity. This insight he needed to be able to lead *his* people in the right way as an initiate.

The highest power working in the ether world that the Egyptians knew about was Todt/Hermes/Mercurius.[5] *Hermes Trismegistos*, Hermes of triple greatness, was the original hierophant and the founder of the Egyptian mysteries. In the Bible he bears the name Henoch, which simply means 'the initiate'.

The Egyptian initiate, therefore, was initiated in these 'hermetic' mysteries – in the first place in the mysteries of the ether body, of the time stream, of development.

Whoever today, involuntarily and without preparation, feels the forces of this organ-ether world breaking out falls prey to forces that overpower the consciousness. The victim of these forces, torn apart, will experience himself in his schizophrenia as two (or more) persons who address him in a hallucinatory way, give him commands, enrage him – depending on the organs out of which these forces break through. Those who only experience astral forces will be plagued by depressive feelings, which, ultimately, can lead to suicide. Not without good reason can psychosis be called 'a failed initiation', as we shall explain later on.

In all ancient eastern mysteries there was the need for a leader, guru, or hierophant to guide the pupil step by step. The mantras, which the leader gave during the period of preparation, were charged with the personal power of the leader.

In the Middle Ages, in post-Christian times, the mystics were no longer guided by a living guru. They could go their path by permeating themselves with Christ. For them, Christ became the guru, to whom they surrendered themselves totally. This path, however, required withdrawal from ordinary life.

Modern man should not surrender his ego to a guru. With his already so much more strongly individualized ego, he must himself be responsible for his progress. He should follow the advice of someone with greater wisdom or of an initiate, but he must himself carry out the preparation in full consciousness, and determine when he is ready for further conscious steps. No submission to another person may take place. This would nullify development of the modern ego and mean regression to immature stages of ego development. We shall come back to the role of the guru or teacher in both chapters on inner development (Chapter 6 and 7).

Chapter Three
THE PATH OUTWARD: THE NORTHERN MYSTERIES

Because of its sensory nature, our day consciousness is confined to the surface consciousness that has been mentioned before. Each night, when falling asleep, we break through this surface consciousness and enter the spiritual reality that hides behind the surface. That it remains hidden is due to ourselves; we concern ourselves only with that which the physical senses reveal to us.

At the moment of falling asleep, when we give up this sensory consciousness, we enter the world of the elements and of the beings that populate this world, of whom in the sense-perceptible world we only experience the effects. But at the moment of falling asleep we lose our day consciousness. Of the world of night we normally perceive nothing.

A path of initiation 'outward' means that we retain our consciousness when falling asleep, that we cross the threshold consciously.

The Germanic-Celtic mysteries[1] were mysteries in which the pupil was led not inward into his own subjective world, but outward into the cosmos, into the world of the hierarchies,[2] which guide the development of humanity. These mysteries of the far North expanded all over Europe and southern Russia, and even into the old Persia of Zarathustra.

While the path inward leads to a hallucinatory experience of one's own organic forces, the path outward leads to *ecstasy*, to becoming one with the forces of the cosmos. This means an ego dilution, an expansion of the ego in the cosmos, which has the result that the ego becomes weaker and weaker. The preparation, therefore, has to consist of strengthening the ego, of the development of extra ego forces. In the northern mysteries this took place with the development of *courage*. The many years of preparation of the pupil consisted of a series of trials of courage, physically as well as morally.

Thus the journeys of the vikings in their small ships on the open sea were a good preparation. Courage also had to be practiced in battle and through the endurance of terror. When you visit the central Germanic sanctuary of the 'Externsteine' in Germany (between Paderborn and Detmold) you see a formation of sheer cliffs rising to 45 metres in height. Between two cliffs, above a yawning chasm, one can still see the anchor points of the so-called 'schwankende Brücke' (swaying bridge), which consisted of two ropes with wooden crosspieces. The disciple had to traverse this swaying bridge to the other side, without getting dizzy; for those who didn't pass this test, life was over. Something similar took place nearby at the 'sacred chariot race', which wasn't exactly a genteel affair.[3]

For the actual initiation, a surplus in ego courage forces had to be accumulated. Heavily armed, battle-hardened Roman legionaries started to shake with fear when they heard the battle cries of the onrushing hordes of Teutons. The Celts even did battle totally naked, their bodies painted blue, and armed only with a small shield and a long sword. The surplus in ego courage forces that manifested itself in this 'wildness' had a magic effect on the southern people, who did not know of these forces in this form.

Once the pupil had passed all trials, there came the moment of the initiation. For this, the pupil had first still to experience an intensive connection with the course of the year.

Then the priest brought him, fully conscious, in contact with the elemental world. In a sense, this world had always been accessible for the Nordic peoples of that time. Nature was populated by elves and trolls, and fog and storm giants. The last remains of this can still be found in Sweden, Norway, and Ireland. But in the initiation the entry into this world was no 'encounter', as in the daytime world, but a *becoming one* with the elemental world. The ego dissolved in the storms, was then flung back into the depths of the earth, and passed through the icy rigidity of the forces of coldness and through blazing fire.

The first release of the ego was experienced as a feeling of bliss and lightness and a release from earthly ties. This meant there was a great temptation to remain in this condition. When neurosis is discussed it will become apparent that this excarnation experience of levity is still a temptation.

But then, with a shock, the transition to the cosmos took place, with the elemental world as the first level, resulting in the sense of being torn apart by the forces of earth, water, air and fire.

In these mysteries the priest also had twelve helpers. They had prepared themselves for this helping role by imbuing themselves completely with the forces and the character of the seasons of the year. Respectively, three helpers had connected themselves with each of the four seasons: three with spring, three with summer, three with autumn, and three with winter. Because of this specialization – the result of a voluntary sacrifice they had made – these helpers had developed one-sided, concentrated ego forces. Together, they could protect the pupil from being torn apart by the elements. They consciously went through the experiences of the pupil in their own soul, remaining steadfast in their ego consciousness. Because of this, the pupil could pass through the elemental world and go on to his next experience. He became conscious that behind and in everything there are spiritual beings present. A veil fell away; earth, water, air and fire *became being*.

Into this elemental world the pupil took his soul qualities, and these could, to a greater or lesser degree, disturb the cosmic order. Also, what now became visible for the pupil was that the elemental beings are not only helpful nature beings, but that there are 'evil' beings too. He became aware of luciferic and ahrimanic beings.[4] These immediately associated themselves with the negative characteristics of the pupil, and reinforced these. Should the pupil now have returned to day consciousness, his negative characteristics would only be amplified.

For that reason, the guiding priest now brought the pupil to a vision of what the human being would eventually have to become, at the end of his development. Before his spirit eye there appeared a being of overpowering luminosity, a being that radiated at the same time sternness and goodness. In the language of the mysteries he is called 'the greater Guardian of the threshold', in distinction to the lesser, 'subjective' guardian who is encountered on the inward path. The greater Guardian is the ego of humanity, which appeared in the world as Christ. The image of this greater guardian, this pre-Christian Christ figure, gave an awareness of what man will become once he has fully permeated his being with the Christ force. The Celts, therefore, spoke of Christ as 'the king of the elements'.

For the pupil, this encounter represented an almost devastating blow to his self-love. He now saw what he was, and what he had to become. In his soul he vowed that for the rest of his life he would continue to fight against egoism and the lust for power.

When he had endured the encounter with the greater Guardian, he could, via the elemental world, reach a further spiritual world. In the Germanic mysteries this was called the crossing of the Gjallard Bridge. Behind it was the world that in ancient Indian terminology was known as Kamaloka, in medieval terms called purgatory. Here, he met the dead, in that phase where they did penance for their earthly astral deficiencies, and tried to overcome these deficiencies.

Behind this, furthermore, was the world of order and harmony of the planetary forces, in which high hierarchical beings held sway. Having first lived through the lower astral forces in the immediate hereafter, the pupil now learned about the higher astral forces in the realm of cosmic order and harmony. These forces also work in our astral body and determine our health. For the ancient Greeks these pure astral forces were represented by the Golden Fleece; to be in search of the Golden Fleece meant to search for a path of initiation. The northern Germanic people experienced this world macrocosmically as a large 'clock' with twelve groups of spiritual beings (our zodiac) and seven planet 'hands' that went around, continuously forming new constellations (our clock, with twelve numbers and two hands, is a reduced image of this; the small hand is the sun, the large hand the moon, which is depicted on some old clocks). With the seven 'hands' numerous constellations could come about in the totality of the world harmony.

This cosmic clock formed words in a spirit language: the signs of the zodiac as the consonants, the planets as the vowels. To understand this spirit language meant: knowing what *the moment demanded of humanity.* This was the fruit of a succesful initiation.

Finally, the pupil was led through still higher worlds, and learned to know the world in which the forces that build up our brain and make our thinking possible are at work (in German: *der Vernunftwelt*). And eventually, one gained access to the world of archetypes (Urbilder) where the highest hierarchies are at work. (Jung found an image of this archetypal world in the human archetypes each human being carries within himself, but which, as Jung rightly notes, are in principle unrecognizable for our day consciousness.)

Not every pupil underwent the same initiation. In the elemental world, the way through the macrocosm was varied according to the pupil's temperament. The choleric experienced a blazing fire world, the sanguine a world of blowing winds, the phlegmatic sank in a swamp, and the melancholic experienced a bone-chilling cold. (See also Christian Anderson's fairytale of the Snow Queen; and in Nordic folk tales many other initiation images are living.)

For contemporary humanity, entry into the elemental world without preparation means a depersonalization through ego dilution, which is often experienced as a sense of freedom and lightness, as a liberation from one's every-day troubles. When modern man then suddenly crosses the threshold, however, he can hardly find the way back. (A penetrating description of this phenomenon can be found in the book *Snapping*, by Conway and Siegelman, to which we shall return in Chapter 12.)

The encounter with the great forces of nature gave the northern initiate an intensive experience of self-knowledge. Without a preparation aimed at self-knowledge, and at learning to endure the insight 'That is how I am', the meeting with the ideal human image would be crushing. Those, however, who had learned to maintain their self-confidence in spite of this self-knowledge, who had learned to accept their double, could, because of the encounter with the greater Guardian, receive the encouragement: This is what man can become! He who has had this encounter, knows how imperfect he is, but has at the same time acquired the everlasting power to keep striving for perfection under all circumstances of life, and knows that he is helped by Christ, 'the king of the elements'.

Of the northern initiation a remnant has been preserved by a stroke of good fortune. It is the Song of Olav Åsteson, 'he who once slept so long'. This song will be discussed below, and then the text itself will be reproduced, as an example of an initiation experience.[5]

The Dream Song of Olav Åsteson

In about 1850, a Norwegian clergyman named Landstad recorded the 'Dream Song of Olav Åsteson' in a remote valley in Telemarken from the oral memory of the local population. The song, in the old Norwegian language, became a factor in the linguistic controversy of Norway in which Old Norwegian eventually won out over urban Norwegian, which is Danish.

In 1919, the Norwegian author Ingeborg Möller-Lindholm brought the Dream Song to the attention of Rudolf Steiner during a visit to Oslo. On his request, she made a literal translation, which later he worked out further himself. From then on Rudolf Steiner referred to the song several times. On such occasions Marie Steiner-von Sivers always recited the text in German. Rudolf Steiner's lectures have made the importance of this old legend clear also for our times.[6]

What is special about the Dream Song of Olav Åsteson? It is only a fragment of a much larger whole, but has nevertheless preserved all elements of the northern path of initiation.

Who was Olav Åsteson? In order to make a historical connection, we have to go back to about the year 1000, when Norway, then still Germanic-pagan, came into contact with Christianity through two great kings, Olav I and Olav II. Olav the First, 'Tryggveson', lived from 969 to 1000. He came from Estonia as a slave, spent his youth in

Novgorod, and later, as a viking, sailed to France and England.

Through a hermit in the Scilly Islands he became an Irish Christian, and later married a Christian Irish princess. Back in Norway, he became king in 995, and started conversion of the country to Christianity. He also wanted to conquer Sweden, but was killed in the year 1000 during a sea battle in his ship the Great Snake, the largest ship of that time. Olav Tryggveson was the archetype of the viking king and viking initiate, with all the courage and wildness of the northern path of initiation. For him who had met the 'greater Guardian' the conversion to Irish-cosmic Christianity was a natural step.

Olav II, 'Haraldson', was born in 995, the year Olav I became king. He therefore met Christianity already during his youth, but, as becomes apparent from the song, he had also undergone a northern initiation path, which, however, was not in conflict with western Irish Christianity. He, too, went to England as a viking when still a youth, and returned to Norway in 1015 at age 20. In 1016 he did battle against the ruler then in power and became king of Norway. The conversion to Christendom of Norway was then carried through forcibly, which created much resistance. In 1029 there was a rebellion of nobility under the leadership of Knut the Great. Olav fled to Russia, returned again in 1030, and was killed in the Battle of Stiklestad, fought against his fellow Norwegians. His cruelty and wildness were soon forgotten. His grave became a pilgrimage, where miracles of healing occurred. Already in 1164 he was canonized, and is venerated to this day as Saint Olav.

Olav Haraldson's mother was called Åste. This name has two meanings: firstly, 'love', and secondly, 'the hereditary stream in which clairvoyance still lives'.

Olav Åsteson, therefore, had a hereditary connection with the old courage mysteries through his mother, and, via his environment, made a connection with a cosmic Christianity, in which, according to Irish tradition Christ was experienced as 'the king of the elements'. In his soul lived the duality that is typical of such a time of transition, and his biography can certainly not be judged by middle-class standards.

Besides the historical context there is, as always in matters of this kind, a spiritual background. Rudolf Steiner pointed out that the name Olav Åsteson can also be seen as a mystery name carried through several generations (as with the name King Arthur), and also that the *content* of the song has an older origin than the version that was handed down, which dates from the Thirteenth Century. In conversations with Ingeborg Möller he gave further information about this, which she wrote down. A passage from her notes reads as follows: "The content of the Dream Song is much older than is commonly asumed; it dates from about 400 A.D. A great Christian initiate then lived in Norway. His mystery name was Olav Åsteson, and the song describes his initiation. He founded a mystery school in the southern part of Norway; the name of the place was not mentioned. Originally, the song was much longer, and had twelve parts, one for each sign of the zodiac. This song described Olav Åsteson's journey through the world of stars, and related what he saw there and what he experienced. What has survived today contains only remnants of the original song. The above-mentioned mystery school continued to exist until early medieval times, and the leader was always called Olav Åsteson."

This information from spiritual research (of Rudolf Steiner) also throws some light on Olav the Holy. Perhaps this king was also in this sense an Olav Åsteson. The essential thing is that the song is the 'sediment' of a genuine initiation path.

In the song as we know it now, Olav is described as the initiate who in the twelve holy nights between Christmas and Epiphany experiences a mystery sleep. On January 6, he can tell the churchgoers about his experience. His 'song' contains all the elements of the northern cosmic path of initiation, but in a later period; as a result, Christian elements are mixed in with the images.

The stages of this path are marked by a changing chorus. Following an introduction, the ether world is mentioned: "The moon shone bright, and far ahead the ways led." This is the passage through the elemental world – high through the clouds; he is pushed into turbid swamps, crosses divine streams, travels over the thorny moors, and sees the icy masses as blue flames!

Then he comes to the Gjallard Bridge, which leads to the next region. The bridge is guarded by three beasts: 'hound' or dog, 'serpent', and 'bull' – a kind of Nordic sphinx – or spirit serpent, spirit hound, and spirit bull. Only those who honour truth may cross the bridge.

Again the path leads through swamps, through the earth, through ice masses. He chooses the winter road, and from far the light of paradise already radiates. Then he sees the Mother of God, who sends him on to the area of purgatory – the area of kamaloka here called Brooksvalin. The chorus then changes: "In Brooksvalin shall stand the throne of doom." Olav subsequently experiences all of the consequences of earthly guilt. It clearly is already an astral region: from the North, evil spirits came riding, led by the Lord of Hell himself. But from the South came Saint Michael, at the side of Jesus Christ. Christ is still the world judge here, the greater Guardian, who watches Michael weigh the human souls.

Then comes the last part: the blessing. The chorus then is: "The scales have spoken and truth gives tongue on doomsday." The pointer of Michael's scale speaks, and wisdom resounds in spirit being. This part, incidentally, gives the impression it is of a later date; it lacks the stricter form of the previous parts.

During his journey over the thorny moors, Olav tears his scarlet mantle. The scarlet mantle indicates Olav's royal status – also in the world across the threshold, which means: he was fully initiated.

Next follows Benedict Wood's translation of the Dream Song.[7]

The Dream Song of Olav Åsteson

I

Would you hearken to the song I sing
And to the tale that I shall tell?
Hear then of Olav Åsteson
On whom a slumber deep fell.
    Ay, that was Olav Åsteson
    Who slept a sleep so deep, so long.

II

He lay down in the Holy Night
And slumber deep on him lay;
He woke not till the thirteenth day
When folk to church did wend their way.
    Ay, that was Olav Åsteson
    Who slept a sleep so deep, so long.

He lay down in the Holy Night
And slept so sound upon his bed;
He woke not till the thirteenth day
When little birds their wings spread.
    Ay, that was Olav Åsteson
    Who slept a sleep so deep, so long.

He woke not till on the thirteenth day
The sun shone forth o'er the lea;
Then saddled he his horse in haste
And to the church forth rode he.
    Ay, that was Olav Åsteson
    Who slept a sleep so deep, so long.

There the priest at the altar stood,
His reading from the book was long.
Olaf sat down by the door
And there began his dream song.
    Ay, that was Olav Åsteson
    Who slept a sleep so deep, so long.

On the folk both the young and old,
On all a great silence fell;
Meantime Olav Åsteson
His dream did unto all tell.
    Ay, that was Olav Åsteson
    Who slept a sleep so deep, so long.

III

I laid me down in the Holy Night;
Deep sleep upon me fell.
I wakened not till the thirteenth day
When folk to church did go.
    The moon shone brightly
    And far ahead the ways led.

Lo, I have been in cloudy heights
And deep in ocean depths;
And whosoe'er will follow me,
No laughter gladdens his lips.
    The moon shone brightly
    And far ahead the ways led.

Lo, I have been in cloudy heights
And deep in miry sloughs,
And I have seen the blaze of hell
And one part seen of heaven.
    The moon shone brightly
    And far ahead the ways led.

I fared forth o'er the Holy Stream
And over valleys deep;
The waters I heard, but saw them not,
Where under earth they run.
    The moon shone brightly
    And far ahead the ways led.

He did not neigh, my faithful horse,
My hound, he did not bark;
The bird of morning did not sing;
And wonder lay over me.
  The moon shone brightly
  And far ahead the ways led.

With sense enchanted forth I fared
Across a thorny heath.
My scarlet mantle was all torn
And e'en the nails on my feet.
  The moon shone brightly
  And far ahead the ways led.

I came unto the Gjallard Bridge,
That hangs in the wind on high;
T'was covered o'er with rich red gold
And pointed nails in each bar.
  The moon shone brightly
  And far ahead the ways led.

The Serpent stings, the Hound, he bites,
The Bull, he bars the way;
Three creatures of the bridge are they,
Fearful and crooked are they.
  The moon shone brightly
  And far ahead the ways led.

The Hound, he bites, the Serpent stings,
The Bull sets to his horns.
They suffer none to cross the bridge,
Who have condemned without cause.
  The moon shone brightly
  And far ahead the ways led.

I journeyed on across the bridge,
A hard and toilsome way;
I had to wade through Murkmire Moor;
But far behind me now it lies.
  The moon shone brightly
  And far ahead the ways led.

I had to wade through Murkmire Moor;
My feet no ground could find.
And so I passed from the Gjallard Bridge,
The dust of death in my mouth.
  The moon shone brightly
  And far ahead the ways led.

So came I to those waters there,
Where ice burned with flames of blue.
But God did put it in my heart
To turn my feet therefrom
  The moon shone brightly
  And far ahead the ways led.

So went I on the winter way
That lay at my right hand;
And lo, I saw there Paradise,
Its light shed o'er that fair land.
  The moon shone brightly
  And far ahead the ways led.

God's Holy Mother there I saw;
No wonder could be more fair.
"To Brooksvalin now wend thy way.
There judgement shall be given."
  The moon shone brightly
  And far ahead the ways led.

IV

There was I in the other world
Full many nights and long.
Only God in heaven can know
How deep was the suffering I saw.
  In Brooksvalin
  Shall stand the throne of doom.

First I saw an evil man
As ne'er before I saw.
In his arms he bore a boy,
And he walked in the earth to his knee.
  In Brooksvalin
  Shall stand the throne of doom.

Then I came unto a man;
His cloak was all of lead.
His poor soul in earthly life
Ever fettéréd was by greed.
    In Brooksvalin
    Shall stand the throne of doom.

Came I then to men who bore
A burden of fiery earth.
God grant mercy to their souls
Who have moved their neighbour's landmarks.
    In Brooksvalin
    Shall stand the throne of doom.

Came I then to children too
Who stood upon brands of fire.
God forgive their sinning souls
Who their father and mother have cursed.
    In Brooksvalin
    Shall stand the throne of doom.

Then came I to the house of shame,
And witch-wives were therein.
Lo, they churned, they churned in red blood,
And a heavy task it was.
    In Brooksvalin
    Shall stand the throne of doom.

Hot it is in the pool of Hell,
So hot no man could believe.
Over a pitchy cauldron they hung,
And they pounded a scoundrel's hide.
    In Brooksvalin
    Shall stand the throne of doom.

From the north there rode a host;
With a rout and a clatter they came.
Grutte Greybeard rode before
And around him his turbulent horde.
    In Brooksvalin
    Shall stand the throne of doom.

From the north came forth that host;
No blacker horde was e'er seen.
Grutte Greybeard rode before,
And he rode on a coal-black horse.
  In Brooksvalin
  Shall stand the throne of doom.

From the south there rode a host;
In holy calm they came.
At their head rode Michael,
Who stands at Christ's right hand.
  In Brooksvalin
  Shall stand the throne of doom.

From the south came forth that host;
No nobler host was e'er seen.
First rode Michael, Lord of Souls,
And he rode on a snow-white horse.
  In Brooksvalin
  Shall stand the throne of doom.

From the south came forth that host;
So great it seemed without end.
First rode Michael, Lord of Souls,
And a hórn hé héld in hís hand.
  In Brooksvalin
  Shall stand the throne of doom.

That was Michael, Lord of Souls;
A blast he blew on his horn.
Now must every soul go forth
Before the judgement throne.
  In Brooksvalin
  Shall stand the throne of doom.

Trembled then every sinful soul
Like an aspen leaf in the wind;
And what soul soever was there
Full sorely he wept for his sins.
  In Brooksvalin
  Shall stand the throne of doom.

That was Michael, Lord of Souls;
And there in the balance he weighed,
Weighed the souls with all their sins
Before the face of Christ.
  In Brooksvalin
  Shall stand the throne of doom.

V

How blessed he who in earth life
Gives shoes unto the poor;
He can indeed on the thorny heath
Walk e'en barefoot without harm.
  The scales have spoken
  And truth gives tongue on doomsday.

How blessed he who in earth life
Gives bread unto the poor;
He feareth not in the spirit land
The fearful baying of the hound.
  The scales have spoken
  And truth gives tongue on doomsday.

How blessed he who in earth life
Unto the poor gives corn;
He feareth not on the Gjallard Bridge
To meet the bull's sharp horn.
  The scales have spoken
  And truth gives tongue on doomsday.

How blessed he who in earth life
Gives clothes unto the poor;
He feareth not in the spirit land
That frozen waste of ice.
  The scales have spoken
  And truth gives tongue on doomsday.

VI

All the folk hearkened to his words;
They hearkened well, young and old.
That was Olav Åsteson,
Now has he all his dream told.
  Stand up, O Olav Åsteson,
  A sleep you've slept, so deep, so long.

Chapter Four
DAY-MAN AND NIGHT-MAN

Everyone is familiar with the conflict between the needs of one's 'natural' being, formed by heredity and education, and one's *second, inner* being, which has ideals, sets goals, and judges one's deeds according to inner norms. The poet Schiller declared in his *Letters about the Aesthetic Education of Man,* that every individual has, so to say, an ideal person within. To be like this ideal person is the highest task of life.[1]

For our present culture, this is a typical romantic-idealistic statement, for this so-called higher man is for many an artificial product of obsolete ethics, and the cause of needless inner conflicts and of many neuroses typical of our culture. Many people regard the unbridled indulgence in the drives and desires of 'first', natural man as good therapy for the damage caused by any 'social conscience'. That is what many popular forms of group therapy are about.

Those, however, who do not reject the possibility of the existence of 'second man' out of hand can, as it were, see with their own eyes the birth of second man by objective observation of the development of children to adolescence and adulthood. Already when the child starts to say 'I' at about 2½ years of age, and experiences its first ego consciousness, second man announces himself. Towards the tenth year, an intensive ego experience is added, which occupies the emotional life to such an extent that the child reacts against its environment. In the following years, feelings of loneliness and doubt are experienced. This signifies doubt about the legitimacy of the hereditary human being, which often is expressed by the question whether one is really the child of one's 'so-called' parents.

In the years of adolescence – the period of about 17 to 23 – second man unfolds fully. The young person awakens to more or less conscious questions: Here I am, with certain hereditary tendencies and with a certain conditioning by the culture in which I live. The former is evident in my constitution, temperament and character, and the latter in the diplomas I obtained. That is a given fact, in which I am unfree; certain things I can do, others not. But what am I to do with these gifts? Continue my education? Look for a job? Explore the world? Or perhaps just wait and see what life will bring me? (These questions often are not asked consciously, but are expressed in the form of protest; the adolescent starts reacting against his parents, against his upbringing, his school, society, etc.)

These are existential questions, which from that time onward are part of life. They surface in the consciousness as an 'inner voice' and demand that one should live one's own life, according to one's own objectives, one's own norms, one's own conscience – often against one's aptitudes and upbringing; for the inner voice that speaks so clearly at about 19 is the voice of one's own higher ego, which is the bearer of a striving towards the future. Everything that was developed up till then is old, has arisen out of the karma of previous lives. Now the ego that in this life wants to add something new to the old breaks through. It is the new that makes sense of the present life.

A comment may be made here. Our Western culture has since about the year 1700 split into two streams. The first clear exponents of these two streams were two contemporaries: Locke and Leibnitz.

The Englishman John Locke (1632-1704), theologian and physician, fled during the English religious wars to the Netherlands, and there wrote his world-famous *Essay concerning Human Understanding*. Well known from this is the thesis that at birth man is a blank page, a *tabula rasa*. All that we have within us later, as a conscious life, has, according to Locke, entered via the senses: "*Nihil est in intellectu quod non prius fuerit in sensu*". The experiences of life fill in the blank page. Man is *passive* and is formed *from the outside.*

Moreover, Locke took the position that complex ideas such as friendship, loyalty, love, honesty, etc., are suspect. Only simple ideas can be investigated scientifically. Complex concepts, therefore, must be reduced to simple components. The simplest ideas, after all, are the building blocks of the human psyche. Human *behaviour*, the only aspect of the psyche that is observable and of which we have any objective knowledge, must, therefore, be investigated in terms of the simplest basic drives. Everything higher is speculative and subjective. According to this mode of thought, the rat is regarded as a simplified model of a human being. That is why scientific research into the behaviour of rats is supposed to be more dependable than investigation of the complex behaviour of people.

Gordon Allport, the nestor of American psychologists, determined that Anglo-Saxon thought stands in what he calls the *Lockian tradition.*[2]

Thus, behaviourism is based on *tabula rasa* and on passive formation of the personality from outside.

The other leading figure was Gottfried Wilhelm Leibnitz (1646-1716). He was a child prodigy; at age 20 he was offered a professorship at the University ofNurnberg, Germany and there he also became acquainted with rosicrucian alchemy. At 26 he was at the court of Louis XIV as the ambassador of the German sovereigns. Here he wrote his *Consilium Aegyptiacum*, in which he suggested that the task of Louis XIV was to conquer Egypt, and not the European countries. During the years of this ambassadorship he occupied himself out of boredom with mathematics, after a meeting with Christiaan Huyghens, because it was a field that was still new to him. After a short time he invented calculus.

When Leibnitz read the essay of Locke, he immediately wrote a reply, *Nouveaux essais sur l'entendement humain*, in which he laid down his vision of the human being.

According to Leibnitz, man is motivated actively by his central 'monad', his personality. Observation is already an active individual process, taking place differently for each person in any given situation. For Leibnitz, man is a being who lives towards the future, forever 'on the way', or, as Allport expressed it later, forever 'becoming'. For Leibnitz the so-called world is not material, but consisting of condensed spirit, conglomerations he calls monads. The mineral world consists of the greatest condensation of spirit monads – these, therefore, have a deep trancelike state of unconsciousness. Life in the plant world consists of less condensed monads, sleeping, but more active. The monads of the animal world are in a dream state, where consciousness arises. The central human monad is barely condensed and awake.

Man has the task to raise the natural consciousness to such an extent that at the time of death he can dissolve in the divine consciousness. For Leibnitz, therefore, man had a high task, which he could fulfill or neglect.

Allport points out that European thought had long held on to this active human image. After the Second World War, however, through the worship for everything that came from America, the Lockian tradition became predominant in Europe as well, and now dominates education, the humanities, and medicine.

Frankl[3] has pointed out that this tradition is a case of selective blindness, of colour blindness, you could say, for everything that has to do with the spirit. In an extreme way and in popularized form, this reduced human image is described in *The Naked Ape* by Desmond Morris.[4]

Proponents of the Lockian behaviouristic image of man call the acknowledgement of second man 'ideological', 'world-conceptional', and therefore unscientific. That can be countered by the fact that their own choice of human image is as ideological and world-conceptional. Materialism, after all, is also based on a pre-scientific postulate; in that, it is not very different from a 'faith'.[5]

As soon, however, as 'second man' in us is seen not only as an adaptation, but as our own identity, which we call the self, the ego, the individuality or, with Aristotle, the *entelechy*, then a colourful, dramatic image of man arises. Then, that which in my book *Phases* I stated as a motto becomes a reality: the human biography is a symphony composed by ourselves.

'Hymns to the Night' by Novalis

Second man, in the tradition of Leibnitz, can be described in various ways. The German poet *Novalis*, pseudonym of a lawyer and mining engineer by the name of Friedrich von Hardenberg, a contemporary of Goethe and Schiller, described this second man in the language of romanticism as *night-man*. Of this night-man, this second man, Novalis became aware with a shock as a result of the death of his fiancée Sophie, a girl of 15. Because of her death he could write his masterpiece, the *Hymns to the Night*. We shall present a translation of part of this, as an example of an inner experience of 'second man in us'.

Novalis was, in a sense, ahead of his time. Because of his particular disposition he was able to experience something which only now is starting to become a reality for larger numbers of people. This conscious experience of 'night-man' was for Novalis not the result of a deliberate inner path of development, but resulted from a shock, which was the effect the death of his beloved had on him. At the same time, Novalis did possess the rare capacity to be 'woken up' by this shock experience, and he did not, as is mostly the case, become dull and insensitive as a result of his sorrow.

Preceding the translation, first a few more notes on the life of Novalis and the creation of *Hymns*:

Friedrich von Hardenberg was born in 1772, son of a Saxon baron, who was director of a salt mine at Weissenfels in Germany. A few years earlier, after the death of his first wife, the father had become a member of the Hernhutter Brotherhood, a very pious, even pietistic group.

Young Friedrich was a delicate, sensitive child, but after a severe illness at age 9 he grew up to be an energetic, cheerful youngster. He had a classical education at a *Gymnasium*, and then studied law at Jena, a famous German university in those days. An important experience there was a meeting with Schiller, who taught history at Jena. He also met Goethe and other important figures in the cultural life of that time.

When in 1794 he had started work as a lawyer, he met the twelve-year-old Sophie von Kühn during a business trip. Immediately he was filled with a deep love for her, a love that would determine the entire course of his further life. After a short time, an official engagement with the girl took place.

It is not easy to get a good picture of her, of this extraordinary being. What is certain is that she made a deep impression on everybody who was acquainted with her. All describe her as a heavenly creature, an enchantingly innocent soul, who in her gaze suggested great depth of soul.

For Friedrich she became the 'cornerstone' and at the same time the main motivation of his life. Even her untimely death, in 1797, did not change that. To the end of his own short life (Hardenberg died in 1801, almost 29 years old) he felt connected with her and, through her, with the 'other world', the 'world of the night', in which he came to experience the image of Christ.

The *Hymns to the Night* are the precipitate of the process the poet experienced as a result of the death of his beloved. He himself experienced the crossing of the threshold inwardly. Hardenberg's artistic work (which he published under the pseudonym 'Novalis', that is 'he who clears new land, and sows') falls largely in the short period between the death of Sophie and his own. Clothed in the language of German romanticism, it is entirely pervaded by the experience of how the night 'lights up as our true homeland'.

Hymns to the Night was completed in 1799.[6]

Hymns to the Night

What living being,
Gifted with feeling,
Bestows not his love
On the all-joyful Light?
Loves it before
All of the wonders
Spread out before him
Through regions of space—
Light undulating,
Colour-filled, raying
Its mild omnipresence
By day?
As life's inmost soul
It is breathed
By the giant world
Of restless stars
Who swim in its blue ocean,
By the sparkling stone,
The peaceful plant,
By the creatures'
Many-fashioned
Ever-moving life.
It is breathed by the clouds
Many-hued, by the zephyrs,
And, above all,
By the glorious strangers
With the thoughtful eyes,
The swinging gait
And the sounding lips.
As a king
It summons each power
Of terrestrial nature
To numberless changes,
And alone doth its presence
Reveal the full splendour
Of Earth.
Downwards wend I my way
To Night, holy, inexpressible,
Secret-filled—
Far away lies the world,
Sunk in deep vault;
How dreary, forlorn her abode!
Deep Melancholy
Stirs in the chords of the breast,
Far-off memories,
Wishes of youth,
Dreams of childhood,
Short-lived joys and vain hopes
Of the long endured life
Come in grey garments,
Like evening mists
After sunset.
Far off lies the world
With its motley of pleasures.
Elsewhere doth the Light
Pitch its airy encampment.
What if it never returned
To its faithful children,
To its gardens
In its glorious house?
Yet what flows so cool,
So refreshing,
So full of hid tidings
To our hearts,
And absorbs the soft air
Of Melancholy?
Hast thou too
A human heart,
O dark Night?
What holdest thou
Under thy mantle
Which steals unseen
Upon my soul,
Giving it strength?
Thou seemest but fearful—
Precious balm
Drops from thy hand,
From the bundle of poppies.
In sweet intoxication
Thou unfoldest the soul's heavy wings,
And givest us joys
Dark, inexpressible,
Secret as thou,
Joys which are promise of heaven.
How poor and childish
Meseemeth the Light
With its varied affairs.
How joyful and bless'd

The departure of day.
It is but because
Night withdraws those who
serve thee
That thou sowest
In the wide realms of space
Shining spheres,
to proclaim in the times of
thine absence
Thine omnipotence,
Thy returning again.
More heavenly than those
flashing stars
In those wide spaces,
Seem to us the infinite eyes
Which the Night
In us opens.
Farther see they
Than the palest
Of that numberless host.
Unneedful of light,
They look through the depths
Of love-enfilled heart
Which fills with unspeakable joy
A loftier space.
Praise to the world's Queen!
To the lofty proclaimer
Of holy world,
To the nurturer
Of blissful love.
Thou comest, Beloved . . .
The Night is here—
Rapt away is my soul—
Finished the earthly way,
Once more art thou mine.
I gaze into the depths of thy
dark eyes,
See naught but love and
blissfulness therein;
We sink upon Night's altar,
Softest couch—
The veil is shed,
And kindled by the warm impress
There glows
The pure flame
Of the sweet sacrifice.

Must ever the morning return?
Endeth never the thraldom
of Earth?
Unhallowed affairs swallow up
The heavenly coming of Night?
Will never Love's offering burn
Eternal and hid?
To the Light was appointed
its time,
A time to its watching—
But timeless the rule of the Night;
Without end the duration of sleep.
Holy Sleep!
Bless not too seldom
Night's consecrated ones—
In this Earth's daily round.
Only the foolish mistake thee
And know of no sleep
But the shadows,
Which thou in compassion
Castest upon us
In that twilight
Of the true Night.
They feel thee not
In the golden flood of the grape,
In the almond tree's
Magic oil,
In the brown juice of the poppy.
They know not
It is thou
That hoverest over the breast
Of the tender maiden,
And makest her bosom a heaven—
They guess not
That out of old histories
Thou comest to meet us,
Opening Paradise,
And bearest the key
To the dwellings of the bless'd:
A silent messenger
Of infinite mysteries.

Once, as I shed bitter tears, as my hope, dissolved in pain, melted away, and I stood lonely on the barren mound which in its dark, narrow compass hid all that formed my life – lonely as none other had ever been, moved by unspeakable anguish, bereft of strength, no thought but of grief – as I looked round for succour – could go neither forward nor back, and clung to the fleeing, extinguished life with unending longing—there came out of blue distances a twilight shower from the heights of my former bliss; and in one moment burst the bonds of birth, the fetters of Light. Away fled the glory of Earth and my tears therewith. Melancholy flowed into a new unfathomable world; thou, O Inspiration of Night, Slumber of Heaven, camest o'er me. All that lay round me softly arose, and above it hovered my unbound, newly-born spirit. As a dust cloud became the mound; through the cloud I beheld the glorified features of the Beloved. In her eyes rested eternity. I grasped her hands and my tears became a sparkling indestructible cord. Thousands of years drew away down into the distance as a thunderstorm. On her neck I wept enchanted tears for the new life. That was the first dream in thee. It passed, but its image remained – the eternal, unshakable belief in the heaven of Night, and its Sun, the Beloved.

Now know I when the last morning will be – when the Light will no longer scare away Love and the Night, when slumber will be eternal and only one inexhaustible dream. Heavenly weariness deserts me now no more. Long and toilsome was the way to the Holy Sepulchre, and the Cross was heavy. He whose lips have once been moistened by the crystal wave which, unseen by common sight, has its source in the dark womb of the mound at whose foot breaks the earthly tide, he who has stood above upon this boundary of the world, and has looked across into the new land, into the dwelling-place of the Night – he, of a truth, turns not back to the affairs of the world in the land where Light holds sway, and eternal unrest makes its home. Up above he builds himself tabernacles, dwellings of peace, he longs and loves, gazes across, until the most welcome of all hours draws him down into the wells of the fount. All that is earthly floats on the surface, and is washed down from the heights; but what has become holy through contact of love runs released into hidden ways in yonder realm, where cloud-like it mingles with the slumber-wrapt loved ones.

Still thou awakest
The weary to work,
O cheerful Light—
Thou inspirest me with joyful life.
But thou allurest me not
From remembering
That moss-grown monument.
Willingly will I
Bestir busy hands,
Look on all sides
Where thou needest me,
And praise the full pomp
Of thy splendour;
Unwearied, pursue
The beautiful sequence
Of thine artistry's work;
Glad will I watch
The course fraught with meaning
Of thy mighty,
Shining clock;
Fathom the symmetry
Of the forces
And the laws
Of the magic-play

Of numberless spaces,
And their times.
But true to the Night
And her daughter,
Creative Love,
Rests my innermost heart.
Canst thou show me
An ever true heart?
Has thy Sun
Friendly eyes
Which know me?
Do thy stars grasp
My longing hand
And give me in turn
A tender pressure?
Hast thou bedeckt her
With colour
And light outline?
Or was it she
Who gave to thine adornment
Higher and lovelier meaning?
What delight
And what pleasures
Offers thy life
Which outweigh
The enchantments of death?
Doth not all that inspires us
Bear the colour of Night?
She beareth thee as a mother,
And to her thou dost owe
All of thy splendour.
Thou wouldst vanish
Into thyself,
Thou wouldst dissolve
Into endless space
Did she not hold thee—
Not bind thee,
So that thou grewest warm,
And flaming
Begottest the world.
Verily I was, ere thou wert.
With my race
The Mother despatched me
To dwell in thy world,
Make it holy
With Love;
To bestow
Human meaning
On thy creations.
Not yet have they ripened,
Those thoughts of the Gods.
As yet are the traces but few
In our age.
One day thy clock will depict
The ending of time,
When thou wilt become
As one of us,
And full of longing,
Melt away and die.
Within me I feel
The busy affairs
Draw to an end;
Heavenly freedom,
Blessed return.
I discern thy removal
In wild grief
From our home,
Thy resistance
To the glorious
Ancient heaven.
In vain is thy fury,
Thy raging.
Indestructible
Stands the Cross,
Triumphant Banner
Of our race.
I wander across
And every pain
Will turn to a pricking
Of joy again.
But yet a short while
And free am I
O'ercome with the love
In my breast to lie.
Unending life
Comes over me,
And I look from above
Down below upon thee.
Thy brightness fades
On that little mound,
A shade is bringing
The chaplet cool.

Oh, drink, Beloved,
Of me drink deep,
That soon I be wrapt
In eternal sleep.

I feel Death's encroaching,
Youth-giving wave,
And wait through life's stresses
Full courage and brave.

With these last words "I feel Death's encroaching, youth-giving wave, and wait through life's stresses full courage and brave", Novalis gave expression to his entire attitude in life. Because of the crossing of the threshold by the grave of his beloved, he goes through his initiation. From that moment on, the life of night is for him present *during* the day.

Hymns to the Night is more than an autobiographical expression; it is at the same time a documentation of the development of humanity, a vision of the future. What *life* yields to Novalis, and what he subsequently assimilates, modern man must consciously incorporate into his biography: the double consciousness of a life of day and a life of night, connected with a courageous stand in the storms of life.

Chapter Five
SECOND MAN IN US

The fragment of *Hymns to the Night* by Novalis presented in translation in the last chapter is an image of what Rudolf Steiner often called 'the experience of the dawn of a new age', in which the darkening of spiritual life will come to an end, and in which the true spirit-soul being of man (our 'higher ego', or Schiller's 'ideal man in us') can more and more consciously determine the meaning and goals of life. Rightly, the Romanticists would still refer to this true spirit-soul being as 'night-man' for at that time it could only make itself felt from out of the unconsciousness of the night and appear only as a dream reality during the day.

The purpose of the path of development described in subsequent chapters is to make this higher ego the guide in our life during the day as well. But the higher ego also has an important role to play in the life of the human being today even when inner development is not yet pursued consciously.

At the zenith of life between death and a new birth, in the so-called 'world midnight hour' (we shall come back to this later[1]), the human being makes the decision out of his higher ego to seek a new incarnation in order to make it possible to take a further step on the path of development. This higher ego then has the rewards from previous lives at its disposal as well as the liabilities. Moreover, the ego has a memory of the vision of cosmic man, the image the divine world has in mind as the goal of the development of humanity, which is shown to the human being between death and a new birth. This 'memory' is the creative force that is able, as a 'spirit' principle', to build up the physical body in all its complexity.[2] It is as it were the drawing of the architect, according to which the life forces of the ether body can build up the physical body. This spirit principle is active particularly in the first phases of embryonic development.

The ego itself, however, is much more concerned with the future, with the tasks to be set for the coming life. The ego can accompany the incarnating human being before birth, during his 'descent' from the spiritual world, until birth. Then it remains behind in the spiritual world, and, from above, provides impulses for the biography.

Every night we meet our own higher ego in the spiritual world and are judged by it. In the morning, we wake up, half consciously feeling positively or negatively disposed towards our deeds and intentions. Should we do nothing further, these feelings of satisfaction or unease, which we call our 'conscience', simply remain.

At death we meet this higher ego with our soul being. Then, during the time of purification, it presents us with the 'bill' for the past life.

What is described here is that which is behind the well known parable of the 'talents'.[3] A master, before setting out on a journey, gives a talent to each of his servants with instructions to look after it. When he returns home, he demands that each of the servants account for what they have done with the talents. The answers differ: One has buried the talent, and can now return it unchanged; that, however, displeases the master. Another has squandered the talent, and now comes empty handed; the master isn't pleased with that either. The third has traded with his talent, and returns it with interest; that pleases the master. In one's imagination one can enrich this parable with yet other possibilities, but always the master will be satisfied only if one returns with more than one has received. Our own higher ego demands, as master of its servants, that the talent one has brought with one is increased and developed. In other words: the servants – the astral, etheric and physical bodies – must be enriched during life.

That which during our ordinary life we address as 'I' is not yet the true higher ego. It is the *reflection* of the higher ego in the soul – in the astral body and in the sentient, mind, and consciousness soul.[4] The modern scientific image of the human being, therefore, recognizes no true ego. It wishes to explain man entirely in terms of the animal functions in him. "Man is just an intelligent animal, and nothing more", a student called out to me during a lecture at Boston University when, speaking on the subject of curative education, I talked about the spirit being of the child than can not express itself because of a deficient 'instrument'.

Indeed, the actual spirit being of man is not yet noticeable as a matter of course; one has to undergo inner training in order to make conscious during the day what occurs during the night. The higher ego lets go of the incarnating human being at the moment of birth, as it were, and accompanies him from the outside from then on. But there are moments in human life when the higher ego can give renewed 'birth impulses'. At certain moments, the gate to the higher ego reopens, and earthly man can reinforce his intentions for the present incarnation. These moments are determined by the cosmic constellation, namely by the relationship of sun, moon, and earth.

As said before, the higher ego accompanies the incarnating soul during its descent through the planetary spheres, down to the moon sphere, from where physical birth takes place. We enter life on earth through the 'gate of the moon'. The ego then withdraws to the sun sphere, where it belongs.

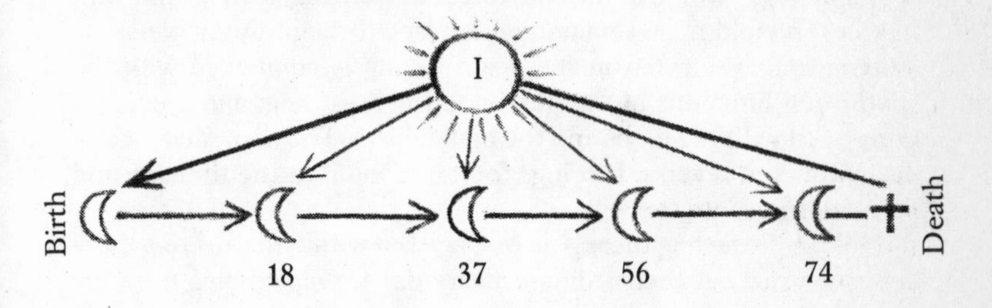

Just 18 years, 7 months and 9 days later, the birth constellation with respect to the 'aspect' of the sun, moon, and earth returns (the so-called first 'moon node'. At that moment, the gate of birth reopens momentarily, as it were, and the ego can renew its impulses for the incarnation. This process repeats itself with the second moon node (another 18 years, 9 months, and 7 days hence), and so on. (These moments should not be seen as limited to a certain day, but rather be regarded as a period in which the influence of the higher ego increases and then decreases again over a period of some years centred around the moon node constellation.[5])

The first repetition of the birth constellation occurs towards age 19. That is why the years between 17 and 20 are of the greatest importance for the future intentions of young people. They face important study or vocational choices, or it may be a case of confirmation or rejection of choices that were imposed on them too early. The young person then wonders: Who am I? What do I want? What am I able to do? To be actively involved with these existential questions between age 17 or 18 and 19 or 20 is an important task for post-secondary education.[6]

The second 'moon node constellation' is of great significance too; it comes at age 37, shortly after the mid-point of life, at a moment that many people experience as a dead point. Two of the greatest dramatic works of all time, the *Divine Comedy* of Dante and *Faust* of Goethe, start with this situation of desperation of age 35, in which it becomes apparent that if the thread of life can be picked up again, the actual fulfilment of the incarnation can take place in the second half of life.

The third and fourth moon node constellations also have a special place in many biographies.[7]

If one visualizes the image of one's higher ego, as it accompanies the course of life from spirit heights, one takes the first step on the path of imaginative development. A further step is to form a picture of how the higher ego works in the soul forces of thinking, feeling, and willing. In threefold man, thinking takes place through the nerve-sense system, mainly located in the head; feeling is connected with the rhythmical functions of the heart and the breathing; and the will is connected with the limbs and the metabolism. The higher ego, however, works in reverse. It brings forces of will into the thinking and consciousness into the will.

Only in the feeling there is an overlap. But within this overlap there is the contrast between ordinary, every-day feeling coming from the past, and the feeling related to the higher ego pointing at the future. Our ordinary thinking, feeling, and willing, after all, are the fruit of previous lives and of the upbringing we had up till now. Our higher ego is future-oriented, and aims for what we should add to our talents. Thus, one can clearly observe how in adolescence between 17 and 21 the feeling, which previously still was secure, gets mixed up. The tasks for the future, sensed vaguely, cause everything out of the past to be rejected to the point of the unreasonable: parents, social structures in which one has grown up, middle class morals, etc. The awareness of one's higher ego, of ideal man, or second man in us, arises in the life of feeling first, and then in the other soul forces. New impulses enter the thinking, making it *creative*, opening up new ways of looking at things and opening up new interests. When the sleeping will becomes more conscious, this expresses itself on the moral plane. Old morality, taken for granted, becomes problematic. New norms, new values, new moral goals emerge from unconscious depths, and confront the developing human being with an existential life crisis.

In conversations with people in their first half of life, Rudolf Steiner pointed out that it is of the greatest importance not to sleep through these fruitful, but often difficult, years, in which an intensive encounter with one's own ego takes place; one should be awake to new impulses, which can then be taken up in a fruitful development of one's own biography.

Thus far we have spoken about the biographical development from past to future as it unfolds naturally, culminating in the full encounter with the ego at death, when it will be apparent whether the master is satisfied with what his servants have done with their talents.

At present, however, in the period of the consciousness soul, this naturally occurring meeting is no longer sufficient. The counterforces, and Ahriman[8] in particular, will do everything to prevent the meeting with the higher ego, or at least to see that it passes unnoticed. The materialistic image of man and the world leaves little room for the concept of a spiritual figure as the ego of the human being. When then the experiences arise, they are pushed aside as undesirable feelings of uncertainty, as weaknesses, or as frightening experiences that must be suppressed. 'Tranquillizers' in many forms are readily available in order not to allow any experience of the ego impulses for the future to come through.

One can only be certain about what exists, about the past. Everything future brings by definition uncertainty. Ahriman's ideal is for man not to add anything new to his talents, but only to build on his innate capabilities by the rules of logic; let life be run off like a computer program. Predictable man, in a technical environment – that is the ideal of Ahriman and of all dictatorships inspired by him. The human being who works out of his ego is unpredictable, and therefore a dissident. He belongs in a psychiatric institution. His ego must be extinguished, or at least rendered inaccessible.

That is why those who want to live out of their ego must do more than merely taking a waiting attitude. They can seek a path of inner development, and open themselves to the awakening of second man within.

In the next chapters we shall deal with paths of development as they were given in the past as well as with the requirements of an inner training suitable for the consciousness soul age, in which particularly the will and individual problems of morality play a role.

The animal only knows a past, programmed by heredity. Man has a future as well, of which he can become conscious through his higher ego. The more conscious this 'second man in us' becomes, the more one can take oneself in hand. This is the result of pursuing a path of inner training.

Chapter Six
PATHS OF DEVELOPMENT IN THE PAST AND NOW

Right from the beginning of Rudolf Steiner's activities in what was then the German division of the Theosophical Society, he made clear where he stood. In the series of lectures *At the Gates of Spiritual Science*, held in Stuttgart in 1906, he says: "There are three paths of occult development: the Eastern, the Christian-Gnostic and the Christian Rosicrucian, or simply the Rosicrucian. They are distinguished above all by the extent to which the pupil surrenders himself to his teacher."[1]

In this chapter we shall briefly describe the most important aspects of the three paths, which leads to a description of the path of anthroposophy in the next chapter.

The eastern path of development

In order to get an idea of the eastern path, we have to return to the situation of ancient India, more than 6000 years before Christ. It was in the Indian regions that the first post-Atlantean culture took its course.[2] Mankind at that time was hardly individualized. The human ether body did not yet have the sharp outlines it has now, strongly as it is tied now to the the physical body. At that time it merged gradually with the surrounding ether world. For the consciousness of the time this meant that what we now call atavisitic clairvoyance, which some people experience spontaneously, was than commonplace.

The holy Rishis, leaders of the Indian culture, could direct this clairvoyance at the divine world (the higher hierarchies) in order to give the still cosmic ether bodies of people form and definition in the right way, with divine help. This was necessary as a first step towards individualization. It required paths of development adapted to the consciousness of that time. This meant total dependence on, and at the same time reverence for, the teachers. This path was called later the path of the royal yoga (*raja yoga*). It was a purely meditative path.

In addition, there arose *hatha yoga*, which had the purpose of making the body (and particularly the breathing) subject and 'obedient' to the meditative path. This was a further step on the way to individualization, by giving more definition to the ether body, and tying it more closely to the physical body. Because the ether body is the carrier of all life rhythms, in the breath, the blood, and the metabolism, the training of hatha-yoga consisted of learning how to control these life rhythms.

In much later times, in the first century after Christ, it was the great yoga teacher Patanjali who, from remnants of the Sankhya philosophy and what still remained of memories of the 'original' yoga, founded his yoga school, which became the most important example for all subsequent yoga schools. It was only here that the aspiration arose to attain peace and bliss by means of a strengthening of the soul, after purification and ennoblement. This ideal arose at a time when ether bodies were already more defined and 'natural clairvoyance' was already on the wane. The objective was no longer an encounter with the gods (the higher hierarchies), but the education of one's own soul and a blissfull merging into an undifferentiated All.

The yoga path of Patanjali leads to the desired bliss (Samadhi) in eight steps:[3]

1. *Yama*: no lying, no killing, no stealing, etc.
2. *Niyama*: following religious customs and rituals (yoga does not know *dogmatics*, but *rituals*, which through repetition become part of the pupil).
3. *Asana*: assuming certain positions during meditation.
4. *Pranayama*: controlling the breathing, to such an extent that the meditant no longer exhales (poisonous) carbon monoxide.
5. *Pratayahara*: control of the sense impressions.
6. *Dharana*: being able to shut out all sense impressions.
7. *Dhyana*: meditating on images that have no equivalent in the sense world.
8. *Samadhi*: empty consciousness, without falling asleep; thinking without thoughts, so that the spiritual world can reveal itself.

These are the eight areas in which the guru gives the pupil his assignments. The guru determines for how long the pupil has to do the exercises of each stage.

In essence, all yoga schools after Patanajali follow this pattern.

In order to understand these yoga schools and the power they had over their pupils, the following should be mentioned: The content of the meditations was (and still is) in the form of the names of Hindu gods, who are invoked in reverence. In antiquity these were Brahma (Father), Vishnu (bringer of life) and Shiwa (divine spirit, divine consciousness). Shiwa is the one invoked most; '*om namah Shivaja*' ('I bow before Shiwa') is repeated endlessly in the Hindu meditation. In true yoga, the sacred words must be accompanied by thoughts of Shiwa and the desire to be united with Shiwa. (Thoughtless meditation as is learned in certain schools is already a decadent form, which puts the pupil in a position of greater dependence on the guru).

Swami Mactanandra, who brings Siddha yoga to western people, says: "Shiwa is your own inner self. He is the self of All. Shiwa is bliss, unlimited love. Shiwa is almighty."

About the role of the guru he says the following: The guru is not the human being you have in front of you. The guru is the merciful power of God; the guru is your own higher inner self. 'Om' is the consciousness penetrating All. The guru is this 'Om' . In the mantra the guru gives you, his 'shakti' (spiritual force) vibrates. Such a mantra can give liberation because the entanglement of your karma is dissolved. Kundalini, the Mother of All, who encompasses all yogas, is the form and content of the mantra given by the guru. So, repeat the mantra all the time. Through the mantra, the guru enters within you and opens the new world of yoga for you. He brings it to realization, and dissolves all that is negative. Those who seek are led to total liberation by the guru. Repeat the mantra, don't be tempted by the world. In the course of the meditations the personal ego disappears, and the experience of your ego leaves you! What remains is the pure, eternally blissful consciousness, the highest being, and it is you! Inside and outside are one. Seek yourself. Hari, Shiwa, Sjakti, Allah, Jesus, Buddha, all live within you!"[4]

This means, therefore: inside and outside are one; the individual existence is cancelled.

From this quote, the total dependence on the guru is evident. Via the mantra, the guru himself enters the pupil. He frees the pupil from his karma; the pupil no longer has to do this himself. The pupil allows himself to be developed by the guru. The goal of this development is the extinguishing of the personal ego, of the individuality, and the guru then brings you bliss. The pupil does not have to understand the mantra himself.

Only a living guru can give this kind of leadership. Here the view is: book knowledge stays in books; personal wisdom can be transferred and work for you.

In ancient times the suppression of the ego was necessary. The ego was still permeated by Lucifer with egoism, and this egoistic ego had to be eliminated.[5] Only by the Christian force of love, which works in a germinal form in the human ego, a non-egoistic individual development becomes possible. That is why in our time the relationship between pupil and teacher must change. Dependence must make room for *freedom.*

The human being of today who strives for a conscious path of development, may accept the advice of an initiate. He himself, however, is responsible for his path. This is possible only when he himself has insight into what he does.

It is the task of the modern initiate to make this insight possible. All of anthroposophy can give us insights, which, through a lot of effort, we can make our own by studying and verifying.

This path of meditation, therefore, is a different one from that of the east. In the east, the original ancient language has a magic power of its own. The invocation of the gods means more than the mere sound of words and the accompanying emotions. But the 'mantras' (or verses) given by Rudolf Steiner are always formed in such a way that the content is understandable and clear. The meditating person connects himself with the content.

That is why anthroposophical verses and mantras can be translated into other languages, although this isn't easy; it is difficult to express the same content in different languages.

But Rudolf Steiner emphatically rejected all guru relationships. He did not want reverence. He wanted people who understood what he had to say – people who understand him, and make their own decisions, and take responsibility themselves for their own path.

The medieval Christian path

Since the ego of man has received the force of unselfish love as a *possibility*, through Christ, every form of dependence on a living guru means a backward step on the path of development. The Christianized ego must learn to become his own guru, to choose his own tempo, his own content – in short, to be responsible.

The follower of eastern paths of initiation regards this as arrogance, as mortally dangerous. For him, the ego is still the villain, made selfish by Lucifer. 'I' is equivalent to 'egoism', and can only be eradicated by pursuing the 'not I' and by having the astral body, as the carrier of consciousness, cleansed under the leadership of a master.

In the Middle Ages, an intermediate form could still arise: the mystic-Christian path of development. For this, too, the pupil had to withdraw from every-day life and go his lonely way as a monk or a hermit. One could go this path without a living master, but one had Christ as one's guide along the way.

This required that one connected oneself with Christ in such a way that one actually experienced His passage to Golgotha in seven 'stations'. Each station took several years of lonely struggle.

The first station was the *washing of the feet.* All that is higher bows in gratitude for that which is lower, which, because it has made the sacrifice of existing on that level, makes the life and work at a higher level possible. Thus Christ knelt before his disciples and washed their feet.

The second station was that of the *scourging.* One had to learn to remain steadfast despite all the blows life might deal one. One said: I will remain steadfast under all the sorrow and all the pain life can give. This went as far as experiencing physical pain over the entire body.

The third station was the *crowning with thorns.* One had to learn to endure the mockery and the taunts of the world. The imagination of the crowning with thorns became so intensive that one had unbearable headaches. To learn to endure these was the result of the third station.

The fourth station included the *bearing of the cross* and the *crucifixion.* The body becomes like the wood of the cross we carry, and we ourselves are the carriers. This meditation led to the vision that one hung on the cross oneself, and caused the stigmatization reported to have been experienced by many medieval saints (among others Francis of Assisi).

The fifth station was the *mystical death.* In this, all became darkness, and one joined in Christ's 'harrowing of hell'. One experienced all aspects of evil, until darkness was split asunder and the light of Christ illuminated all that was in darkness. This was called: the tearing of the veil in the temple.

The sixth station was the *burial.* One's earthly incarnation is no longer confined to the limitations of one's own body; the entire earth becomes one's body, in which one follows the deed of Christ.

The seventh station was the *resurrection,* which can not be described in words. One was then wholly united with Christ. The words of Paul, "Not I but Christ in me", had then become reality.

This Christian path of development flourished in the Middle Ages. The medieval soul had the capacity to intensify and deepen the inner life to such an extent that the way of Christ on earth could really be lived through. Since the beginning of the New Age, it has become less and less possible to do this to the same extent and in the same manner. The present soul condition as well as the circumstances demand something new from a conscious path of development.

The Christian Rosicrucian path

In addition to the path of the Christian mystics, which was followed within the church, there also was a Christian tradition outside the church. We do not mean the dozens, indeed, perhaps even hundreds of sects and splinter movements since the first century after Christ, but a tradition that runs like a thread through history and comes to the surface in the ninth century as the *grail stream.*

The symbol of the grail is connected with the blood mysteries and the blood relics that played a role until the later Middle Ages. Often the 'rose-coloured blood of Christ' was mentioned in this context. There are many stories relating how blood relics were brought from the East to the West (see, for example, the book *The Ninth Century*, by W.J. Stein).

The most important blood mystery is the grail. This is not the place to discuss this mystery in detail (my booklet about 'the four mystery streams' deals with the grail mystery in part.[6]) What can be indicated briefly is that the grail was seen as the stone that Michael, in his heavenly battle with Lucifer, knocked out of Lucifer's crown. The stone then fell to the earth. Via the Queen of Sheba and King Solomon this stone, ground in the form of a chalice, came into the possession of Joseph of Arimathea who collected the blood of Christ in this chalice under the cross.

This blood had undergone the effects of the Christ incarnation, and was cleansed of all desires. The turbid red blood, bearer and symbol of the lower, animalistic passions, had become innocent and of a 'rose-red' colour, as the bearer and symbol of the penetration of the human being with the purifying force of Christ.

Many are the legends in which it is told how the grail blood was carried from the East to the West. According to some, angels brought the grail to Spain; according to others it was Joseph of Arimathea himself who brought the grail to the south of England; and according to still others the 'Sons of Bron' brought the grail to France. Among the knights of the Round Table of King Arthur it was only Sir Galahad who, because of his faith, was able to make the grail visible in the circle of Arthurian knights.

Rudolf Steiner pointed out[7] that these grail legends are an image of the Christ force itself, which gradually travels from East to West in the hearts of men, cleansing the astral body of the lower passions and transforming it into spirit self. This was experienced in the rose colour. When over the centuries the number of people who could still keep the 'grail' alive in their hearts dwindled more and more, an 'important leader of humanity' came forward, under the name Titurel, who received the spiritual task to build a protective castle and to found an order of grail knights who had to protect the grail. But already in the third generation after Titurel, the grail king Amfortas failed to maintain purity of heart and was wounded by the (luciferic) magician Klingsor.

Then the grail is saved once more as Parcival follows an arduous path towards becoming grail king. Parcival can be seen as the one who prepared a future humanity, which (in the time of consciousness-soul development) could become grail bearer – bearer of the spirit-self blood – by its own power, starting from nothing (that is, without any tradition from the past).

But the entire grail episode, as it was written down centuries later by Chretien de Troyes, Wolfram von Eschenbach, and others, is situated in the time of the mind soul. Knowing and knowledge were then still connected with the *heart*, and penetrated the entire feeling life of man. The new age, the age of the consciousness soul, has brought a form of knowing and of knowledge that is carried only in the head, and expresses itself in abstract formulations, which on no account should have any personal, emotional content.

In the consciousness-soul age it is infinitely more difficult to experience something of the all-pervading force of the grail. With Parcival as the grail king, the tradition of the grail as the giver of life, kept in a castle to be entered only at night, comes to an end. Even night-man can in this time of abstract thought no longer behold and experience the grail as the symbol of the risen Christ.

Parcival, according to tradition, takes the grail with him at the end of his life, and sails 'eastward', where he keeps the grail until the West can once more, out of its own forces, receive it. Accordingly, since the tenth century the mystery of the blood – the grail – is no longer accessible in that form.[8] 'In that form' means that the direct 'certainty of heart', which previously came about through merely beholding the grail (or beholding a blood relic), could no longer be experienced by man.

With the dawn of 'the New Age' at the beginning of the fifteenth century a break in the continuity of Christendom based on the Resurrection, which for centuries had been represented by the symbol of the grail, became a real threat because of the intellectualization of thinking and the drying up of 'heart experience'. New forms of human development were needed to save the resurrection mystery, the old blood mystery. These new forms became known as the *Rosicrucian stream.* A new symbol came to the fore: the rose cross. The black cross, symbol of the physical body, was surrounded by seven red roses, symbol of the plant-like, purified blood. This, too, was a symbol of resurrection, which was built up meditatively in the spirit,and could thus permeate human beings in their thinking, feeling, and willing.

Indeed, it is not a matter of just one path, but of many, for the Rosicrucian stream flowed in many ways and in many forms below the surface of traditional, dogma-bound Christianity as if through hidden veins.

Thus, there were genuine (Rosicrucian) alchemists, who in the medium of combining and separating chemical substances sought the '*quinta essentia*', the fifth form of matter besides the familiar forms of the solid, liquid, gaseous, and warmth elements. This fifth form was the etheric world in which the blood of the resurrection was to be found. Also the philosophers' stone, carbon, the carrier of all forms of life, was sought in its pure form as the substance of resurrection.

In addition, there were traveling physicians and simple craftsmen who by means of wood-cut prints spread their resurrection message, and gave people the images that brought sustenance to thirsting souls, just as once the grail had done.

But there were also sovereigns and diplomats who, inspired by the rose cross, attempted to avert wars and to spread culture. Then there were industrialists, well into the eighteenth century, who by means of Rosicrucian alchemy found new ways of making things – for example the manufacture of noble porcelain, to replace rough stoneware. There were also academics at universities such as Upsala, Sweden, who were adherents of the 'Theophrastic' movement, a cover name for the Rosicrucians. And, finally, there were individual scholars such as Leibnitz, who as a young man became familiar with the teachings of Rosicrucianism while at university, where he wrote his philosphy of divine monads (see also Chapter 4).

Below the surface of the externally confused history of the beginning of the New Age flowed an invisible stream, which here and there came to the surface. It was the stream that carried the striving towards resurrection – heartwarming and head-warming. Then sounded the call for liberty, equality and fraternity in the French Revolution, inspired by the Rosicrucian movement. Even in the present day it can make people enthusiastic.[9]

How could this Rosicrucian movement come about? Who was the founder and guardian of this stream, as Titurel had once been the guardian of the grail stream? That must have been an individuality who, like Titurel, was a leader of humanity and who was very closely linked with the mystery of death and resurrection. Rudolf Steiner spoke about this leader of humanity in a lecture in Neuchatel, France.[10] It was an individuality who in the middle of the thirteenth century prepared himself by an initiation under exceptional circumstances for an incarnation in the following century, in which he would bear the name Christian Rosenkreuz. Subsequently, this individuality was almost continuously incarnated, with short breaks between death and the next life. However, he still had to work under cover, which meant that each incarnation could only become known 100 years after it had been terminated by death. The individuality Christian Rosenkreuz stood, so to speak, fully consciously below the cross, and worked out of the power of the resurrection of the purified blood. His symbol was the black cross, ringed by seven red roses.

But in addition to this genuine Rosicrucian stream, there was also a great deal of charlatanism; alchemists, who instead of inner change sought gold; leaders of sects who called themselves Rosicrucians, and used the symbols, but no longer understood them. Thus, by the end of the last century and also in this century, real Rosicrucianism had gone entirely underground, and only those Rosicrucian groups and societies that merely continued the outer forms had remained at the surface.

On the level of the 'underground' streams, working quietly, lies the connection of anthroposophy with the grail stream as well as with the Rosicrucian stream. Each of these, like anthroposophy, had created forms for resurrection Christianity in a certain phase of western development, so that this 'esoteric' Christianity of resurrection could live among people. Already from his first public appearance in (what then still was) the Theosophical Society, Rudolf Steiner mentioned this connection with Christianity of the resurrection. The first cycle of lectures, *At the Gates of Spiritual Science*, the book *Christianity as a Mystical Fact*, and the later book *Occult Science – An Outline*, in which at the end it is stated that this book can also be called '*Science of the Grail*' all speak of the new form in which, after the period of darkness is over, the light of Christ can shine for humanity. That which earlier on still took place as a nocturnal experience of the grail or as an 'underground' activity of the Rosicrucians, can now be made fully public through anthroposophy, in the conceptual form as well as by practical realization in the inner life and in outward work.

It would take a separate book to explain the metamorphosis of the 'grail stone' into the 'foundation stone' of the Christmas Foundation Meeting.[11] What can only be indicated here is that it is possible to demonstrate that anthroposophy, particularly after the Foundation Meeting in 1923-24, is in the forefront in the battle for esoteric Christianity, and that it can give humanity the forms and symbols possible for the present age. Rosicrucianism, as it worked on well into the nineteenth century, the individuality called Christian Rosenkreuz works together with the individuality we call Rudolf Steiner on the continuing task of awakening resurrection Christianity in human beings.

Chapter Seven
THE PATH OF ANTHROPOSOPHY

In the old spiritually based cultures, man experienced the world of night as his true origin. To wake up in the morning he experienced as something that was like a recurring imprisonment from which he gradually had to free himself, not by committing suicide, but by overcoming all earthly desires and merging with the spiritual world, with the 'All', the 'nirwana'. In actual fact, this was a return to the state of being as yet unborn, to existence before birth.

In the course of evolution, the night world became less and less conscious, and finally was experienced only in dreams, which required interpretation in order to give any impulses for daily life. In the Old Testament we find an example of this: Joseph could still interpret the dreams of the Pharaoh, who himself lived entirely in the daytime world.[1] In the dream world, indications could still be found for leading the people. But the Greeks already had the saying: "Better a beggar in the land of the living than a king in the realm of shadows". For the Greeks, the day was life, the night death. They were the first to be daytime individualities in the full sense; they trusted their own day-thinking, and as a result they could develop philosophy. Since then, night-man has been exiled to the realm of faith.

We mentioned Novalis-Hardenberg as an example of modern man. Although a poet, he was able to do his work as a mining engineer in the salt mines during the day, and in addition to make his night individuality conscious to his day-individuality. He was one of the first to go a modern path of development because he did not withdraw in order to further his own inner development, like the Indian yogi or the medieval mystic, but he went this path in the fullness of life.

Modern inner development is possible *while* man lives a social life according to his aptitudes, education, and his own individuality – a daily life devoted to others.

Working for others can be a conscious choice, and in some vocations this stands out clearly. Unknowingly, however, *every* person is at work for others in his vocational life. With the division of labour in our society he can not do otherwise. He does not bake bread for himself, he makes screws and machines for others, he does 'public' administration, or administers justice in the name of laws made by others and applied to others. Thus we are in our daily life constantly part of a network of human relationships.

Our day-individuality is caught in paradoxes within our own aptitudes and education. This either furthers or hinders our outward achievements. In this struggle we are largely un-free. Our day individuality is the result of our past, from this life as well as from previous lives.

But on the strength of his own individuality, man can make a decision to seek a second kind of life, a spiritual life, besides the daily life. There are opportunities for doing this, to begin with, by taking an interest in the products of the life of the night, for instance in the areas of art and religion. But those who try this will soon become aware of certain limits. These are limits of knowledgeableness, artistic sensibility, and past religious experience.

He who wants consciously to awaken his night-individuality in his day individuality must make a decision to follow a path of *inner development*, comparable with the path of the pupils in the ancient mysteries. However, instead of looking for old forms, one will have to ask oneself: What is the path for a pupil of the *new* mysteries?

The new mysteries are no longer tied to a certain time or a certain place. One can not go somewhere to a mystery place and then stay there for a while. The new mysteries are present everywhere, at any time, in the *fullness of life.* We have to learn to live at two levels of consciousness continuously – one directed at daily life and the other at the awakening second individuality, at the night rising to consciousness in us. The night-consciousness runs like a thread above our ordinary consciousness, as it were. We can at any moment seize it and live with it, or we can release it when life demands, only to seize it again afterwards and continue with it.

Ordinary life offers plenty of opportunities to do this. We have to wait for a bus; instead of pacing up and down impatiently, we can direct our attention inward and for a few minutes fill ourselves with thoughts and feelings we have built up at other times in our meditative life. The pavement is full of people, it is noisy, but quietly the mind is turned inward, for as long as the situation allows. This is possible only when at other times we have worked systematically on our development.

The path of anthroposophy has been described by Rudolf Steiner in a number of books, the most important of which are: *Knowledge of*

Higher Worlds and How to Attain It and *Occult Science – An Outline* (chapter on 'Knowledge of Higher Worlds – Concerning Initiation'). Furthermore, indications for inner development can be found in many (printed) lectures of Steiner.

For a comprehensive description of the anthroposophical path of inner training, we refer the reader to the relevant literature.[2] In this chapter the intent is to indicate what is characteristic for this path. Of course, the author is led by his own preferences and experience.

Outline of the anthroposophical path of inner training

There is nothing compulsory or binding in this modern mystery path. The preparation consists, among other things, of practicing a number of soul qualities that are familiar to everyone, and everyone can acknowledge the importance of this. Moments of inner peace; intensive observation of the world; quiet inner observation of one's own actions; impartiality towards other people; tolerance with regard to others' opinions; warm feelings for the positive in other people; gratitude for what the world and people have given one in youth and afterwards; equanimity of feeling without being cold-hearted. All of these qualities must be practiced for a long time and brought into harmony with each other. The forces that are developed in this preparation gradually become part of our character. Many people find in their destiny the incentive to develop one quality or another; the person who has in freedom taken the decision to pursue spiritual development does this systematically and with perseverance.

A further step is *meditation.* This consists of an intensive immersion in a content one has chosen or an image one builds up. Meditation is: to absorb a content of one's own choice, intensively and repeatedly, in full awareness of what one is doing. This is not mindless repetition of words without knowing what they mean, even though these words in themselves are the names of higher beings in the language of another culture.

In such a spiritual training of his own choice, the pupil will gradually find the way to the content that at a certain moment can bring him further. In anthroposophical literature one can find a wealth of content suitable for meditation.

The first benefit of this inner path, which awakens the night individuality in the day, will be a beginning of imaginative vision. Starting with unprejudiced, intensive observation of nature, one becomes gradually aware of characteristic images that connect the human being with the creative forces working behind or in the natural sense world. This starts with simple exercises, for example: Can I experience the characteristic difference between a birch and an oak so intensely that I can express this in a drawing or in words? Do I see '*the* birch' and '*the* oak' before my inner eye as two archetypal images?

Goethe had acquired this imaginative vision by years of intensive observation of the plant world, which enabled him to come to the inner vision of the archetypal 'plant'. Before his mind's eye he could see this plant's metamorphosis into all existing plant forms and, as he expressed it, even in plant forms that perhaps occur nowhere, but which *could* exist.[3]

The developed imaginative ability is the first step on the way to modern 'exact clairvoyance'. Many an artist has already developed this ability in part.

The next step (which does not necessarily always have to follow the one described above) leads to the ability of *inspiration.* This supersensible activity is related to what in the sense world we know as *listening.*

As an exercise, we can concentrate on intensive listening to sounds in nature, to the human voice, and to music. More and more we will hear what is behind the sounds, behind the words, behind the tones. We acquire a subtle feeling for qualities.

Some people have an aptitude that brings them into close contact with the audible world in daily life. A friend of mine, who was a cellist and conductor, told me once that as long as he could remember he had always been surrounded by music. The big problem of the composer, however, so he told me, is the technique, mastered only with the greatest effort, to place himself outside this stream of music, and then to transform it and write it down in the form of an orderly piece of music. Only with improvisation, music may flow freely.

Another example that indicates the attitude and life experience required to be able to really listen is a children's song, in which a child complains that father and mother have so little time to listen to him. The child then goes to the grandmother, who *can* listen, and the song then ends with the words: 'Apparently you have to be quite old to be able to listen'.

In ordinary life this 'empathetic' listening is a professional attribute of the psychiatrist and the social practitioner; to practice impartiality, tolerance, and equanimity are prerequisites for this kind of listening. Thus, there are professions that in the present time already necessitate a step in the direction of a path of inner development, but here, too, one can follow this path systematically and with perseverance. Then there will be moments when the *inner voice* speaks and says more than one knew already. A higher world breaks through, which can be distinguished from one's own fantasy or half-conscious aims. This path can be described as a conversation with one's own higher ego.

At a higher level inspiration leads to the ability to distinguish between that which emerges from our conscious inner world and what objective powers outside ourselves speak to us.

Inspiration leads to an inner certainty that can't be shaken by anything.

In imagination, *thinking* becomes a spiritual organ of perception, and in inspiration *feeling* becomes a spiritual organ of perception. The third soul force, the *will*, can be developed into *intuition*. Here, too, one has to learn to distinguish during preparation between wishes and desires that give rise to actions of the day-individuality, and the deeds of the second, or night-individuality. As a preparatory exercise it is necessary to practice courage and fearlessness in ordinary daily life as well as what is so aptly called 'presence of mind'. The latter enables one to recognize the moment for intuitive action when it comes, to jump into the course of events and do one's higher duty.

Taking action out of intuition (and this does not mean intuition as it is often understood, which is related more to an emotional-instinctive sense for doing the right thing) is not something that can be mastered at the drop of a hat. For years one can struggle with the question: 'If only I knew what I should *really* do' . If one is not prepared to suffer through this and to have sleepless nights, while being tormented by this question, one can not develop the ability to take the bull by the horns when it becomes apparent what one really has to do.

Intuition speaks to us out of the 'opportunity'. He who is unprepared lets the opportunity slip past, possibly unnoticed; he who is prepared, grasps the opportunity because it is an answer he has been waiting for. In intuition, soul-spirit man, the night-individuality, speaks to us through the world; intuition approaches us from outside! In a final conversation with a friend from his youth, Rudolf Steiner said: "Pay attention to the questions you are asked. *In the questions your karma expresses itself*".[4]

The path of development that leads to intuition requires that you prepare yourself to *recognize* questions, for they are mostly asked not in words, but out of situations. Only a few times in life it may happen that on awakening in the morning, intuition, appearing to come out of sleep, stands before you, worked out to the last detail. You are then shaking like a leaf, permeated by a will that far exceeds your own will, and in dismay you wonder: 'Why must *I* do this? It interferes with all my plans and wishes, it is too much for me'.

The highest intuition is described in the Bible as the episode in Gethsemane, when Christ becomes aware that He has to face the crucifixion and exclaims in desperation: 'Take this cup away from me'. This cry can sound in everyone's life, to a much lesser degree, but for oneself as real: 'Take this cup away'. If one drinks it anyway, one becomes aware that taking action out of such a situation also generates powers that far exceed one's own abilities.

In intuitive action, man knows himself to be the instrument for higher powers. Personal destiny has to be put aside. One makes oneself available for that which has to be done at that particular moment in cultural history.

What has been described here is concerned with the first steps towards imagination, inspiration, and intuition. What these three mean to a modern initiate, one can glean from the work and the biography of Rudolf Steiner. Many people are somewhere along this path, but in the twentieth century there has been no one who stood as fully within the culture and the knowledge of his time and at the same time lived as consciously in a spiritual world as Rudolf Steiner. His entire life's work, as well as his biography, are witness to the fact that he stood fully consciously in both the day and the night world.

We have already mentioned that intuition comes from outside, as opposed to inspiration, which comes from inside. The other person expresses for me my karma, my task in life.

The human being does not have to attempt this path alone. It can also take its course in a group of people who are connected in their life of will through working together, which at the same time signifies a shared destiny. I once called such a community a 'responsibility community'.[5] Each alone takes his own path of development in such a community, but in this he depends heavily on the others. All consider it *their* path of development to be awake to what the *other* could and should do. This can be expressed in words or by creating situations in which the other can become creative, and this applies mutually. An archetype of such a community is the Pentecostal community of the disciples, or the community of the Round Table of King Arthur.

Attention is directed not at oneself, but at the other. One helps the other, carries the other, and stands behind the other when he is carrying out his task inside and outside the group. Whoever has had the privilege to work in such communities, has experienced that he can work out of a totality even when he has to work alone somewhere in the world. He is, as it were, 'covered'.

Such a group has nothing to do with sectarianism, with giving up one's own identity in order to be relieved of one's own ego in the group spirit; on the contrary, it demands the greatest degree of alertness to the needs of the world, and a deep commitment to giving answers to the questions of others. Every insight, every skill of the individual is available to the entire community. It is the opposite of what I experienced in some universities among the people who worked there. They kept their thoughts and their results to themselves because they were afraid that someone else would publish these under his own name and thereby would steal their thunder. On the other hand, I also got to know research teams that worked closely together, at least within their specialism. The difference still is the common objective: What is your commitment? What is the task of the group in the world? In how far do you support each other outside the work situation, as striving human beings?

The new mystery path, which takes its course in imagination, inspiration, and intuition – this path on which the instruments of day-man, thinking, feeling, and willing, become the instruments of second man, or night-man – this is the way to the higher ego, to the 'self', which out of the world of night accompanies us on our life's path in search of the next step on the path of development, all the way through many lives.

The first individuality, day-man, has been formed from the past, from the karma of previous lives. That is why man is unfree as a day-individuality. He must accept his own past and take it as the starting point for going further in this life.

The strength to go on comes from the second individuality, the spirit-soul being in us that during the day is connected with the first individuality, but frees itself at night and from the spiritual world draws the impulses for setting its objectives. Each night there is a judgement of our deeds, each night we renew our goals in life. With that we wake up in the morning, but are distracted by the visual impressions and sounds of the sense world.

To become aware of the impulses from the night in day consciousness is a necessity for modern man if he is to keep sight of his life's task in this tumultuous world and if he is to receive the strength to keep realizing this life's task.

The external life history of day-man we call the *biography*. The inner life story, brought into the life of day by the night-individuality, we could call the spiritual history of man, or pneumography, analogous with biography. In this inner pneumography, karma becomes visible, not out of the past, but into the future. Man, who 'forever striving makes great effort', creates *his future*, which in the next life is again the point of departure.

This consciousness can awaken enthusiasm for going along the path of development described here. This is the more true the more one knows that every human being is being called upon to make his contribution to the development of the consciousness soul not for himself alone, but as part of humanity. The task in the consciousness-soul age is doing the good, and particularly in small matters of social life, between people. The driving force that inspires us to do this is the power of the heart, which unites with the world in love. The path of development is a path of the middle, borne by heart forces. Each step that one really 'wills', however small, is important, not only for ourselves, but for humanity as a whole.

A few people have the calling to perform historical deeds. We all have the calling to spread light and warmth in ordinary daily life. That is the culture of the heart that counts here and now.

He who lives in *Imagination*, sees in all forms the archetype.
He who lives in *Inspiration*, develops the culture of the heart.
He who lives in *Intuition*, acts out of the moment, and accomplishes the good.

Some practical viewpoints

In order to be able to go the meditative path described above it is necessary to create in the soul life conditions for a healthy development. Rudolf Steiner speaks about the 'preparation', which, however, consists of exercises that always have to be done *besides* the meditations too.

A few of these we will mention below. In the literature referred to earlier, they have been described in much greater detail. Moreover, the *way* Rudolf Steiner describes them is such that the reading itself is already part of the training. That is another reason for recommending that these books themselves be consulted time and again.

First of all it is necessary to develop *patience*, being able to wait for the inner processes to take their full course.

It is of importance, too, to ensure there is rhythm in one's life. One has to give new meaning to one's daily and weekly rhythms. To experience the rhythm of the year can result in a meeting between the ego and the world. Rudolf Steiner's week verses, which follow the course of the year, are of help in this.[6]

One has to find a new relationship not only with nature, but also with human culture. Without study of human culture, man today does not make progress in the consciousness soul. It is important to take note of human thought in subsequent stages of development, and to get a sense of the development of world conceptions and images of man. Only then you know where you stand spiritually as a modern human being, and where more work has to be done.

In this way, a feeling can arise, which gradually becomes inner certainty, that you are part of a large spiritual cosmos, in which each human being, with increasing freedom, also has an increasing responsibility for further development. This applies not only to ecological problems and abuse of natural forces, but in particular to the further development of human thought and the morality of the actions resulting from it.

In preparation for imagination, an attempt can be made to make *pictures* out of *thoughts*. Images are more meaningful than abstract definitions. Images always have a thought content, an emotional value, and a moral symbolic value. What our time suffers from is that it is these values that have been eliminated from our thinking. We must consciously recapture them. Then the images speak to us, and nature and the arts speak a new language, too.

Important exercises are those of the 'six-fold path'. They are often called subsidiary exercises (referred to in German as *Nebenübungen*) because Steiner recommended that they always be done alongside the specific meditative exercises. But you can also consider them as the *core* of the anthroposophical path of development because they have to do with the *human soul*, which is the 'stage' of the entire path of development. There they act in a health-giving way on the relationship between the ego and the soul forces of thinking, feeling, and willing.

The six exercises are:

1. Control of thinking
2. Control of willing
3. Control of feeling
4. Inner tolerance
5. Open-mindedness
6. Equanimity of the entire soul

When these exercises are carried out (they are described in detail in *Knowledge of Higher Worlds and How to Attain It*) it will be discovered that the first three can be practiced consciously as individual activities, but that the last three have to be practiced as part of life itself. Open-mindedness, for instance, can only be practiced in social life with plenty of human contact, in which again and again you are unexpectedly placed in situations in which you have to question your own prejudices.

On this modern path of inner training you may follow the advice of an initiate, but you are responsible for your own tempo, and for the sequence and content of the path. Gradually, an organ is developed that gives warning when you want to forge ahead too fast, or when you are too lazy to do what is necessary. This organ one could call the 'esoteric conscience'; it is our *inner guru.*

Once on this path, one meets subsequent steps and forms as if they suggested themselves, and one is always totally free to use them or not. If, however, you have decided on a step, you have to hold yourself to this decision (persistence); giving up frivolously causes severe setbacks and severe crises of conscience.

In our present western society, materialism has caused such emptiness of soul that many people are looking for 'fulfilment'. That is why our spiritual life is inundated with many old forms of spiritual development, from India, ancient Persia (Mazdaznan), Islam (Sufi) and Japan (Zen). They all offer, with more or less justification, solace for thirsting souls, or more peace, and success in business.

The position of anthroposophy in all this must be clearly stated, in as far as it is the only path that ties in with the development of thinking in the western consciousness soul. The aim of this path of development is not greater personal happiness or more success in business, but the awakening to an awareness of the responsibility we have for the evolution of humanity as a whole. That is why this path starts with our present capacity for clear thinking, as it has evolved for the development of natural science. From there, it leads to a future-oriented spiritual-scientific thinking.

Chapter Eight
ABOUT THE HUMAN 'DOUBLES'

If one can gradually give more form to one's life out of one's ego – be it as a result of conscious inner training or because of life experience – one will start to take more inner distance from some aspects of one's own inner being. We can start to experience all kinds of habits, character traits and 'inabilities' as something that is not part of our higher ego, but something we are stuck with, and which sometimes is quite annoying. All of these aspects of ourself can be added up imaginatively in a figure, a kind of shadow figure, which is not us, but which follows us on our heels. That is how the experience of our 'double' (*Doppelgänger*) arises.

The theme of the double has always played a role in world literature. Writers have given expression to the human double in many variations.[1]

In daily life, too, the double plays an important role. Not only are we up against our own unsympathetic shadow figure, this sinister partner plays tricks on us in social contact as well. How often are we blinded by someone else's double, so that we do not see his real being. Many misunderstandings and conflicts in social life are the result of the unconscious activities of doubles, and sometimes the most vehement and painful confrontations in marriage or at work are nothing but 'double-quarrels'.

In psychological counselling the same problem arises, of course. Client as well as therapist first show certain aspects of their double during the first meeting, and much has to be straightened out before the spiritual individuality appears on both sides. (We return to counselling in Part II.)

If one wishes to follow a path of inner development, insight into the manifestations of the double is of great importance; it is a necessary piece of self-knowledge. Such insight is possible with the help of anthroposophy. Rudolf Steiner spoke more than once about the double, each time from a different viewpoint, from which it is already apparent that it does not suffice to speak of 'the' double, but that we are dealing with several *aspects* of the double. All these aspects have one thing in common, and that is that they involve parts of our bodily make-up and our soul being that are not fully penetrated by the ego, if at all – in other words, something on which we do not have a hold with our (higher) ego.

We will describe seven different aspects. This overview is perhaps not complete, but it can be of help in distinguishing different aspects of our double.

Perhaps this approach can also make another contribution. The feeling that the double is something exclusively negative in character that has to be overcome, may be replaced by an entirely different feeling, which could be described as follows: 'My double is not part of my higher ego, but still belongs to me. It does not accompany me for nothing. The cause of its existence lies in my own being, in my karma. By turning its presence into a learning experience I can reach the next step in my development'.

We may distinguish the following doubles:

a. Our hereditary tendencies in *constitution*, *temperament*, and *character*.
b. Our *upbringing*, the indoctrination with a cultural background and cultural values (comparable with the *persona* of Jung).
c. The double that is formed out of undigested *remnants from previous lives*, which work in this life as a kind of interference pattern.
d. *Unredeemed nature beings* as doubles.
e. Certain *geographic* forces that have an effect on us such that certain (soul) structures considered typical for a certain area or continent arise (typically European, American, Asian, etc.)
f. Incarnation as a *man* or as a *woman* as an aspect of the double in us (compare the animus-anima issue characterized by Jung).
g. The double as '*guardian of the threshold*'.

All these instrumental variations are not what we 'are'. We 'have' them as a result of our individual past. Only on the basis of this 'crystallized' past a new incarnation begins, which every day again is a struggle to come a step closer to the ideal of man – man as we will eventually be. And this ideal of man is going to be an individual variation within the totality of humanity, just as in an orchestra harmony arises from many variations in sound.

This open future, aiming for an ideal image of man, goes with the future of man as the bearer of freedom.

a. Constitution, temperament, and character

What do we experience when we meet a fellow human being? First of all, there is the appearance, the physical body. In the appearance, the *constitution* becomes a picture in space. At the beginning of the century, the French physician Sigaud[2] described a number of constitutional types arrived at phenomenologically. He did this for the benefit of family physicians to enable them to recognize at a glance how their patients would react to acute and chronic illnesses. He distinguished four types; one of his students drew them schematically as follows:

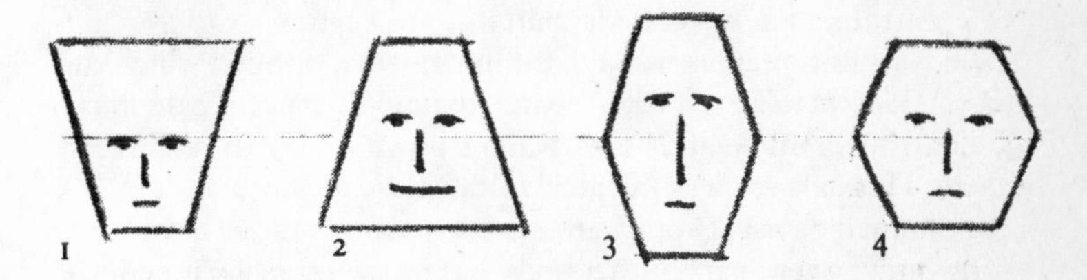

1. The *cerebral type* has a high forehead and a broad skull. The cranium dominates over the face. A line drawn through the root of the nose, above the eyes, lies below the mid point between the lowest point of the chin and the top of the cranium.
   The cerebral type is sensitive to all sense impressions, and has a tendency to digestive weakness. It is the intellectual type (Einstein!) or, with less gifted individuals, the administrative type. At a more advanced age the body has a tendency to chronic illnesses. Acute illnesses take a violent form, particularly in childhood.
2. The counter-image is the *digestive type.* The line through the root of the nose lies far above the middle. The jaw structure dominates. The belly and the trunk dominate, and the person likes to eat a lot and eat well. Obstruction calls forth explosive anger. The soul life is simple and oriented towards the material. The capacity for work can be enormous. Life's aims are egocentric, and particularly directed at gaining power.
3. The intermediate form is the *respiratory type.* Here, the long, frequently flat chest, and the middle part of the face with the nose structure dominate (Charles de Gaulle!). Respiratory types are socially difficult, wilful people. As children they are already exceptional.
4. Finally Sigaud distinguished the *muscular type,* with a balance between the three previous constitutions. The eyeline is slightly above the middle. There is a harmonious appearance with good

musculature. This type is lively, athletic, practical, a doer, and infrequently ill and healing quickly.

In these four 'housings' we meet the actual individual human being. At first contact and during relationships the constitution plays an important role. It determines the first impression of someone – an impression that can evoke sympathy as well as antipathy. It is an impression that makes the 'timbre' of the incarnation instrument apparent. The constitution determines, so to speak, whether one will go through life as a violinist, flautist, or trumpeter. What one will play on the instrument is, however, a matter for the ego.

The constitution is, as we said, the appearance through which the physical body manifests itself in space. This appearance is essentially threefold: head, trunk, and limbs. Rarely, however, are these three in balance. This balance was the ideal of the ancient Greek arts.

The human physical appearance is not a marble statue, but a functioning body. Every part of that body has its own specific functions; in case of one-sidedness in the appearance, the function concerned also dominates. Because the appearance is visible to everyone, one can draw immediate conclusions about the constitutional functioning of the total human being from the one-sidedness of the appearance.

The constitution, as an expression of old karma, dominates behaviour, health, and developmental tendencies in the first seven years. In kindergarten one should look especially at the constitution.

The biological functions express themselves in the soul as the four temperaments: choleric, sanguine, phlegmatic, and melancholic.[3] These qualities, too, are functional, and are not related to the personality. The temperament is noticeable a little later than the constitution, in the behaviour and in the manner of acting and reacting. The temperament is also the fruit of a karmic past.

The human temperament is caused by the structure of the ether body. The temperament is a 'figure in time', or a pattern of movement and reaction.

One can find out about the temperament by looking at the movements of a person. It is most striking between ages 7 and 14. The lower (elementary or primary) school especially must look at the temperament. Knowledge of the possibilities in temperamental tendencies is highly important for the learning process, as part of the total behaviour of the child. In their fourfoldness, the temperaments are an expression of the dominance of one of the four ether forces in the etheric body. The temperament is thus an expression, as it were, of the physiology of the etheric body.

The temperament comes to the fore once the constitution has matured. Constitution and temperament can reinforce each other or conflict with each other. In the first instance (for example phlegmatic-digestive, or melancholic-cerebral) extreme onesidedness can arise. The second instance can result in inner conflict situations that can manifest themselves in the behaviour. One has to recognize these conflicts for what they are in order to be able to deal with them pedagogically (and sometimes even medically).

The third element, which comes to the fore specially after puberty, is the character type. The character is the 'colour' of the soul structure, caused by the dominant forces in the *astral body*. This develops individually between 14 and 21. In this phase the inner life, and therefore also the behaviour, is determined to a high degree by this unfolding astral body as it has been passed on out of old karma. The astral body unfolds according to the sevenfold planetary qualities. That is why there are seven character types. In my book *Phases* they have been characterized as: the inquisitive, the thoughtful, the organizing, the caring, the innovative, and the conserving types. These six appear in two modalities, the active and the passive, or extrovert and introvert. The seventh quality is a balancing one. (In Chapter 9, about the planetary processes, we return to this typology.)

The astral body lives outside space and time; it is a *qualitative* structure, which is the basis of the life of soul and gives it 'colour', in the same way the key gives a certain character to a piece of music, regardless of how the music itself goes.

Between 14 and 21 the character then breaking through dominates over the structures of the constitution and the temperament formed earlier; they become more recessive, but continue to make their influence felt in the unconscious layers of the personality. They can also reinforce certain character structures, or work against them.

In the secondary school, and in the higher classes of the Waldorf schools, a working knowledge of the character types is needed in order to be able to evaluate and help the pupil pedagogically.

From the above it is apparent that constitution, temperament, and character have to do with the three bodies, the physical, etheric and astral bodies (called the 'sheaths' after the German word '*Hüllen*'). Behind these three veils, the individuality – the ego or 'self' of the human being – is hidden, having set itself new goals in this life. Most of the time this individuality is concealed. One gets to know the true spiritual human being only after some time, through many conversations, or in the course of regular contact. Sometimes, on the other hand, the personality shines through the veils and speaks to us directly.

Constitution, temperament, and character are formed out of the past, out of old karma. The individuality strives for a *new karma.* It is not content to rely simply on old attributes. It wants to add something new. This happens in life when the ego influences the three sheaths so that gradually they are 'transformed'. The result is that in the psyche, in the human soul, something comes about that is totally new. This striving of the ego to give the soul a character of its own is realized between age 21 and 42, in the middle phase of life.

When the ego works actively on the *transformation of the astral body,* something comes about comparable to fertilization of an ovum. The 'ovum' in this case, the astral body, grows into something new, the *sentient soul.* The astral body is directed inward towards the build-up, the maintenance, and the functioning of the internal organs, and becomes noticeable in the soul in the form of desires. The ego then directs this astral body to the world, and has it 'fertilized' by the sense impressions. This results in a rich inner life that frees itself from the egoism of the astral body, tied up as it is with the organs. With this, the ego has created its own soul instrument.

The sentient soul unfolds in the period from 21 to 28.

In a similar way the ego can have a fructifying influence on the *ether body.* The life forces are thereby partly detached from the physical body and form part of the soul formed by the ego. These ether forces bring yet different qualities into the soul, depending on the organs from which they have been withdrawn. This is how the *intellectual soul* arises from the side of the nervous system, and the *mind soul** from the side of the rhythmic system.[4]

'Mind-soul' forces have to be developed alongside the 'intellectual' forces, otherwise the intellect becomes abstract, dry, and bureaucratic. The intellectual-mind soul unfolds between 28 and 35.

Finally, the ego has to transform the (formative) forces of the *physical body* and make them available for the soul. From this, the consciousness soul is born, which particularly has to do with the moral objectives that can direct the will, so that the unconscious will can come to moral and meaningful actions. Between 35 and 42 this consciousness soul can start its development.

A separate chapter will be devoted to the development of sentient-, intellectual-mind-, and consciousness souls (see Chapter 10).

* In German '*Gemütsseele*'. No exact translation of the German word 'Gemüt' exists in contemporary English.

From the above it may have become apparent that that which initially has the character of a 'double' in our constitution, is gradually formed and transformed in the course of life, so that it can become the instrument for the development of the soul.

b. Upbringing and culture as a double

The small child awakens in its humanity through the forces of imitation. Totally open, it takes in all the influences coming from the outside: language, thought, judgement, cultural forms, climate, and nature; the buildings and living spaces created by man live on in the memory pictures and the patterns of behaviour.

Because of all these impressions in the first phase of life, a 'tentative' soul structure is created. The same individuality would form different soul structures in a western family from those it would form in a village in the interior of Africa. This tentative soul structure then has to be individualized in the middle phase of life (between 21 and 42) by transformation directed from the ego. The degree of success in doing this is, of course, different for every individual.

In the encounter with another human being, this (tentative) 'cultural individual' plays a very important role. Someone can appear quite attractive, but the moment he opens his mouth, the cultural pattern is revealed in the voice, and 'places' the person in question in a certain culture, class, or generation. The conflicts with strangers and minorities do not have nearly as much to do with race as with these cultural doubles, which manifest themselves in different habits, in language, etc.

Since the cultural double is tied up with the etheric body, in which patterns of behaviour are to be found as memory pictures, actions and reactions at this level are instinctive. The astral body, with its desires, can be controlled and changed by the ego. The ether body with its habits and drives can only be changed indirectly, via the astral body, which takes a great deal of time.

c. The interference pattern from a previous life

Constitution, temperament, and character are results of previous lives, 'processed' in a cosmic metamorphosis. Upbringing and culture have influenced the soul aspects in the present life. In addition, there is an aspect of unassimilated forces from previous lives that 'prowl around', as it were, in the present life.

At death, the physical body is abandoned to the elements of earth or fire. As a consequence the form the spirit has given to matter disappears.

After death, the soul-spirit being of man still lives in the ether body. This ether body is the bearer of memory pictures. These pictures are now displayed before the soul as one great life 'tableau' for about three days. Then the ether body (Rudolf Steiner speaks in this connection about the ether 'corpse', analogous to the physical corpse) starts to dissolve in the ether elements, just as the physical corpse dissolves in the physical elements.[5]

But just as there is physical matter that is not dissolved by the earth, specifically synthetic materials such as plastics, there are also ether structures in the life tableau that are so foreign to the cosmic ether world that they are refused and do not dissolve. These are, particularly, conceptions and feelings of a technical-material nature. Like plastics, they are the result of materialistic conceptions and actions. They remain in the ether sphere, undigested, but retain their link with us as their creators.

With the descent to a subsequent incarnation, the human being must pass again through the sub-lunar ether spheres, where he gathers an ether body for his new incarnation under the direction of the formative forces of the soul-spirit being. The soul-spirit being then finds the undigested 'package' from the previous life, which, because of its affinity with us, creeps into our ether body as it is formed, and there forms a disturbing element for this incarnation.

The soul-spirit being experiences this intruder during its incarnation path; again and again it acts as a sort of interference pattern. For ourselves, this double is experienced as tendencies, impulses, notions, and emotions of which we have the feeling: 'That is not me, but they still belong to me, I can't get rid of them. They interfere and they are annoying, and time and again they interpose themselves between me and others. These others see this double before they see what I really am, and judge me accordingly. I feel misjudged, I suffer from it, but always they come between me and my fellows even though I don't want it!'

This package is an island in the soul that the ego can not penetrate. For it has not been worked over in the metamorphosis between death and birth. By rejecting this island, by denying it, I only fix it. It brings grief to my present life, and only by acceptance of this grief can I eventually dissolve this piece of old, undigested karma.

In practical social life this means that for every person one gets to know better a second, unsympathetic person is experienced. This unsympathetic person has the unpleasant habit of appearing just when one thought that a positive relationship had been found.

Ether structures of this kind are real beings, in this case real 'ghosts' (as opposed to the astral beings, who are demons, these ether beings can be called ghosts). If one sees through them as *ghosts from the past*, which are most of all bothersome to the person concerned, one can push them aside in the encounter and begin to see the true human being of this incarnation.

These ghosts bring about discord, quarrels, and hatred between people in marriage and in situations where they work together, and hamper mutual understanding. They can be dissolved only when we can see through them and lovingly accept them as someone else's cross, which we can then help them to bear.

To learn to accept one's own interference pattern is a step on the way to maturity, and at the same time the only means by which the ghosts can gradually dissolve themselves.

In exceptional cases, when a following incarnation takes place so quickly that the old astral body hasn't yet dissolved, the remnants of the old astral body can have a disturbing effect. They become 'demons', and lead to possession, which can cause serious psychical disturbances. These disturbances can be resolved by calling on forces that have the power of metamorphosis, for instance through a Christian cultus or an intensively sympathetic meeting with a spiritual fellow human being.

d. Unredeemed nature beings as doubles

In the cycle *Spiritual Hierarchies*[6] (second lecture), Rudolf Steiner describes how during life man is connected with sensible nature, and also with the elemental beings that live behind this sensible nature as forces, as laws of nature, as 'causes' and 'keepers'. When a Spirit of Wisdom, a Spirit of Movement, or a Spirit of Form thinks, such a thought is a being, an astral-etheric form in the elemental world. These thought beings are exiled to nature or to the movements of earth and planets, and we know the effects they have as laws of nature. The banishment of elemental beings to the world of creation takes place for the benefit of the human being, who can develop in the world. Once he has completed his development, this form of earthly life will become superfluous, just as once 'old Saturn', 'old Sun', and 'old Moon' were dissolved in order to make further development possible. The central position in the entire evolution of earth has been occupied by man from the moment he himself became responsible as a result of his ego development. It is his task to relieve the elemental beings of their task through certain forms of insight and by the development of feeling and willing – to liberate them from their exile in the sense world. Because of the densifying process in the earth and the planets, a stream of elemental being continuously passes into a state of 'enchantment', of densification.

Rudolf Steiner describes four kinds of elemental beings, which each have to be liberated in their own way.

The *first kind* of nature beings we know from fairytales as gnomes, ondines, elves (sylphs), and fire beings (salamanders). By looking at nature, we absorb these beings, along with their activity. Then these elemental beings remain connected with us until our death. At death there is a differentiation between those beings that have been liberated through our spiritual work, through our ability to see through the 'Maya' of the sense world and being able to recognize spiritual reality, and those beings that have not been liberated because we have only stared at them with 'photographic' eyes.

The latter stay connected with us, and we meet them in the elemental world on the way down to earth for our next incarnation. We have to take them along, and experience this as a burden that is foreign to *this* incarnation, and yet belongs to us. Through wisdom we liberate them, and through ignorance we keep dragging them along with us, which makes the possibility to break through to supersensible vision more and more difficult for us.

A *second kind* of elemental being is relegated to the task of carrying the earth through the rhythms of day and night. We liberate these by being diligent, industrious, and productive. We tie them to us by being lazy, sluggish, and unproductive.

A *third kind* is connected with the lunar rhythm of about 28 days, with the waxing and waning moon. We liberate them by means of a happy disposition, contentment, and peace of mind. Through discontent and dejection they remain linked to us for the next life.

The *fourth kind* is connected with the year rhythm of the sun. They are summer beings who are banished to the denseness and darkness of winter. We liberate them by living with the course of the year in a religious way (weekly verses given by Rudolf Steiner are a help in this[7]). This means spiritual participation in the course of the year, and piety with respect to the processes of nature. We tie this fourth kind of being to us by living through the year in an unspiritual, godless way.

What does it mean if we have to drag these four kinds of elemental beings along with us – alien as they are, and yet tied to us? They are the heavy burden we have to carry along on our life's path. They give:

First kind: Emptiness in the experience of nature, even fear of nature (think of packaged tourism);

Second kind: Uneasiness, lethargy in the will, feelings of deep reluctance as soon as one has to become active;

Third kind: An undercurrent of discontent, of dejection, of being unable to really be glad and joyous;

Fourth kind: Inability to have any religious experience; this leads to hatred of everything spiritual, to aggressive materialism.

It is clear that the first kind hinders us in our thinking development, the second in our will, the third in the feeling, and the fourth in the ego development as a whole.

Who does not know of people who live in a cloud of melancholy or darkness, and suffer from this themselves; or people in whom an aggressive hatred rises up as soon as there could be a religious spiritual experience? There are those people, too, who project their own burdens and powerlessness onto their environment by blaming others, or circumstances, for their own heaviness and darkness.

This is an aspect of the double – these clouds of unredeemed elemental beings that bother us, weigh on us, and drag us down. While redeemed elemental beings help to reinforce the faculties of spiritual thinking, feeling and willing, these unredeemed beings form an ether configuration that under special circumstances can separate from us, and is then experienced as a being that threatens us, but is at the same time linked with us. In the life of kamaloka, after death, undigested elements of certain experiences also remain behind.

The beings that have been assimilated live in our karma, and bring us to encounters that can lead to karmic adjustment. The unassimilated beings weave themselves into the double, and give this figure its very personal physiognomy and its orientation towards certain kinds of problems, which are different for each person.

Should this story discourage us? No. Exactly by seeing through the being of this double it is possible to go to work and liberate these exiled elemental beings and, in consequence, also ourselves. The first thing that is needed for this is a deep sense of gratitude with respect to these beings who have gone into exile in the laws of nature for our sake. Elemental beings that were banished into the processes of nature are engaged in the material forces, but rightly so. Dragged along in our subconscious, unrecognized, they are a prey of Ahriman, who can wrongly use them in order to call forth materialistic thoughts, feelings and will impulses in man. That is why in this period of the consciousness soul these elemental beings become somewhat dark and coercive.

Yet the ego belongs to a 'hierarchy' that is so much higher, that as soon as it recognizes the double, and confronts it with courage, its sun force sweeps away the darkness and can return the elemental beings to their true cosmic homeland. For this, courage and enthusiasm for a spiritual relationship to creation are needed, which, among others, one can acquire through everything Rudolf Steiner has imparted about this in his *Occult Science – An Outline* and many lectures.

e. About the geographic double

In a lecture on 16 November 1917, Rudolf Steiner spoke in detail about the ahrimanic and luciferic doubles we carry within us.[8] Particularly the ahrimanic double is important to the consciousness soul period.

At the present, an ahrimanic elemental being[9] links up with the human being a short time before birth. It links itself to the bodily 'instrument' and permeates it in the same way it is permeated by the soul and spirit of the human being himself.

This being has a connection with the sub-natural forces of electricity and magnetism, and causes electrical and similar phenomena in us. Our own ether body works with the life forces of nature. This shadow ether body accompanies all etheric processes with electrochemical parallel processes.

What kind of being is this that makes a connection with us before birth, and has to leave us again before death? Through these beings, Ahriman hopes to permeate man with his cold, mephistophelian intelligence, and to inspire a technical world in which everything is controlled mechanically and electronically. These beings have an incredible intellect and a strong will, which works almost as a natural force. But they have no feeling, and no morality.

In 1917, Rudolf Steiner already said that these beings would inspire an electronic world. Now, 65 years later, we have this world all around us. These are the beings that inspire inventors out of the subconscious at moments of fatigue or illness.

All electrical phenomena associated with our nervous system, although they make the rhythms of the nervous functions visible in the electro-encephalogram, actually take place in this double, and not in our ether body. Yet it is true that they say much about the etheric rhythms, for they reflect the light world of the ether body in the subphysical world of electricity. Our entire biochemistry, too, is in fact a science of the function of the ahrimanic double.

All so-called 'cold' chronic illnesses, which arise in us from inside, are caused by this double. Chemical medicines, which themselves are the result of inspiration by this double, call forth reactions and side reactions that cause the symptoms to disappear. They do assist certain processes, but they have no effectiveness in actually restoring the functions of the ether body with respect to its light quality. These medicines are most effective against 'hot', feverish, luciferic illnesses. They are justified where they remove the immediate threat to life in acutely dangerous situations. The actual cure, however, still has to follow later, and that is a matter of the ether body proper.

Ahrimanic doubles are different in different regions of the earth. It is they that call forth geographic differences in the constitution and behavioural characteristics.

In the West, on the American continent, they have a particularly strong effect on the constitution, which manifests itself, among others, in the elongation of the limbs and of the lower jaw. The technological advances in the United States of America should also be seen against this background. Other influences come from beings that work geographically in Europe, Asia, or Africa.

The same goes for luciferic doubles, which do not at the present create such a spectacular technical culture, but are of great importance for our considerations because they call forth neurosis in the human being. They draw man away from his task here on earth, and cause him to float away, searching for personal liberation. They try to extinguish the ego by arousing a longing for old paths of development, a flight from this world. These are the forces that lead to sects, drugs, alcoholism, etc.

One meets the ahrimanic double on the way inward. It works in the unconscious organic processes, particularly in the nerve-sense system, and calls up an obsessive will aimed at intelligent control and exploitation of natural forces.

The luciferic double one meets on the way outward, in the temptation of ecstasy. In old, pre-Christian cultures the luciferic double was the most important. In our time it is the ahrimanic double. This double only connected itself with man during the Egyptian epoch as a result of the culture of mummification. This forced man to remain connected with the physical world after death, which in later incarnations led to materialism.

One should not look upon this only in a negative way; materialism *had* to come, as a legitimate world conception, in order to form the resistance necessary for the development of the consciousness soul. One must see these ahrimanic elemental beings that act as doubles in our lives in the same light. They are necessary for the development of the consciousness soul. This development is realized in overcoming this double. This means we may accept the stimulant for the intellect, but must at the same time develop a warm feeling life as a counterbalance, and a sense of morality for that which we accomplish in the world by means of our will. Only a culture of the heart, which results from the six-fold path in the anthroposophical path of development (see Chapter 7), lays the foundations for overcoming and liberating the ahrimanic double. What has to be avoided during this process is to come under the influence of the luciferic double, which wants to draw us away from our earthly and social tasks.

In psychotherapy, it is important to be fully familiar with these doubles, the more so since they work in the unconscious realm and often cause fanaticism in either direction.

f. Male-female problems

There are in our time many emotional viewpoints about being man or woman in a certain incarnation. This issue has to be removed from the realm of emotions in order to be able to throw new light on it out of spiritual science.

Many emotions already disappear when one knows that as a rule the human ego passes alternately through male and female incarnations. This means that in each cultural period one experiences the opportunities for development proper to that period twice – once as a man, and once as a woman. The choice of a male or female incarnation, therefore, is a meaningful decision of the (higher) ego, which is determined by the experiences in the previous incarnation.[10] To protest against this during life on earth is unfruitful, and denies us the possibility of really experiencing that which in this incarnation we *can* experience as man or woman.

The separation of the sexes took place in ancient Lemuria, the period during which the human being received his astral body, as a gift from the hierarchies.[11] Previously, in Hyperborea, man was still etheric-vegetative, with a head that was open to the cosmos like the calyx of a flower. Man was still asexual then, physical-etheric, and still in a situation where the physical still worked as a force and not yet as solid matter.

The division of the sexes signified the creation of two kinds of astral bodies: one more extrovert, directed outward, and the other introvert, directed inward. This was how lucifer could increase his power over human beings and make them more egoistic. But as a counter-balance benevolent gods created the necessity of a connection between human beings of the opposite sex for procreation. To this end, physical attraction was created as a first learning experience towards spiritual love later on, which is the objective of earth evolution.

In the course of evolution, the relation man-woman has acquired a three-fold aspect: Firstly, there is *sexuality* as an outcome of the physiological necessity for procreation at the physical level. Next, there is the *eros*, the soul aspect, awakening with the first infatuation, which changes the entire world; the eros pervades the entire soul and stimulates the sentient soul to have an experience of a rich inner world. And, finally, there is *love*, the spiritual aspect, which manifests itself when one has met the ego of another human being and wishes to connect oneself with the other's incarnation task. This encounter is the basis for loyalty to the other human being.

Man-woman relations based exclusively on sexuality are short-lived, for soon the novelty has worn off, and one starts to get annoyed with certain habits, i.e. the double, of the other.

Relations based on the eros last longer, but most of the time they founder after age 42, when the spiritual aspect of the incarnation comes to the fore more strongly.

Only a relationship built on a meeting of egos has durability and can stand the storms of life. But such a meeting of egos transcends the fact of being a man or a woman, and in principle is possible between any people. An encounter with a human being who touches one in one's ego is the greatest gift one may receive.

There are men in whom the female existence of the previous incarnation still has a strong after-effect, and women for whom the male existence still works on. This phenomenon should not be put on a par with homophilia in men or women. Homophilia has much deeper origins; it has its root causes in the creation of the physical body.

In the first weeks of embryonic development, the 'archetypal' kidney starts to form, out of which male as well as female organs can develop. Initially, both possibilities are there, but from a certain moment on, between the 20th and the 30th day, one of the two possibilities prevails, and the other possibility is held back. The remainders of the other possibility stay undeveloped for the rest of life.

The ether body is the formative, activating force that brings about growth. Wherever this occurs, the ether body unites with the physical body. There where a potential exists in the ether body that has not expressed itself physically, the ether structure remains as such.

Thus, every (physical) man has a female ether body and every (physical) woman has a male ether body – that is, physically one is man or woman, but etherically the opposite sex is present potentially. It depends, then, on whether in one's *soul life* one is oriented more towards one's physical incarnation, or whether one does not descend all the way and experience one-self more in one's ether body.

Homophilia is a problem of the human *soul* in its relation to the physical body and the ether body. Many homophiles feel themselves superior to others because they experience themselves (mostly unconsciously) as a bit less earthly. On the other hand, the incomplete descent into the physical incarnation impoverishes the possibilities for development in this life. But in fact, these choices and inabilities have a deep karmic background, which one could only judge if one were able to perceive the karma of someone else in a sesponsible manner. For as long as that is not possible, one does better to refrain from speculation and particularly from general statements about possible karmic backgrounds.

We already said that as a rule a male incarnation alternates with a female incarnation. Rudolf Steiner pointed out that individualities who receive a developmental task related to humanity in general, which may override their personal karma – i.e. leaders of humanity – do sometimes deviate from this rule because in a certain culture they can only carry out a certain task either as a man or as a woman.

In the ancient Lemurian development period, the woman, with her tendency towards the inner life, was the mainstay of the culture of that time, while the man was wild and boisterous. The last remnants of this can still be found today among peoples that still have something of Lemurian humanity in them. For instance, among the Papuans of New Guinea the matriarchy is still alive.

A transition from matriarchy to patriarchy can be observed in Crete, where the ancient culture was ruled over by female gods. The abduction of 'Europa' by Zeus – the beginning of a dominance of male gods – is a mythological image for the break-through to a patriarchical society, which continues until today.

There is certainly no future in a 'revenge of woman' or a reintroduction of the matriarchy. What the future calls for is the creation of parity in all social organs. Rudolf Steiner himself took the lead in this by composing the executive of the first General Anthroposophical Society on the basis of parity. Since then, unfortunately, this precedent has been deviated from, and all too easily it is said this is because 'no suitable women can be found'. Are there none, or are they not seen by the men?

Anyway, great changes are in the wind for male-female relations, particularly there where human individuality, the human ego, which transcends the incarnation that happens to be male or female, is concerned.

As spiritual man develops further, the moment approaches that the human being will no longer be born out of the metabolism, but from the creative power of the word. This also means that incarnation in hardened material bodies will no longer be necessary, and that the separation of the sexes will end.

g. The guardian of the threshold

In one of Rudolf Steiner's fundamental books, *Knowledge of Higher Worlds and How to Attain It*,[12] (which originally appeared as a series of articles), the 'guardian of the threshold' is dealt with in the last two chapters. The first of these chapters starts with the sentence: "The important experiences marking the student's ascent into the higher worlds include his meeting with the 'Guardian of the Threshold'." Strictly speaking there is not one, but there are two guardians of the threshold, a 'lesser' and a 'greater'. In the two chapters mentioned, these two guardians are described in detail, first in a narrative form, and then in an explanatory form.

When one wishes to go deeper into the guardian of the threshold, one would do well to read both these chapters, and also Chapter 5 of a subsequent series of articles by Rudolf Steiner, published under the title *A Road to Self Knowledge*.[13] The theme of the guardian of the threshold comes up throughout the work of Rudolf Steiner in many forms. In the third Mystery Drama, for instance, which is entitled *The Guardian of the Threshold (Der Hüter der Schwelle)*,[14] the figure of the guardian occupies a central position. But also in many lectures there is mention of both guardians.

For our purposes the following may suffice:

That there are two guardians will not surprise the reader who has come this far in this book. The world to which the consciousness of today is accustomed is situated between the two boundaries. Man lives in between two worlds that are each of a totally different character: an outer world with objective laws, and an inner world that is subjective-real for man. If one breaks through the outward boundary, in ecstasy, one 'sees' images; when, as a mystic, one experiences the inward ego condensation, one 'experiences' feelings.

The lesser guardian of the threshold meets the human being on the way into his own unconscious realm. It is a real spirit figure, one we have created ourselves. It is the sum total of our negative past, created in past incarnations as well as in the present one. In this experience, this figure appears as a frightening, spookish being, which bars the way to conscious descent into the unconscious parts of our being. If we should meet this being in full consciousness, he would impress upon us that we only have to look at him to know all that we have to change before we can meet the forces of the unconscious, dionysian world without being enslaved by these forces.

A half-conscious approach to the threshold already gives a hint of the imminent encounter. This expresses itself in feelings of repulsion, of depression, of disgust, and of fear. Since this half-conscious approach of the threshold is now part of our culture, these feelings are epidemic.

The guardian impresses on man that, should he wish to pass him, man has to be able to assume the task hitherto fulfilled by the guardian. He will now have to take responsibility himself for his own development, free of fear, and permeated by the 'mystical vow' (as it was called in the Middle Ages) to make every effort from then on to control drives and desires, and to apply himself only to positive tasks.

If one passes the threshold consciously, the guardian remains visible, and every error and every relaxation of a firm self-discipline become visible in a demonic malformation of this figure. The lesser guardian is the conscience accompanying us, but now becomes a deeply moving experience.

Rudolf Steiner places the lesser guardian before us, speaking: "Hitherto I only emerged from your personality when death recalled you from an earthly life; but even then my form was veiled from you. Only the powers of destiny who watched over you beheld me, and could thus, in the intervals between death and a new birth, build in you, in accordance with my appearance, that power and capacity thanks to which you could labour in a new earth life at the beautifying of my form, for your welfare and progress. It was I, too, whose imperfection ever and again constrained the powers of destiny to lead you back to a new incarnation upon earth. I was present at the hour of your death and it was on my account that the Lords of Karma ordained your reincarnation. [. . .]

"Visible do I thus stand before you today, just as I have ever stood invisible beside you in the hour of death. [. . .] I am indeed the Angel of Death; but I am at the same time the bearer of a higher life without end. [. . .] But I myself must provide your first acquaintance with that world, and *I am your own creation.* [. . .] You have formed me, but by so doing you have undertaken, as your duty, *to transform me.*"

When one has but the slightest experience of the lesser guardian, one becomes shockingly aware of the fact that all thoughts, feelings and impulses of will are realities, which together form an image (*Gestalt*). In the world behind the threshold, this image becomes a 'being', which shows its character in its physiognomy. Abstractions here become 'real' there. In Chapter 2, we pointed out that the path inward is a path 'back into one's own time'; the guardian now reveals to us the moral content of our past.

If we were to get to know only the lesser guardian, we would become mesmerized by our own past, and only find escape by avoiding further incarnations and in an egoistic aim for perfection and dissolving in a 'being-no-more', a nirwana. The path inward always has the danger that one is only concerned with oneself in one's subjective-real existence. This is what often happens.

On the path otward we break through the boundary with the world around us. That includes nature, but also our fellow human beings and the culture they have created together. The greater Guardian of the threshold now points out the world and the future. Without him there is no future. The greater Guardian meets us as a lofty figure, of a beauty that is difficult to express in words. This being gives us an inkling of what man will have to become in the far future; and this being speaks approximately as follows: "Hitherto you have sought only your own release, but now, having yourself become free, you can go forth as a liberator of your fellows. Until today you have striven as an individual, but now seek to co-ordinate yourself with the whole, so that you may bring into the supersensible world not yourself alone, but all things else existing in the world of the senses. *You will some day be able to unite with me . . .* "

The greater Guardian is the image of the being who strives to redeem all of humanity and all of nature. Behind that image we can experience the spirit image of Christ, who brings the redemption of the world. "An indescribable splendour shines forth from the second Guardian of the threshold; union with him looms as a far distant ideal before the soul's vision." (Thus Rudolf Steiner describes the encounter with the greater Guardian of the threshold.)

The first steps on this path towards redemption of the world are taken by having an interest for everything around us, which culminates in a penetrating, loving observation of this world. The phenomenological approach of Goethe is a shining example.

For the psychologist, both paths are of equal importance. His own path inward teaches him the language in which the lesser guardian speaks in dreams and sudden inspirations, in the 'organic language' of the inner experiences he is entrusted with by his fellow human being. He will then be able to take the frightening aspect away from this 'language' by eliminating the sense of alienation that the entrance into an unknown world calls forth. His own path outward, the intensive interest in and observation of the world, give him the opportunity to liberate his suffering fellow man from egocentric imprisonment by making visible to him the many tasks in the world.

The hierarchical beings man encounters in this Apollonian world outside us were called 'gods' in pre-Christian cultures, and the 'host of angels' in Christian times. Against the background of the nine hierarchical levels as given in Christian teaching, the guardian points out to us the task of humanity to become the 'tenth hierarchy'.

Every modern human being finds himself in the position where both boundaries are no longer absolutely closed, and that the 'guardian experiences' occur in many forms, often unexpectedly. One may take into consideration that each of these experiences is always an admonition to reconsider life from the viewpoint of eternity.

In daily life, a word spoken unintentionally, or an unintentional deed of another, can call forth a guardian experience. One recognizes this by the fact that such a word or deed touches us to the core and stays with us for some time. But all too easily we blame the other for having done this to us; mostly it is ourselves who use the situation to let our guardian speak. If one takes such situations to be an occasion for gaining a little self-knowledge, the following experience can arise: 'What was said there hurt – it is untrue, for that is not how 'I' am. But at the same time I know that is how I am, too, even though I wish not to be. What was said was so hurtful for me because it was partially true, but this partial truth I will accept, and I will work towards improvement.'

Not only inside and outside, but also past and future are covered up for us by our guardians. That is how we are allowed to see and to deal with only as much as at a given moment we can cope with, even if we think it is too much for us.

For both threshold crossings we need plenty of courage. Thus, there is a large kernel of truth in the statement by Adler that 'encouragement' is a central aspect of psychotherapy.

Chapter Nine

PLANETARY PROCESSES IN THE COSMOS AND IN MAN

Starting points

In the previous chapters we spoke again and again about human development, on a historical as well as an individual basis, and as a process taking place unconsciously as well as in the form of a conscious path of inner training.

In the rest of this book we will bring under discussion a number of *problems* of development (and possible solutions to them). These problems arise specifically in our time, as the result of the human situation described here. This makes it necessary to consider certain aspects of anthroposophical knowledge regarding the human being in some detail first; that will then form the basis for insights with respect to the psychical phenomena we wish to investigate.

This chapter about the planetary processes gives the necessary background for subsequent chapters, in which the viewpoint of the planetary influences will be further applied (specifically in Chapters 10 and 15). The concept of the so-called 'double planetary processes' was elaborated by the author in the early Fifties for bio-dynamic agricultural preparations, and was shortly thereafter also adapted to the needs of anthroposophical medicine. This resulted in a few publications in which, on the one hand, the activity of agricultural preparations was elucidated, and, on the other hand, the connection of the processes of illness and therapy in internal medicine.[1] Now, the same points of view will form the basis for a rational-spiritual approach to disturbances in spiritual development.

In every living organism, physical, etheric, astral, and spiritual formative forces are at work. Before we get into the activity of the planetary forces, it would be good to distinguish first once more, as simply as possible, the activity of the different forces we call 'physical', 'etheric', and 'astral', and investigate them with respect to their fundamental character.

When we speak about an organism with organs, such as a plant, an animal, or a human being, one already assumes that, besides life, there has been a still higher principle at work, an organ-forming principle. If one speaks about the plant, one speaks in the first instance about something *physical*, which is permeated by something *etheric*, so that it is elevated above the mere physical; from the fact that this living substance is constituted such that it has organs, that it is an organism, we can conclude that this living substance assumed a form through something astral.

One can say in general that every organism, from the physical point of view, appears to be threefold. In the plant this threefoldness manifests itself as root, leaf, and flower (fruit). This threefoldness is comparable with the physical structure of man as it appears in head, chest, and limbs.[2] In this threefold organism the etheric formative forces work as follows: in the root area 'head' the so-called life ether is active, in the fruit 'limbs' the warmth ether, and in the leaf 'chest' the light- and the chemical ether. The activities of the etheric formative forces are always generalized. An organ is never created through the etheric activity alone. This happens only when something of an astral nature is imprinted in the etheric.

The archetype of the physical configuration of an organism is therefore *threefold*, composed of a polarity and a middle part that brings the poles into rhythmical connection. This occurs only in a living organism; in a dead organism only the opposites are left, such as in a magnet. The living organism, however, is permeated by the etheric, which manifests itself in a *fourfold* way, as has been described in a book about the etheric formative forces by Günther Wachsmuth.[3]

The astral operating principle brings about a flow in this living physical-etheric totality, which in its archetype shows itself to be *sevenfold*. The basic principles of the astral activity are the forces of the planets.

These seven force principles are in a sense still of a general nature; they only tend to form the organs, in which they manifest themselves. In these organs, however, they usually have their termination, having pervaded the entire living organism.

The spiritual forces, finally, that express a certain species or *individuality, are twelvefold* in their archetypal formative nature – a configuration that is revealed cosmically in the *zodiac*. Only as the result of this spiritual activity 'the plant' becomes a rose or a lily, 'the animal' a lion or a wolf, and 'the human being' a certain individual.

The sevenfold activity of the astral forces relates to the activity of the planetary spheres. In human life they act on the organs of the body in a formative and supportive way (every night the astral forces help to restore the body processes[4]). At the same time they determine the soul structure. The seven planetary forces can be considered as specific qualities that permeate human soul life.

The origin of these qualities lies in the life before birth, or to put it more precisely, in the life the human soul has between death and a new birth.

From various lectures by Rudolf Steiner about life between death and a new birth one gets the following picture[5]:

When the human soul passes through the planet world in the life between death and a new birth, it absorbs in each sphere the specific qualities of that sphere. This occurs twice, once on the ascent, after death, through the spheres of Moon, Mercury, Venus, Sun, Mars, Jupiter, and Saturn, and once on the descent on the way to a new incarnation in reverse order.

Each time on the way up, man discards certain specific characteristics as far as the form these have acquired during the preceding life on earth is concerned. On the return journey he reaquires these characteristics, but now in a form that is required for the impending earthly life in order to give his future karma its instrumental foundation.

Midway between two incarnations an experience occurs beyond the planetary spheres; this moment is called the 'the world midnight hour' by Rudolf Steiner. This is when the decision for the new incarnation is taken. The higher ego of the human being is then at a point in his development where all ties with the earth have been cut. The higher ego is in a situation in which it has to make a free decision either to remain in the spiritual world as an incomplete spirit being in the state of development thus far attained, and to forget about further, arduous development, or to seek a new life on earth, and thus go a step further.

The former is the temptation brought to man by Lucifer. No one would at that moment be able to resist this temptation if it were not for the fact that at that moment the good hierarchies serving the high Christ-being present the human being with an image. They reveal to the ego the image of cosmic man. This is the image of what the human being will be eventually, at the end of his evolutionary path. This archetype of humanity, as the hierarchies imagine it, the human being now carries further with him as a memory. The discrepancy between that which one *is* and that which one *should become* gives the strength to resists the luciferic temptation and to decide to begin a new incarnation on earth. The human being then comes to realize that the path of development *on earth* is the only way to come a step closer to this archetypal image.

A spiritual memory picture, however, is not a mere image, but a creative force that accompanies us as a spirit-seed during the entire descent and also during embryonic development. This memory picture, this spirit seed, crystallizes, as it were, in the form of our bodily configuration, and sees to it that the fertilized ovum becomes a human being.

The qualities of the planet spheres together form our 'star body', our astral body. During its descent the ego gathers in each planet sphere as many qualities as the stage of his karmic development permits. Once the ego has gone all the way from the saturn sphere to the moon sphere, a new astral body has been formed for the coming incarnation. In it are embedded our possibilities and limitations at the psychical level.

In the subsequent earthly incarnation process (to age 21), the *character* is formed by a gradual release of this astral constellation, in our consciousness on the one hand, and in our tendencies to health and illness on the other. But at the same time the ego also works on the transformation of the astral body to the sentient soul and, ultimately, to the beginnings of a spiritually purified astral body in the form of the spirit self.

This means that in this transformation process a loosening from the earthly incarnation already takes place, and that in, and because of, this loosening process the transformation of the astral body can occur. In other words, man starts to die from birth onwards, and this death process becomes stronger and stronger, particularly in the second half of life, until finally it has gained the upper hand to such an extent that the spirit can free itself from the incarnation in death. This death for the earth is at the same time a birth for the spiritual world.

Thus we distinguish a descending astral stream that takes form in the world of space, and an ascending stream, which detaches itself.

Both streams are described below in their qualitative aspects for each planet separately, and also in connection with the activity of polar qualities. Finally, everything will be summed up in a picture of the incarnating and excarnating human being.

In further chapters, as mentioned before, we shall refer back to these streams.

The seven planetary processes

The seven planetary processes can be arranged according to the sequence of their activities as follows:[6]

		according to activity in metals
1 Saturn	outer planets	1 lead
2 Jupiter		2 tin
3 Mars		3 iron
4 Sun		4 gold
5 Venus	inner planets	5 copper
6 Mercury		6 mercury
7 Moon		7 silver

With respect to the inner activity of the planets, where we can distinguish three pairs of opposite influences, with each time the sun in the middle as a harmonizing, rhythmical element, we deal with the planetary forces as four processes:

First process: polarity 1 – 7	Saturn – Moon Sun in the middle
Second process: polarity 2 – 6	Jupiter – Mercury Sun in the middle
Third process: polarity 3 – 5	Mars – Venus Sun in the middle
Fourth process:	Sun in the middle by itself

The seven planets represent seven qualitative worlds, seven qualities, seven working principles. In order to get to know these, one has to entirely immerse oneself inwardly in the specific qualities, and get a feel for the impulses of the planetary movements in an inwardly sensitive way.

Saturn and Moon

Firstly, the *Saturn activity* will be described. As seen from the earth, Saturn is the planet that is furthest away, just as the moon is the closest. Both are gates, as it were: Saturn is the gate between the astral planetary activity and the spiritual influences of the fixed stars, and the moon is the gate between the planetary spheres and the etheric, earthly influences.

Wherever spirit wants to make its imprint into substance, Saturn has to give direction and incarnation forces. Saturn works from above downwards, accompanying each incarnation process from the world midnight hour through the gate of birth, working on throughout the first 30 years of life. It is a lofty process, for with the help of Saturn, spirit manifest itself down into dead matter.

In man, the saturn process works in such a way that, raying in via the back of the crown of the head right down into dead substance, it wants to make man into an image of his individual spiritual ego. It rays through the body from above and behind, and terminates in the skeleton. With that, the skeleton has become a dead image of the ego. The skeleton is so magnificent because it reveals to us this image of the ego. Should Saturn work alone, man would after 30 years have become a magnificent, beautiful stalagmite.

Saturn places us as a spiritual being in the world of space. He is at work during the entire development of man before birth. Helped by Saturn, the human ego turns to the earth again following the world midnight hour, and completes the painful journey of incarnation, becoming more and more densified.

During the embryonic period and during youth, it is Saturn who crystallizes the skeleton out of the watery organism. Saturn has a differentiating activity in the warmth element, which is the most spiritual element. Where Saturn dilutes warmth, crystallized substance (bone) is created. Where he densifies warmth, the birthplace of the carrier of the warmth element, the blood (bone marrow), is created.

Right down inside the physical, almost dead skeleton, the blood is born in the red bone marrow. This red blood then lives as such for about three weeks, and then disintegrates in the spleen. This makes the spleen the termination of the saturn process, and therefore the saturn organ as such, in which the saturn process dies.

We can, therefore, distinguish two saturn processes in man:

1. The incarnating saturn process; this leads to the dead image in space. We could say: through this first saturn process, man (the ego) dies *into* space;
2. The resurrection process of Saturn, which offers the ego the possibility to fulfill his karma in *time* in the blood.

Saturn is the planet of death and resurrection. The ego appears twice in the saturn process: once as an image in space, as the skeleton, and once again as a time image, living in the blood and expressing itself in the biography. When we summarize this once more, we can indicate this by two symbols: ↓ ↑ . Saturn brings the spiritual into the physical, but in the course of destiny leads the spirit out of the physical again, and thereby brings about the resurrection, the conquest of matter by spirit.

Saturn is the outermost planet. He encompasses, in fact, the entire solar system as such. He works spiritually out of the most distant periphery towards the centre. He can be active when he can work all embracively out of the periphery, not if he works out of the centre.

In the astral body, Saturn works formatively on the character. The saturn character is oriented to the memory of the original source of things, the arch-origin. One can call it the investigative mentality. It wants to know in regard to all phenomena what their essence can reveal. Saturn people are diggers for truth who have difficulty taking an interest in everyday matters. The danger is that they lock themselves up in their area of interest, in what in academic circles is called the ivory tower. They see the world with blinkers on.

The excarnating force of Saturn works in the phase of life that follows age 56. What counts then is whether one can gather up one's entire biography and run for the finish. This means sacrificing all that is not essential. The saturn force in our character brings resurrection in the spirit.

The second process to be characterized – the one opposite Saturn – is Moon. Moon lives wherever certain characteristics work through several generations. Moon processes work in procreation and in the hereditary stream. Moon lives in reproduction, wherever a new organism is brought forth from an old one, wherever one cell produces another, wherever there is development of cell upon cell, ever-growing, that is where the moon forces are at work. With Moon the essential thing is endless recapitulation of the same, the recollection of what has existed before. This is the ideal of heredity. It is the chain of generation, streaming out horizontally over the earth, living on in time, one after another.

Wherever there is expansive growth, Moon is at work – in the individual organism in the form of growth through cell division, in several organisms through reproduction. If in the human organism only moon forces would operate, man would be rolling around as a soft protein ball; the forces of growth would continue *ad infinitum.* The moon process in man, however, finds its limit in the skin; outside the skin its activity ceases. Raying in from the front in the region of the bladder, it works in the reproductive organs, and radiates through the entire human being from the inside out, through the skin.

Just as the Saturn process is the carrier of individual spirit forces and becomes visible in the skeleton, Moon is the carrier of heredity and becomes visible in the skin (notice how heredity manifests itself in the colour of the skin, above all else!).

People with strong moon forces have beautiful skin and are very attractive sexually. The movie star is the ideal moon type. The skin as 'moon skeleton' is the picture of hereditary man.

Moon processes have a differentiating effect in the life processes, just as the saturn processes have this kind of effect in the warmth element. In the embryonic stage the nervous system separates off from the skin. The nervous system is an island-like, internalized skin. This 'internal' skin is the carrier of the second kind of moon process. By means of this nervous system the external world is reflected internally and brought into consciousness as a picture. In order to accomplish this 'dead' reflection, the life processes have to be pushed back. Thus, the brain (a skin island in the human being) appears as the moon organ, where the moon forces terminate.

Physiologically, the force that pushes back the living cell division process manifests itself directly in the activity of tissue differentiation. The nervous system is the most differentiated of all; in this potential for differentiation the organism becomes an image of its spiritual archetype. In the plant, Goethe called this '*Steigerung*' (enhancement).

Moon, therefore, has also two aspects: one in which she flows in the tide of time, as it were, in the hereditary, reproductive stream, enhancing growth, stringing together one individual after another, endlessly repeating the same thing; and a second aspect in which she represses life and becomes a mirror. The moon itself mirrors the light of the sun. Silver is the substance we use to make mirrors, while photography is based on the ability of silver to preserve images from the external world.

In the astral body Moon has a character-forming effect. The moon forces create the philistine, the person who is interested only in externals and in the security of a repetitive routine: the conservative person. As mentioned before, this orientation to externals comes into its own in the world of film and television; 'glamour' on the surface, emptiness inside. The continuous play on the erotic element is also something that remains purely on the outside. The one-sided moon person has difficulty entering into relationships, always stays the playboy or the sex symbol; suicide is often the only escape route from inner emptiness.

The other (excarnating) side of the moon character leads to the reflective, abstract intellect, to the encyclopedic 'know-it-all' without any real insights of his own. Students know them as those who take down and memorize every word, but who cannot answer a question that has not been covered and requires that one think for oneself.

In the life of feeling, Moon can give rise to the wildest fantasies without any artistic coherence. This fantasy, too, remains empty of meaning, while the saturn person, on the other hand, gets stuck in his search for meaning.

The moon type is the *conserver*, the bookkeeper.

If one lives with the qualities of these processes, one sees how Saturn and Moon weave into one another. Saturn places the image of the ego, of the individuality, in space. This imagery represents a death process. Man then attains resurrection by writing his image into time, into his biography. Moon places the non-individual, the hereditary principle, into the flow of time, and the human ego overcomes this stream of generations by forcing back this stream of life and waking up in the image of the outer world.

Saturn I
Incarnation down to the skeleton, therefore death as an image in space

Saturn II
Excarnation – overcoming death by resurrection in time (biography)

Moon I
Reproduction – repetition streaming on in time

Moon II
Repression of reproduction processes through differentiation of tissues ('enhancement'), mirror consciousness in space

Saturn and Moon together weave into the secrets of space and time, of death and resurrection, of floating in the stream of time and awakening in consciousness.

Jupiter and Mercury

Jupiter is in the first place the great sculptor of the world. Just as Saturn creates a naked image of the spirit in the magnificent form of the skeleton, so does Jupiter sculpt around this skeleton the semi-soft forms in flowing beauty. These jupiter forms are the expression of man as a soul being. The plastic jupiter forms are rounded off from above, always imitating the vault of the heavens from the forehead down.

All internal organs are rounded off from above, often concave underneath because the organ lying below it presses into it. The balls of the joints are at the upward end of the bone, the sockets at the bottom end. The jupiter force rays inwards from the forehead, plasticizing the wonderful structure of the brain in childhood, and later forming thoughts. These are especially the kind of thoughts that create order in the great relationships of the world, and make these visible. Then again, the jupiter forces form the organs and muscles deeper down in the body.

Jupiter sculpts the internal organs and the surface of the body in great beauty, but at the same time with a superhuman, cosmic gesture. If Jupiter were to work alone, we would at age 14 all be beautiful Greek statues, which in attitude and gesture would be the expression of the pure soul element. We would all be Apollo and Venus statues. For the sculpting force of Jupiter carries at the same time within it a lofty wisdom. This wisdom in the magnificent structure of our organs is apparent in the forms that come out of the fluid element. But this wisdom-filled sculpting, too, would, if carried through, lead to a general rigidity. The human ego escapes this rigidity through movement in gesture. Gesture is the plastic expression of the soul in the realm of movement. This is the function of the muscles, whose forms give beauty at the surface of the human being, but which in their inward play of alternating stiffening and softening, of expansion and contraction, perform a chemical activity; in its internal chemistry this is closely linked with the liver. (The contraction of the muscles arises through chemical changes in surface tension, and wherever these occur, also in the plant, jupiter forces are at work.)

Thus, the activity of Jupiter terminates in the liver; this is the only organ in man that does not allow itself to be penetrated by the wisdom-filled sculpting forces of Jupiter either in its external form or in its chaotic internal structure, but which instead performs its own chemical activity.

The jupiter type strives for the larger picture in all he undertakes. Details are not interesting, or become important only when confirming the whole. The jupiter type always sits on a throne, so to speak, from where, untouchable, he overlooks and orders the world, symmetrically and according to the rules. This ordering has at the same time a lofty beauty, but in the excarnating stream the Jupiter type has an ensouled gesture, which one finds in great actors and conductors. The subjective soul life has then become spiritually objective and takes on a truly human character. As compared to the saturnian Schiller, Goethe was the epitomy of a jupiter individual.

Jupiter man is the *thinker*.

Opposite Jupiter is *Mercury* and its activities. While Jupiter brings cosmic order, Mercury produces chaos – not ordinary chaos, but a chaos one could call a 'sensitive chaos'. Movement without direction, but prepared to flow into everything where that seems appropriate.

Mercury is flowing movement, adjusting to every resistance, going around either to the left or the right, whatever is convenient, without an intention of his own, but always staying in motion. Movement and flow are the only things Mercury never gives up on. What kind of movement this is and how it flows depend on circumstances.

Mercury adjusts, but flows. That is why in man he is active in an area where there are no fixed channels: in the lymph and the lymphatic vessels. While the blood vessels have their fixed locations, the lymphatic vessels move as they may, as long as they reach their goal, the lymphatic gland.

Jupiter creates symmetrically, according to high cosmic laws. Mercury tends to the asymmetrical, the lopsided. Everything lopsided in the face, in the stature, and also in the plant, is caused by the fact that Mercury has played tricks on Jupiter. Mercury is a joker. He is always in the mood for jokes. He has humour, he enjoys it when the lofty plans of the gods do not quite succeed the way they were supposed to, and that as a result the gods never are finished and everything stays in flux.

A friend once said to me: Jupiter and Mercury can be seen in the image of the king and his fool. The king on his throne orders everything in wisdom. His mantle is symmetrical. At his feet sits his fool, whose attire is asymmetrical – half yellow, half red, just as it happens to turn out – and he makes remarks about the weighty words of the king and shows that things often turn out differently than one thinks.

Mercury is the great realist. He can adapt to heat and cold, to sun and shade. He ensures that in all circumstances life goes on, that the plant continues to grow, and so on. If pressed, he can even become dishonest, and seduce the plant or the human being to parasitism. The ancient Greeks made fleet-footed Mercury the god of merchants *and* thieves. Both ensure that earthly goods do not accumulate in one place but keep moving.

This inner adaptability would eventually lead to an absolute lack of character, however. The ego avoids this by meeting other movements with its own movement. What happens if two flows meet and merge? Swirls and voids are created, which for instance in a river cause the creation of sandbanks.

Thus one can distinguish a second organ-forming principle in the mercury movement. The organs arise through a meeting of two flowing movements. They are of a different form from those that are imprinted on the earth by lofty archetypes.

In the plant world one can clearly observe the interplay of these two formative principles. If one picks the leaf of a beech and the leaf of an oak, one can clearly distinguish the beech leaf as such. If, however, one picks one hundred beech leaves from the same tree, no two are identical. Then one sees the endless variation within the given form. Then one sees Mercury.

Each meeting of two active forces is a 'healing', a cure. True healing takes place only when one activity (the human body, or the plant) can absorb the other activity and turn it into a new one.

The mercury type is marked by what ordinarily one calls 'lack of character' because he adapts to existing trends without principles of his own. Still, there is some system to the lack of system; the mercury type does, in fact, have his objectives, which, one way or another, he tries to reach. The image of the travelling salesman who gets thrown out of the front door, but subsequently gets back in through the back door, illustrates this. In commercial vocations one does, in fact, find many mercurial characters.

In the excarnating stream the mercurial character has an entirely different side. Here, because of the ability to bring about meetings, a healing force arises in the social realm. Situations that have become stuck are brought into development again by making a new aspect visible. The physician brings jammed-up organic and biographic obstructions into movement and development again by bringing about the 'meeting' with the medication in the organism. Through meeting, a new future arises.

The mercury type is in his social dynamics a happy sort. A party without mercurial people doesn't get off the ground! The mercurial character, in its two aspects, keeps community life going.

The mercury type is the *innovator.*

Jupiter and Mercury weave into one another. The prescribed, wisdom-filled forms of the organs find in the flowing mercury movement their unique metamorphosis, adapted to specific circumstances. The chemical expansion and contraction give direction to the flowing movement of Mercury (by surface tension). In this interplay one can find all turgidity problems (state of tension in tissue).

With his plastic activity, Jupiter terminates in the muscle formation. Then this activity shifts to a chemical function, and in movement it conquers the plastic rigidity. In the wisdom-filled chemical activity the muscular movement draws on the liver, in which Jupiter comes to a chemical terminus. (This is contrary to the current view that the liver sends substances to the muscles; from our viewpoint one understands that the muscle draws substance from the liver.) In this fluid flowing activity, Mercury gradually brings the flowing tissue fluid together in the lymphatic vessels, terminating in the lymphatic glandular function. The lymphatic glands, as the terminus of the fluid flow, are the place where this flow leaves the body. Fluid flows throughout the body, except for the introverted air bag we call the lung. The lung is a gland, but a 'negative' gland because it is a void in the fluid body.

Liver and lung are the terminations of the jupiter and mercury activities respectively, and are thus the jupiter and mercury organs.

Jupiter I	*Jupiter II*
Giving rounded-off forms, leading to a rigid soul form	Movement in gesture, movement formed in surface tension

Mercury I	*Mercury II*
Flowing movement, leading to abolishment of any individualized form	Movement as a healing force, form through meeting of movements.

Mars and Venus

Now we shall describe the activities of Mars and Venus. Mars, the last of the outer planets to be described, is the carrier of creative but purposeful movement. He provides the thrust for the spiritual archetypal principle to penetrate the earthly realm, but at the same time to expel this archetypal principle again out into the world. Wherever the plant thrusts into space at its growth points, Mars is at work. He is the force by which an inner activity is carried out into the world, purposefully conquering this world and revealing the inner being. Without Mars there wouldn't be a single plant. Every form of budding and growing in springtime is a conquest of space by mars forces. A good picture of the mars forces is that of the spear thrower at the moment he throws the spear, and is just about to release it. The purposeful concentration of force in that image is a pure mars quality.

These mars forces ray into the human being between the shoulder blades and strengthen the human being in the iron process of the blood. On the one hand, they ray downwards into the blood, on the other hand they ray upwards in the speech. The force by which the word is formed in the exhaled air stream is also a mars force. The mars type, the person in which the mars forces are active in a one-sided way, is in a continuous state of activity directed outwards, but he exhausts himself in creativity and can not maintain that which is created because be cannot stand it that something would be finished and because he does not know how to take care of what has been created. Rather than caring for it, he destroys his creation and builds up something new. Thus the mars type is dragged along, and if one wants to block this driving force, one arouses in him a violent, hot-tempered anger.

The ego that wishes to resist being dragged along in this obsessive activity has to offer forceful opposition to this mars process, for Mars can not be controlled by half-measures. This process of resistance leads to a blocking of the goal-directed force, and then something happens that may be a surprise: when the mars force is blocked, the world begins to resound.

Think of the spear thrower once more: the spear whistles through the air and the driving force is blocked as the spear penetrates the oak or a shield. At this moment of resistance against the driving force the spear resounds. One can study the same thing with a string that is bowed. The force with which the bow is moved is resisted by the tensioned string. While force and resistance vie with one another the string makes a sound. Something similar can be observed by drawing a violin bow on a metal plate. When you sprinkle sand on the plate, sound figures are formed, which show how substance is ordered according to the principles of sound.

This ordering principle one also meets in chemistry. The ordering of the substances in chemical and organic compounds takes place according to these musical laws. Each tone has its own sound form. Because the higher hierarchies speak in the ether world, the substances ordered according to the elements are created on earth out of these cosmic harmonies. This cosmic resounding originates in the mars sphere and is passed on to the earth by means of the chemical or sound ether.

In the animal and the human organisms, Mars works from the inside out in the astral body, also ordering substance.

The forces of iron, working in the iron-carrying blood, in the hemoglobin, come to a termination in the liver. There the iron-free, green-yellow gall is created out of the blood colour, the red hemoglobin. Billirubin is the same as iron-free hemoglobin. In the creation of billirubin, iron is held back, it does not get into the gall. From this holding back this damming up, the structural forces for the formation of protein are created in the liver as 'sound patterns'. The proteins are necessary for building up the human body. Their creation in the liver is a resonant process, in which the substances of carbon, oxygen, nitrogen, sulphur and phosphorus are ordered into 'sound figures'. The driving force in this is the blocked mars force.

The mars type is the *entrepreneur.*

The active mars processes are the opposite of the venus processes, which work entirely behind the scenes. If one wishes to understand Venus, one has to become quite silent and learn to listen. Venus is connected with the deepest levels of nutrition (cell), with the deepest elementary forces, where available substance is absorbed by the life processes by means of a higher principle. Venus is connected with the creation of an environment, with making space for something else to develop. Sometimes one can find this capacity for creating an environment in homes where a quiet, modest, but inwardly remarkable woman is living. In such a home, meetings take place. It is a place for meetings of mind. A quiet warmth prevails there, in which even the shy person dares to express himself. If one wonders how this socially fertile climate comes to be present in this house, the conclusion has to be that it is this modest figure in the background, who speaks a few encouraging words just at the right moment, or only brings in coffee and quickly withdraws again. Venus has the ability to create space for something else to manifest itself.

Just as Mars is connected with speaking, so Venus is connected with listening. 'More precious than light' Goethe calls conversation.[7] Conversation is the harmony between Mars and Venus, with Mars being the speaking partner and Venus the listening partner, reversing roles from one to the other. Where Mars and Venus really meet, a third, new element is created – it is then possible for this third element to be present.

To become entirely Venus, entirely a vessel for receiving something higher leads to a total loss of selfhood; in an absolute Venus attitude the ego could not continue to exist. The process has to revert to its opposite again. The ego overcomes the building-up process by drawing off again that which has gone through the life processes. This is the function of the kidney-bladder system. Out of the kidney and bladder the breakdown and waste processes exert 'suction' on every last living cell. In the kidney (the venus organ) the venus process comes to an end. When ether force and substance are separated in the kidney, dead matter is eliminated, and ether forces radiate upward into the eye and provide the power to turn outward in the act of looking. In pathology, the secret link between kidney and eye is well known.

It is marvellous, this co-operation of Mars and Venus in the living organism. Protein, formed by the mars force in the life process, nourishes the cells via the path of Venus. The venus process, coming to an end in the kidney, brings about the radiation from the kidney, which on the way up unites with the directional mars force, and once more becomes noticeable in the power of vision of the eyes. For the power of the eye to turn to the outside world derives from the kidney radiation.

A wonderful example of Mars and Venus is presented in the musical instrument, for instance the violin. The bow provides the directed movement, the string resists this movement and resounds. The tone acquires real quality, however, only from the sound post of the musical instrument, which creates an environment in which the resounding tone can live; only then is it born as a living quality.

The venus type is the caring type, which comes into its own in the care-providing vocations, from nurse to nurseryman.

Mars I
Directed movement into space

Mars II
Sound as a result of the blocking of movement; protein-forming force; substance-forming

Venus I
Care for nutrition; forming the environment; a vessel for something higher

Venus II
Excretion; separation of substance and ether forces

The sun activity

In the middle between these three sets of polar, opposite forces is the sun process. Wherever Saturn and Moon, Jupiter and Mercury, and Mars and Venus are in balance – not in a dead balance, but in lively interplay – the sun activity is present. The archetype of the sun activity is *diastole* and *systole*, expansion into space and contraction into a point. This expansion and contraction, however, are not radial, but spiralling processes. The movement from centre to periphery takes place in ever widening spirals; the basic orientation is out towards infinity. In the contraction from the periphery, on the other hand, the movement is one of every narrowing spirals towards the centre; the centre is the orientation point. Those among the readers who have done eurythmy will understand what is meant by this kind of orientation.*

Thus, the sun has a dual action: now gathering up and centring, then drawing out to infinity. We can also call these activities 'winter sun' and 'summer sun', or 'night sun' and 'day sun'.

This sun rhythm can be seen in a particularly beautiful way in the human blood circulation when the blood moves from the heart to the periphery of the body, where it is atomized in the tiniest capillaries. It leaves the heart in a great arc, from where it flows to the periphery. On the return, it flows, first slowly, and then faster and faster, back to the heart. It then enters the heart in a swirl through a funnel in the right chamber. In the so-called small circulation the same process occurs, in which the blood flows to the capillaries of the air sacs (in the lungs). The amount of blood in a single heart beat, 35cc, is spread over a surface of about 120 square metres in the air sacs (a field of 10 by 12 metres). There it comes in contact with the air. The blood thus alternately meets the outer world in the lungs and the inner world in the body. Alternately the sun rhythm densifies the cosmos to substance, and again transforms substance to cosmic quality.

This physiological sun activity manifests itself in the soul in the form of extrovert and introvert soul activities. The human sun being irradiates the soul with *warmth* and *light*, directed alternately at the soul life itself and at the world. This breathing life leads to the 'conversation' in the polarity of Mars and Venus, to the process of knowledge in the polarity of Mercury, always present everywhere, and order-creating Jupiter, and to incarnation in the polarity of the spirit realization of Saturn and the mirroring, receptive forces of Moon.

The human sun being works in social life, reconciling opposites, radiating warmth and bringing light through insight.

*From satellite photos shown on television with the weather forecast, one can see how a depression fills up. The cloud pattern shows the direction of the airflow, in a narrowing spiral movement towards the centre of the depression. In the same way the airflow away from a high-pressure area moves in a widening spiral (although this is not usually visible because of the absence of dense cloud in high-pressure regions).

Summary

The activities of the planets are summarized as follows:

Saturn I: Out of cosmic distance, spirit works inwards and densifies to an impression in the physical, a process leading to crystallization. In the soul: the *investigator*.

Jupiter I: The jupiter forces play around these severe spiritual forms, rounding them off to plastic beauty according to great, high examples. In the soul: the *thinker*.

Mars I: That which is created is forcefully placed in space, and becomes visible in its growth. In the soul: *entrepreneur*.

These three together are the incarnation of a living organism. These great archetypes would like to place themselves in the world this way without reckoning with earthly circumstances. But the world answers, and receives and cares lovingly for what comes from above, meeting it with an opposite stream, rising up from below.

Venus I: opens the etheric formative forces as a vessel, and nourishes that which Mars thrusts into space; the *caring* soul attitude.

Mercury I: sets the semi-fluid living world in flowing motion, adapting to earthly circumstances as they happen to be, and changes rigid jupiter forms into forms that are feasible, adapted to circumstances. In the soul: the *innovator*.

Moon I: looks after reproduction, on a small scale (cell division) as well as on a large scale (procreation); it sees to the creation of chaos on both a small and a large scale in which Saturn forces can impress their imprint and in which in each cell the spiritual archetype can be received. In the soul: the *conserver*.

Together, the inner and outer planets under I result in birth and growth of the organism. The driving force through which these planetary forces come to intimate co-operation is the systolic, contracting *force of the sun*, which out of the wide periphery whirls through all of the planet spheres and leads into the earthly. It is the path of man before birth, and it is the spring and the summer for the plant world.

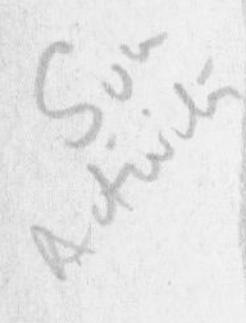

There is not only growth and ripening in the cosmos, however, but also wilting and withering. In this, the planetary forces are scattered by the diastolic, expansive sun force. This is man's path after death, the journey of the soul through the planet spheres. For the plants it is the autumn and winter.

In a wider context, this dying process is time-dependent, but on a small scale it continues at all times even during growth. For one cell, or one organ must die in order to let another grow. Life is a continuous process of decay and growth. Indeed, the excarnating forces are of as much value to the organism as the forces of growth.

Planet	Path of incarnation	Path of maturing
♄	Spirit seed incarnates; *the investigator*	Earth experience; is *sacrificed* to spirit becoming
♃	Plasticising of the form in beauty; *the thinker*	The *ensouled* gesture (i.e. the arts)
♂	Directed activity; inner world manifests itself; *the entrepreneur*	*Ordering force* through power over the word
☉	Giving warmth and light in the social sphere; *the balancing* human being	Will to excarnate to *spiritual striving*
♀	Hidden cell nutrition; the *caring* human being	*Excretion*; Discrimination with respect to the essential
☿	Flowing activity; undirected *the innovator*	Encounter; creates *something new*
☾	Repetitive cell division; *the conserver*	Cell differentiation; the *intellect*

♁

Earth: *resistance*

Incarnating and excanation planetary processes. At the left path of incarnation. At the right the path of maturing

The incarnating processes of the planet world are active particularly in the embryonic period and in childhood until puberty. The latter phase Rudolf Steiner called *earth maturation.* Only during puberty does the incarnating soul consciously meet the resistance of the earth. By overcoming this resistance of the earth, the metamorphosis from incarnating to excarnating planetary forces takes place. This is the process of becoming mature, which starts during puberty and becomes ever stronger throughout life.

This is why each (planetary) character type has a double aspect. On the way through the planetary world, after the 'world midnight hour' mentioned before, the soul stays for a certain time in each of the planetary spheres. The duration of this stay depends on the capacity, determined karmically, for affinity to the planetary quality in question.

Someone who stays in the jupiter sphere for a long time, and permeates himself entirely with this quality, will in life have the capacity for thought. Others pass through this sphere half asleep, and later on have little tendency to a life of thought. And so it goes with all planetary spheres.

Our longest sojourn before birth is in the sun sphere. There we create the design, as it were, for our physical heart with its individual, 'own' rhythm and the capacity for working in life with a 'sunny' disposition.

The metamorphosis from the incarnating planetary qualities we bring along with us to the excarnating qualities, in which earthly experience is *added* to what we already have with us, can take place more or less completely. When the metamorphosis is insufficient, or too soon, psychical syndromes occur, which can then be the cause of physical, organic disturbances.

In the second part of this book we shall go into this further.

The metamorphosis of the qualities named under I to those named under II will now be characterized briefly. With the aid of this characterization everyone can work further himself and learn to handle the character types on the path of development, which is life itself. In this way, the characterization becomes dynamic and becomes a key to the phenomenology of biographic development.

Moon II we have described as the process in which the stream of generations working on through time is thrown back out of space into time. This is a mirroring process in which the past can appear in our consciousness as an image. This image consciousness is the foundation of our capacity for combining thoughts in thought images, our intellect. If this intellectual, mirroring thinking activity is too strong, we have the basis for our materialistic, positivist natural science. If this mirroring thinking is permeated by other planetary qualities, however, then that arises which now is still called 'alternative science'.

Mercury II we have described as the form that arises from converging flows. In the psyche, this leads to the ability to have *real encounters* with people and with the world around us.

From this kind of meeting something new arises in the biography: a new interest, a new circle of friends, etc.

Venus II has a close connection with this. Physiologically, we described this force as excretion. In psychological terms this becomes *discrimination* on the basis of life experience. This is discrimination between what is of real essence and what is not, for instance in friendships, or choice of areas of interest.

Mars II was described as a blocked resounding process, in which the order of matter becomes visible in the substance of protein. It is a living, substance-ordering process. This ordering process, however, only comes to rest in dying substance. Young protein in full life is a whirling, chaotic process. Only dying protein has acquired its chemical formula. The substances that are created become less and less mobile, and then assume their more dense material character.

The incarnating mars force becomes audible in the word that gives expression to what lives in the human being. In the excarnating stream this becomes an ordering force in the social sphere. It is the ability to make one's intentions known in a few, well-chosen words. If this Mars II force is too weak, you see the appearance of 'phrase-making' and of 'sloganeering'.

Jupiter II manifests itself in *ensouled movement*, in the personal gesture by which man becomes visible in social life as a personality. This ensouled movement becomes visible especially in the arts, for instance in eurythmy and in painting. Drama is based entirely on the ensouled gesture.

Saturn II is the force of resurrection out of the world of space into the world of time. This is completed fully at death. Before this, Saturn II determines the ability to bring sacrifice as a basis for the metamorphosis of earthly experience to spiritualization. Egoism, the inability to make sacrifices, is characteristic for a weak Saturn II activity.

In closing, it has to be said once again that the planet I processes bring forces out of the past, which work on like clockwork. But the planet II forces have to be mastered consciously by man in a spiritual development aimed at the future. This is the process of becoming mature (see also my book *Phases*),

The planetary qualities can be characterized in yet another way, namely as soul moods with which one approaches the world.

This results in the following scheme according to Rudolf Steiner's lectures *Human and Cosmic Thought*.[8]

The saturn individual tends to gnosticism
The jupiter individual tends to logic
The mars individual tends to voluntarism
The sun individual tends to empiricism
The venus individual tends to mysticism
The mercury individual tends to transcendentalism
The moon individual tends to occultism

If one goes deeper into these soul attitudes, one finds the correlation with the characterization given above. If, for instance, one has a moon character, which tends to occultism, one has to be extra careful not to fix the spiritual reality in abstract systems and thereby rob it of life. The ensouled power of Jupiter can in that case bring life again.
We have described the sun process as contracting and expanding spiral movement:

The point of turn-around from the incarnating to the excarnating stream lies there where the sun qualities meet and penetrate the earth. The essence of the earth forces, however, is *resistance.* It is because of this resistance that in a (relatively) short period between birth and death both streams can interweave with one another, and both work simultaneously in rhythmical co-operation (breath and heartbeat).

The secret of bodily and spiritual health lies in the proper interweaving of incarnation and excarnation, which is specific for each age.

Summed up in a drawing:

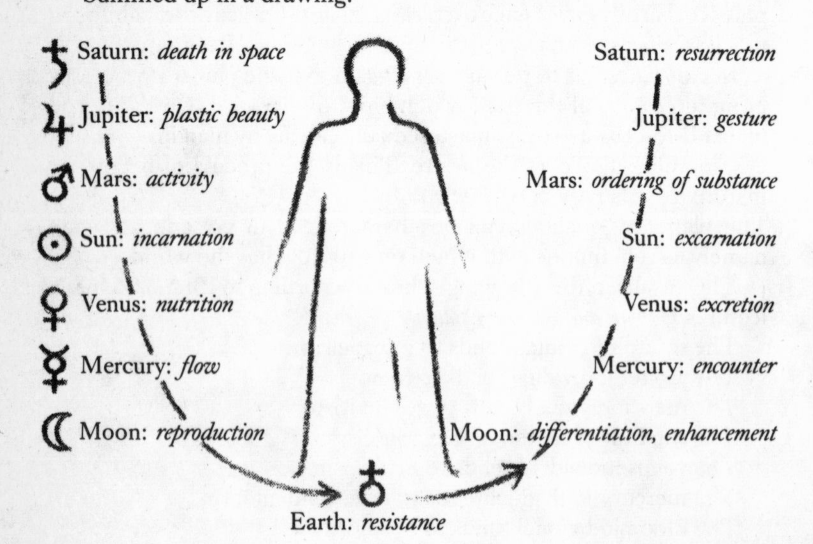

Chapter Ten
THE DEVELOPMENT OF THE SENTIENT SOUL, INTELLECTUAL SOUL AND CONSCIOUSNESS SOUL

In the life of soul, many forms of development occur that are too slow (retarded) or too fast (accelerated). This always results in irregular development of the three soul qualities already mentioned in Chapter 8 under *a*, sentient soul, intellectual-mind soul and consciousness soul. Modern man has to develop these qualities in order to be able to function in his time, 'inward' in the experience of himself as well as 'outward' in the experience of the world and his fellow men.

In a lecture of 1910[1], Rudolf Steiner describes the situation of these soul forces vis-a-vis the bodily forces in connection with the planetary activities in man.

In his conscious life, man is a *being of the middle.* Rudolf Steiner used the term 'self' for the every-day ego experience in the soul. This self is a composition of conceptions, memories, feelings, aspirations, and impulses, in which the memory in particular looks after continuity in the experience of self.

A healthy daily life has its roots in the forces of the middle; in terms of the planetary forces, this middle quality is the activity of the sun, indicated in the diagram on the next page by the word 'sun-self'.

As soon as consciousness deviates too much either upwards or downwards, abnormal states of consciousness arise. These remain abnormal and disturbing as long as the human being is not able to restore the inner balance by means of a strengthening of the opposite pole (through intentional inner development or through life itself).

In essence we can in this representation of the soul qualities recognize the two paths again: the path outwards (the world of planet qualities above the sun) and the path inwards into the body (the world of planet qualities below the sun).

In this chapter we shall throw some light on a few aspects of the development of these soul qualities from the viewpoint of the seven planetary forces dealt with in the previous chapter.

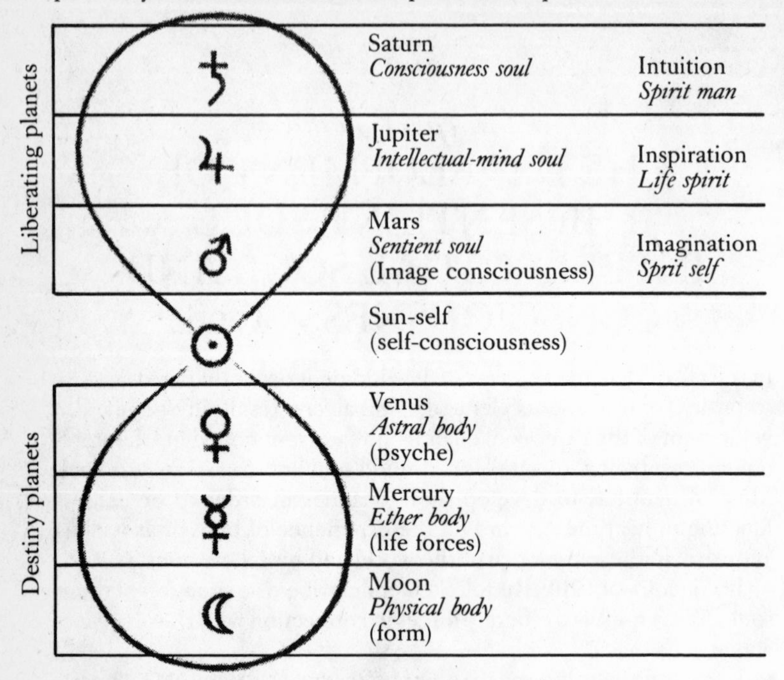

The development of the sentient soul

The astral body, a qualitative '*Gestalt*' (form) outside time and space, is the bearer of consciousness. In this respect it is the microcosmic representation of the planet world within ourselves. When we say: 'That is a nice, pleasant colour', this is an activity of the soul. When this sentient soul has been freed by the ego from the subjectivity of the feelings of sympathy and antipathy, and of the life of desires of the astral body, and has been raised to the level of objective, purely spiritual experience, the day-to-day sun-self has been developed to spirit self. In their culture, the ancient Greeks called this purified astral body and this purified sentient soul the 'Golden Fleece', and they spoke of the 'golden lustre' of the purified astral body.

Astral *body* (or sentient body), sentient *soul*,and *spirit* self are three levels of the human life of consciousness. This also applies to the triad ether *body*, intellectual-mind *soul*, and life *spirit*, and for the physical *body*, consciousness *soul*, and *spirit* man, which we shall deal with later on.

If we now examine the diagram given by Rudolf Steiner, we can see how the astral body and the sentient soul are quite close to the middle, to the sun-self.

The astral body is active in us out of the venus qualities in the metabolism. The venus quality is the 'caring' one; Rudolf Steiner speaks about 'inner cell nutrition' as the bodily venus quality. If connected with the middle, with the self, this is where the sense impressions come to consciousness. This consciousness is still animalistic, and does not rise above what the animals have (a bit of information that will gratify the ethologists, who want to insist the human being has nothing more than this animalistic consciousness).

The consciousness of this astral body is entirely in the service of bodily protection, nutrition, and reproduction. The animal lives totally in this element. In man, however, something has developed we call 'culture'. The consciousness can let go of the exclusively animalistic functions and create an inner world of conceptions, feelings, and will impulses – a *soul world.* To this end the animalistic consciousness has to be permeated with qualities out of the liberating, outer planets. That is why the mars quality connects itself as a cosmic soul quality with the sun-self. This sun-self becomes a first stage in the the development of a psychical or soul consciousness. The sun-self, therefore, has a connection with the animalistic astral body down below, and with the liberating astrality up above. This liberating activity is a mars activity.

The development of this inner soul world took place for the first time in human history during the Egyptian-Babylonian culture period[2] (other cultures developed in parallel at the same time). Previously one still lived exclusively in the forces of the ether and astral bodies. These, nevertheless, were still not animalistic because they were permeated by higher beings in order to prepare the soul for the development of an individual inner world. At that time, the astral body worked 'above', as a function of consciousness in the nerve-sense system, only to provide the foundation for the sentient soul later on, which was to be free of the body, The astral body also worked 'below' in the metabolism, as the force that formed the organs and the impulse for various functions. And it worked in the force of memory – the ability to read earlier sense impressions left behind as imprints in the ether body. The power of recall could not at that time be used at will, but was tied to new sense impressions of a similar nature. Wherever something important took place, a stone was erected, for instance, which called up the memory of what had happened whenever it was seen. (With young children we still know this so-called 'local memory'.)

Only when the astral body becomes 'body-free' in the upper pole, the foundation is laid for development of the sentient soul, in which memories can be called up personally. Still, for a long time, rhythmical repetition was needed to activate this memory. Because of this 'rhythmic memory', the great epics and mythologies of humanity were preserved for a long time; a good example is the Finnish epic *Kalewala.*

Irregularities in the development of the astral body and the sentient soul are, among others, the following:

– The upper part of the astral body, which serves consciousness, intervenes too strongly in the lower part. A heightened consciousness then arises below, and we call this 'pain' .

– The lower part of the astral body works too strongly in the upper part. This gives rise to a lowering of consciousness, dullness, or even unconsciousness.

– The freeing of the astral forces from the physical upper pole is insufficient, and the sentient soul develops insufficiently. This means the human being stays primitive-animalistic, tied to his organic drives. This can also occur partially, as in hysteria (see also chapter 16).

– The freeing of the astral forces from the physical upper pole occurs too early. This leads to accelerated development in children, and gives rise to precocious children and child-prodigies. They run the danger of having their astral forces loosened before the organs are full- grown and mature. Later, this gives rise to insufficiency phenomena up to and including complete collapse of the soul life in schizophrenia.

– The freeing occurs not only 'above' but also 'below' in the metabolism. Then, unfamiliar and frightening experiences arise in the middle (the self) This is when the inward threshold becomes undependable, with all the related symptoms, as already described. The organic forces then experienced are frightening because they cannot be 'placed', just as an unrecognized sound or shadow in the dark is frightening. As soon as one knows what the sound or shadow means, the fear disappears. The therapy related to the crossing of the inward threshold has the aim to make the unfamiliar experiences recognizable. Then they seem less threatening. This is possible only by means of a science that acknowledges the reality of soul and spirit in their bodily manifestation.

– The 'freeing' above goes further than is necessary for the foundation of the soul life. There is a surplus of free astral forces, which merge directly with the cosmic astral qualities of the planets. Then, too, experiences arise, now quite intensive ones, which are described as whirling colours, blinding light, or horrifying darkness and destruction.

The development of the intellectual-mind soul

All of these irregularities in development can arise with the first form of soul development, the humanizing process that raises man above the animalistic level. In the course of human evolution, the process of liberating the psychical forces from the physical has gone further, however.

The next step was to make forces of the *ether body* free in the upper pole. On the basis of these forces, new qualities could be developed in the sun-self – those of the intellectual and mind *soul*. The qualities of the sentient soul are by their very nature a unified whole, bundled, as it were, in the middle, which is close by. In the freeing of the ether body, forces arise that lie further away from the middle. To work on these by means of the day-to-day self requires greater effort.

The intellectual soul develops in the field of tension between the capacity for independent thought in the upper pole and the 'stream of life' of the ether body in the bodily nature of the lower pole – in other words, in the polarity of Jupiter and Mercury. Jupiter represents the ordering cosmic forces that can give the thinking its certainty. Mercury represents the flow of life forces that permeate the All and, if they are not directed, can lead to life running wild.

Order and randomness form the polarity in which the intellectual soul must develop. This is why such a development has a double aspect.

The first aspect is that in which the jupiter forces predominate; this occurred in ancient Greece in a fruitful way with the development of philosophy. In late scholasticism it had taken a withered, abstract form.

The second part of the intellectual soul Rudolf Steiner called the '*Gemütsseele*' (usually translated in English to 'mind soul'). Here the mercurial flow of life predominates, which can mirror itself in all its richness and fruitfulness in the sun-self. The mind soul flourished in the Middle Ages as mysticism. It came to expression in the form of the bourgeois social culture at the beginning of the New Age. The mind soul represents the social pole, opposite the pole of thought of the intellectual soul. Intellectual soul without mind soul leads to intellectualism. Mind soul without intellectual soul leads to social chaos.

From this consideration the importance of the double aspect of the intellectual-mind soul is apparent. *The soul lives in the middle.* The sun-self, the soul, must unite the forces of thoughtful order and life-giving social forces. This does not happen by itself. New, extra forces have to be developed in the self. In ancient Greece, this took place through the arts (especially through music and dance, which were cultivated in educational institutions for adolescents). In the Middle Ages it was done by the church cultivation of piety and the power of faith. Faith and piety had a developmental task during the period of intellectual-soul development. In our times this is still of importance in youth and adolescence. Afterwards, new forces have to be activated to be able to develop consciousness. For this, the power of faith is not enough.

Disturbances in the development of the intellectual and mind soul can show up in the following ways:

— The intellectual capacities are stimulated between age 7 and 14 without the mind-soul forces. This is what happens in an abstract, in-artistic educational approach. Later on this creates unimaginative, anaemic thinking.

— In the second period of seven years, no reverence or religious feeling is called up in the sun-self. As a result, the self lacks the power to unify thought and life forces. Intellectual and mind soul break apart. Random social forces work in the soul in a chaotic way, or can lead to violence or acts of terrorism, led by abstract utopian thinking. These are phenomena we see increasingly.

— The chaotic life forces work strongly in the self, with under-developed thinking forces. Then a vague, mystical quest for the truth arises, which is an easy mark for any kind of mysterious sect. These kinds of people are often seen as well-meaning muddleheads, but they are by no means harmless when they act in groups, which can be organized by characters who are after economic power.

— The life forces are too weak in the middle, the self. In that case a sentient soul still develops, via the astral body, but no mind soul. This is the phenomenon of the psychasthenic constitution, with continual breakdowns in case of any kind of stress.

One can gain a total picture if one understands the interplay of intelligence, social life stream, and middle. From this, the degree to which prevention is needed on the one hand, and therapy on the other, is readily apparent. Many of the basic principles of Waldorf education at the primary level become understandable. Their importance for the creation of a healthy middle sphere, with the intellectual and mind soul as helping forces in life, becomes clear. These principles include reverence and religious feeling, artistic education, and development of the intellect in the right tempo, that is, not too early, but then vigorously in the higher grades afterwards.

The development of the consciousness soul

The development of the consciousness soul has to bridge a still greater span between the saturn forces and the moon forces. Especially here, something has to be done to give sufficient strength to the middle to bring the two extremes together. Strengthening of the middle, indeed, is not enough by itself. Conditions will have to be created from the outside by means of social structures and institutions that will support the unifying powers of the middle. While the intellectual-mind soul could be seen as having a double aspect, the consciousness soul requires a threefold approach to be able to develop in a healthy way. Here in particular, it is a case of the soul living in the middle.

In his *Letters about the Aesthetic Education of Man*,[3] Schiller described his well-known threefold idea of the Drive of Form (*Formstrieb*), Drive of Play (*Spieltrieb*) and Drive of Matter (*Stofftrieb*). These Letters are so important precisely because they represent the first clear exposition of threefold man and threefold society. Previously there had been a theological concept of threefoldness, but only as a basis for faith (dogma) and not as a basis for understanding the threefold nature of the human being.

Schiller was the first to describe *man* as a threefold being, and to link this with the social life in which this threefold being appears: as a barbarian (Drive of Form dominates), or as a savage (Drive of Matter dominates). Since he wrote these Letters during the beginning of the French Revolution, he had a direct demonstration of his vision. He was able to predict that when the savagery of the revolution was spent, the barbarism of what we now call dictatorship would raise its head as a counter-image. He wrote: "The French Revolution has disappointed me. It has deviated – which it did not have to – into two areas in which man loses his freedom. Its demise can, therefore, already be predicted. It is still being applauded, but a man will come who shall tread it underfoot. And he will not only set himself up as a ruler over France, but probably also over the greater part of Europe. I do not know him, but he must have been born already." Thus Schiller foresaw the appearance of Napoleon.

Schiller was of the opinion that the aberration of the French Revolution did not have to occur. From all of his work it is apparent that he blames the fact that the middle sphere was too weak, that the sense of true humanity was too weak. He expresses this in the words: "Man plays only there where he is truly human, and is truly human only where he plays". What this points to is the sovereign importance of the middle, of that part of man where he 'plays' with form and matter, which is where he gains his freedom.

In the middle, man is always an artist. The artists Schiller held in the highest esteem were the 'artists of state' and the 'pedagogical artists', for their medium is that which is the highest expression of creation, man himself.

The consciousness soul has to awaken the saturn force. This is the force that enables the spirit to express itself within matter and make it into a spiritual image. In the human body, this is the formation of the skeleton. "The skeleton is the dead image of the ego", (Rudolf Steiner).[4]

The saturn force works in man from the world midnight hour onwards, and gives the impulse for incarnation all the way to the formation of the skeleton. But at the same time, Saturn does not only lead to death, but also to resurrection, in which the spirit loosens itself from matter again, and strives towards the next world midnight hour. On this path the experience of this life is turned into new capacities for the next life.

On the other hand, the moon forces manifest themselves in the stream of generations, in which life is passed on in time. Saturn and Moon set the limits in the cosmos.

The consciousness soul has to face up to this enormous potential. For this a middle realm is needed that has the forces to reach from one world midnight hour to the next – in other words, the consciousness of an initiate. As long as we do not yet have such consciousness, we need help, but not from hierarchical beings this time, who would make us dependent and unfree, but from social institutions that help to support the threefoldness of the consciousness soul. This is the background for Rudolf Steiner's threefold social order of the social organism.[5]

On a small scale, we can learn to distinguish in our lives between the spirit life, the social life and the working life. We try to avoid one-sidedness, and to involve in each of these areas the other two as well. We also try to see to it that there is a healthy, rhythmical change in our activities.

One-sidedness in this area can cause the following common problems:

— The spirit life dominates in a one-sided way. This gives rise to the fanatic (the barbarian of Schiller), who persecutes all 'heretics' and burns them at the stake.

— The spirit life can be developed too early. This is what one finds in young geniuses, who, unfortunately, are admired by many, and are challenged to high achievement at too early an age. The saturnian force with which the spirit incarnates in these cases seldom leads to a harmonious development later on. It more often leads to disappointment and periods of exhaustion and unproductiveness. If these tendencies are accompanied by a saturnian death wish, the danger is acute. In such cases, a warm encounter in the middle sphere, with loyalty and humour, is good therapy. Subsequently the middle sphere can be strengthened by artistic therapy, although this should not be individual therapy but group therapy. Emotional group therapy, on the other hand, can for these people induce an acutely critical condition, as can LSD and other drugs.

— Saturn activity can also be too weak. Then the spiritual incarnation is hesitant and unsure. This already starts during adolescence and usually leads to existential crises after age 42. Physically, young people experience this condition if they reveal that they 'walk two feet off the ground', that they feel themselves floating, etc. A few injections with lead D20 will usually soon put this right, but more serious cases require lengthy therapy, with a lot of curative eurythmy. They will tell you themselves when they have 'landed'. (See also the chapter on anorexia in Part II.)

— Moon forces that are too strong result in all of the manifestations of the moon type discussed elsewhere: imitative thinking, sex symbol, playboy, etc. This is a great obstacle for the development of the consciousness soul, which in a consciousness-soul society causes these types to be driven to despair. Periods of heavy depression, with attempted suicide, can occur. Here, too, everything depends on whether a human bond can come about in the middle sphere, and loyalty in particular plays an important role. A therapeutic relation must not be terminated too early.

— Moon forces that are too weak are especially a medical problem. The Drive of Matter is too weak in the soul. There is the continual threat of apathy and exhaustion. These people are physically 'minimum sufferers' who do, however, often grow old with all of their ailments and, depending on their environment, are capable of (limited) spiritual activity.

The development of the sentient soul, intellectual-mind soul, and consciousness soul takes place between age 21 and 42, in 'the great sun phase' of life. In this period of three times seven years, the astral, etheric, and physical bodies are partly made free, and provide the basis for the ego activity, which, out of the middle sphere, gives the soul forces form and content.

But the human being, surely, has a soul life long before this! Yes, the soul life is being developed from age 3 onward, but its form and its content then derive from the environment, family, school, and culture in general.

At age 21, we all have these soul forces already, formed by our environment and by the cultural time spirit. That is why there are such large differences between children of different cultures. This cultural difference in soul structure of young people is the central issue for youth in ethnic minorities. There is a lot of talk nowadays about racial hatred and discrimination, but it is not, in fact, race that causes problems, but the totally different (and mutually incomprehensible) soul content. Put in another way: it is the cultural differences that cause the problems, not the racial ones.

At the same time, this is where the hurdle lies. The child from an ethnic minority group already has the stamp of an entirely different soul content and soul reaction at an early age. As a result, education in school is interpreted in the wrong way, placed wrongly. Children of another race who have been adopted from birth give no more problems than any other child. Children from different cultures who are adopted after three or four years often have great difficulties in adjustment.

This first soul structure, absorbed from the environment by imitation, is, of course, a provisional soul structure. Between 21 and 42 it has to be altered by the ego into the soul structure that fits the individuality. Thus the human being is only really mature at age 42. At

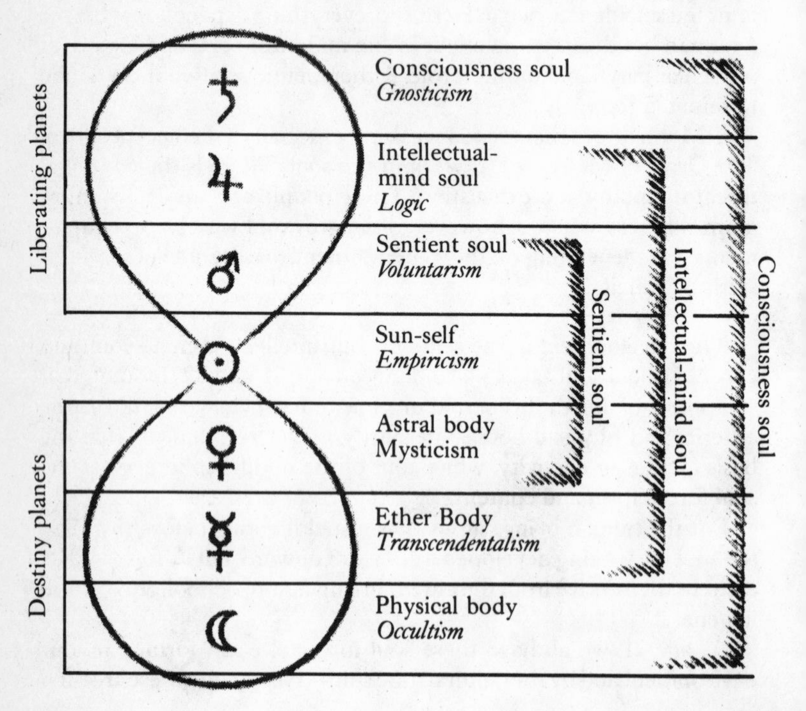

age 21 he is 'tentatively mature'. The 'alteration' in the middle phase of life is the cause of many forms of neurotic and even psychotic disturbances. These are too individual to be dealt with in a general way. With the scheme of developmental problems of the three soul qualities as background, however, the therapist can find the way to a rational therapy. In Part II, a few pedagogical and therapeutic viewpoints with respect to the three soul forces will be discussed (see Chapter 15).

Chapter Eleven
THE SHADOW ON THE PATH INWARDS

In post-Atlantean cultures the human being was initially still open to the spiritual world *outside* him. The outward threshold was still transparent. Beings of the higher hierarchies were worshipped as gods. Elemental beings were seen as helpers of man in day-to-day affairs. A spring, a holy tree, a mountain, or stream was seen as ensouled. In the north, one knew of trolls and gnomes, water beings, elves, and fire salamanders. In the old cultures, people of different regions each gave their own names to these nature beings. They were daily realities. One had to cultivate their friendship by means of certain ceremonies.

After about 800 B.C. these clairvoyant faculties disappeared, which was experienced as a loss. It was the 'twilight of the gods'. During the entire intellectual-soul period (from about 800 B.C. to about 1400 A.D.), people had to make do with the *memory* of these (*spiritual*) worlds, which lived on in epics and legends. We know the last offshoots as fairytales, still popular with children.

In these last two and a half millennia of standing alone in the world, mankind developed intelligent thought. After the fifteenth century, when the consciousness-soul period began, thought in conjunction with scientific experimentation developed.

Since the last third of the last century, however, and particularly since the archangel Michael has become time spirit, and the Dark Age, Kaliyuga, has come to an end[1], a process has started in which the *inward* threshold becomes transparent. This process will become more and more prominent, and if it is not understood it will be a great source of distress to people.

A few symptoms of this process will be discussed in this chapter.

In the discussion of the ancient Egyptian initiation (see Chapter 2) the experiences of the crossing of the threshold were described. What was experienced consciously by a few at that time, now rises up out of the unconscious for all of us. The ego, or self, that gets to know the forces working 'below the midriff', more or less consciously, first arrives in the area of the unconscious part of the astral body, the area of desires, wishes, and longings. This is a process of self-knowledge; all of the old mistakes and all 'sins of omission' come to the surface in the form of pictures. Whatever we neglected to do, but could have, even should have done, appears before us and tints our mood with a faint shade of melancholy. Our burden of sins, everything that has gone wrong, causes more and more self-reproach. Vaguely we sense that with everything that went wrong we have failed ourselves and others. We have become culpable with respect to something 'higher', that these shortcomings have not only held *us* up, but human, and even cosmic evolution as well. One finds this vague sense of uneasiness almost everywhere among contemporaries. People talk of 'doom and gloom', they say life is 'no fun any more', or they cannot 'see it any more'.

The reactions to this cultural phenomenon are varied. Some take refuge in aggression, aimed at a scapegoat outside, others in alcohol or nicotine, in which the uneasiness disappears for a few hours, or for a few minutes.

Aggression against 'society', against politicians, against the police, or hard action against social evils, are often expressions of a search for satisfaction that will displace the malaise, notwithstanding the positive ideals such actions may also represent. Accusations against the marriage partner or the ungrateful son or daughter, or against the boss or the parents, provide the satisfaction that drowns out the self-reproach. On the other hand, this self-reproach may also be nurtured and augmented in a perverse pleasure over one's own wickedness.

Some 20 years ago, the Swiss humorous periodical *Nebelspalter* had a quasi-serious cover story about Swiss prosperity: We are doing fine, things are getting better all the time, etc. but why is everybody so gloomy, then? 'Thank heavens, we have our *Föhn*'.* The *Föhn* is to blame for all the feelings of malaise, it is the villain! This tendency to blame an external scapegoat for one's discomforts is familiar to everyone: blame it on the weather, politics, or the economy!

That many people feel the need to escape from true reality is apparent from the following facts:† Since 1965, alcohol consumption has approximately quadrupled, and exceeds the severe levels of alcoholism at the beginning of this century. The consumption of sleeping pills and tranquillizers has increased to such an extent that the

* Alpine south wind believed to cause physical and psychological distress.

† These facts are based on data from the Netherlands, but apply with reasonable accuracy everywhere in the western world. (Transl.)

authorities are looking for ways to intervene.

Another symptom of the experience of these hitherto unconscious soul forces is a feeling of unrest, of feverish activity that gives no satisfaction and expresses itself, for example, in the search for holiday experiences from which one returns more tired than when one went, because the number of kilometres required to put sufficient distance between oneself and one's daily misery becomes ever greater.

The true cause of this malaise, however, lies not outside, but *within* us. We are approaching an encounter with the lesser guardian of the threshold – that force in us that calls to us: 'Man, know yourself, have the courage to see yourself as you are!'

Many group therapies, encounter groups, and the like, have come about as an answer to this need to come to terms with this sense of uneasiness. The inner distress is, indeed, great, particularly in those sectors of the population where people live in relative affluence and as a result have the time to discover their own inner life. In the winter of 1944-45 these kinds of problems were rare. Everyone battled for survival for his family and himself, a few days at a time. The objectives of survival were close at hand.*

The aggression of young people in a growing number of countries in the western world has its origin, of course, in unemployment and the lack of prospects for a meaningful future. But there have been unemployment and real poverty before over the last few centuries, ever since the beginning of the industrial revolution. The main difference is the form and the violence of the reactions, not on the part of a few, but from entire population groups. Those who condemn these reactions can perhaps afford to find other means of escape from the same lack of prospects for the future and the same poverty – although for them more inner poverty.

In international politics, too, the search for a scapegoat, for an enemy, is a well proven political ploy for diverting attention from the real (internal) malaise and silencing internal criticism.

All these and similar phenomena (everybody can add to them according to his own experience) are the first *symptoms* of the *unconscious crossing of the threshold*, which is now becoming a general problem for western mankind.

The unconscious path inward leads man back in his own time. More and more people start to experience images they can not place in their conscious past. Sometimes these images are so powerful that the individual concerned experiences 'another person' within himself,

* The author refers to the last phase of the Second World War in Holland when part of the population was threatened by starvation. (Transl.)

which he then projects, for example, to a previous life. The literature about *reincarnation* grows rapidly, but is rarely to be taken seriously. All too soon, images of a few centuries, or even only a few decades ago, are explained as memories of a previous incarnation of one's own. This is where it is in the interest of the counter-forces to lead man astray, for a true insight in earlier incarnations can be gained only after a long period of training, in conjunction with earnest self-criticism. In this area, vanity, illusion, and wishful thinking have great power over us.

Of course, our constitution and the kinds of problems we meet are karmically determined, but for the present life they are given starting points from which one has to work onwards. It is more important to get to know this starting point thoroughly and accept it than to have the silent hope that in a previous life one might have been an important personality, indeed. On this point, Rudolf Steiner provides clarity. In one of his Mystery Dramas,[2] the spiritual teacher Benedictus declares that many of us would be ashamed if they knew at what high spiritual level they had once been in comparison with now. But what one could be in previous incarnations before the development of the consciousness soul was not yet supported by a self-responsible ego. Particularly the leading personalities were still the 'persona', mask, or instrument through which the higher world could speak in order to guide the culture of the time. The main merit of the leading personalities was that by means of the mystery path they had made themselves 'transparent' for higher beings. Thus the ancient Greeks knew their demi-gods and heroes – half man, half god. That is to say, a hierarchical being spoke and worked through them. Of Gilgamesh, the hero of a Babylonian epic, it was said that he was one-third man and two-thirds god.

Only after about 1500 A.D. an entirely new situation came about. From the beginning of the development of the consciousness soul, in our history books referred to as the beginning of the 'New Age' , man must go on entirely on the strength of his own ego. And now it becomes clear that this ego, standing on its own two feet, is only starting to learn to walk!

What we were in previous lives, we were by the 'grace' of higher beings. Now we are part of a mankind becoming mature, and we have to learn to walk on our own two feet.

In the situation described here, the longing for dependence on a guru, or on a political leader, or on a system, is particularly strong. Why go the tiresome route of learning to walk of your own will when so many people and organisations are prepared to spare you this difficult road to independence?

This road to independence, however, is not a matter of egoism, as many tempters would have you believe, but leads to development of the ego in order to enable one to help others stand on their own two feet as well. This is also the objective of anthroposophical pedagogy, to teach the child to use the means he has for independent action. This is also the objective of anthroposophical medicine: to give a medicine that activates the constitution itself to conquer the illness, and not a remedy that temporarily takes over certain functions for you. The same principle, finally, is also central to the path of inner development of anthroposophy: not to be *dependent* on a guru, who selects the meditation for you and fills it with his 'shakti', so that your karmic knots are unravelled for you. Rather, *with the aid of* the general insights the initiate can give you, to choose your own inner path yourself.

Mankind is only at the beginning of this process. So-called 'results' of inner development, in the form of feelings of bliss or confusing spiritual observations, are relatively easy to obtain by following old paths, under supervision. Real results, in the form of an ego consciousness that one has really made one's own by oneself, crossing the threshold on one's own responsibility, are less spectacular. They are still fleeting goals, and disappear again when one ceases to pursue them.

The manifestations mentioned above (escape in aggression, in narcosis, or in illusionary images of 'previous incarnations', longing for dependence, submission to authority, etc.) exist on a level at which we ourselves can still take a hand; if we really want to, we can change direction, out of our own ego, develop ourselves, and even take up a path of inner training. It is an entirely different matter in the case of phenomena that, although they are similarly symptoms of an unconscious crossing of the inward threshold, go a step further. Then we are dealing with psychical and even physical disturbances and syndromes that can not be resolved without specific help from outside. We have in mind the different, nowadays quite common *neuroses* and *psychoses.*

A preliminary description will be given below; Part II of this book provides further elaboration, in greater detail, including guidelines for the development of a professional therapy. A number of other viewpoints will be added, consistent with the various levels and the diversity of anthroposophical thought.

Anthroposophy offers a number of viewpoints from which these phenomena can be understood. What we have to do is to describe the 'descent' of human consciousness into its own bodily nature: astral body, ether body and physical body.

On the way inward, awakening half-consciously in our normally unconscious soul levels, we first meet, in a dreamy way, as already indicated, the astral soul realm in the regions of the will. Old and new will impulses become semi-conscious, clothed in imagery in the same way as each dream experience is clothed in imagery. These are shreds of memories, permeated with emotional qualities. Just as in a dream, they come and go, but can nevertheless have a frightening or compulsive character.

This dreamy entry is the first phase. This may be all there is to it. The person in question can then either pull himself together and courageously face the situation, or give in and stay in the mildly depressive mood that has resulted. A third possibility is, as mentioned before, escape into insensibility or into aggression.

Often, however, the descent into one's own 'underworld' continues, and then the consciousness comes into contact with the forces active in the *organs*. These are *astral-etheric* processes, those in which the life forces, ordered by the sleeping soul life, carry out their functions of break-down and build-up.

What takes place here has a compulsive character. These processes can break down substances, dissolve them, and reconstitute and rebuild them into substances compatible with the body. What happens at 37° C, quietly, it seems, can be reproduced outside the body, in the laboratory, only with the aid of strong acids and hydroxides at extreme temperatures, and under high pressure. All this takes place in us quite unnoticeably while we read the paper after dinner.

We can be thankful that these compulsive forces are normally active in a sleeping consciousness. When we intrude into this sphere with our day consciousness, it, too, is seized by these forces, and made unfree. Which organs in particular are the ones to make themselves known, or make themselves known first, depends on the constitution of the person in question. It is important for the psycho-therapist to be familiar with these processes. In the soul life, they take the form of fears, obsessions, real depressions, hallucinations, and even madness.

Four organs play a role in this: the kidneys, the lungs, the liver, and the heart.

The kidney, or, rather, the entire 'kidney process', encompasses the following physiological processes: entry of substances via the intestines; subsequent breakdown and reconstitution to body substance;

distribution of these substances to the body cells (so-called cell nourishment); excretion of the break-down products in the blood stream; separation of the waste products from the blood in the kidney; and elimination of these waste substances in the urine. All this is, from the planetary viewpoint, the physiological *venus process* in man.

If this process, which normally runs its course unconsciously, is mirrored in the day consciousness, in the sun-self, abnormal experiences arise. These have the character of hypochondrial depressions or chagrin, in which self-reproach in the form of chaotic memories fill the consciousness, disturbing the normal functions.

The neurotic conditions of uneasiness at the beginning of the descent were related to moral problems, which still had a basis in reality. The failures were real enough, only the pre-occupation with them was abnormal. With the further descent, however, self-reproach grows all out of proportion and often becomes absurd. The narrowing of the perspective, the absolute fixation on the past eventually leaves only one escape route: stepping out of this unbearable life through suicide. Not only alcohol consumption has increased appallingly as an escape from the sense of distress. The number of suicides, too, has multiplied in the last few decades, particularly among young people. Only the silence kept in newspapers and other publications about suicide covers up this phenomenon.

If the person is a *lung type*, if it is in the first place the lungs that play a role, then other symptoms come to the fore. The lung process also involves more than just the function of the organ itself. From the planetary point of view, it is the *mercury process*. Coming to the surface in the semi-conscious soul life, these processes become stuck, and form dead 'islands' in the soul. These dead islands have been so encapsulated that they are inaccessible to the flowing force of movement of the mercury processes. They are like the sharp rocks in a stream.

A clear symptom of this is that the conceptions become compulsive. Just as with asthma the lungs are full of inhaled air and it is impossible to exhale, so certain conceptions can not be 'exhaled'.

Compulsive neuroses, as experience has taught, are extremely difficult to treat. The person in question knows very well that his obsessions are nonsense, that his fears are unfounded, yet they are there, and they keep coming back against his will.

Some compulsive neurotics are contact-poor people who have not become fully mature during puberty. The compulsion can then take the form of the person's honesty, or of making a note of 'signs' in order to prove the so-called reality of the person's compulsion (particularly with paranoia).

The egocentric fixation on the person's own life, on his own problems, the fear of losing human ties – through *his* fault – cause the thoughts to go around in a vicious circle. Hypersensitivity to sounds or strong light, but also to friendliness of others, cut social contacts more and more. The obsessions can deteriorate into paranoid delusions, although most of the time other organs then play a role as well.

A few examples from my own practice may illustrate what the lung type is like. Many decades ago, I had a patient, a clerk in the post office, who had developed the paranoid delusion that his supervisor was looking for an opportunity to catch him at dishonesty. He didn't let on, but he had designed an elaborate system in which each single postage stamp he sold was recorded. This painstaking performance of duty earned him the highest regard of his supervisor, but he considered the positive evaluations only as dangerous attempts to get him to lower his guard and relax his security measures. When he came to me, this had been going on for years and years. Nobody had noticed anything, not even his wife, but finally it had become too much for him, and he came for help.

Another kind of delusion was that of a night-deskman of a large newspaper, a bachelor, who one night walked off the job, went to the police station and revealed there that he now had all the proof he needed: for 20 years he had been pursued by Sioux Indians, but now it had got to the point where they even left notes in his waste basket. The desk sergeant, very calmly, and with great presence of mind, told him the police had been keeping an eye on these indians for a long time, and sent him on to a psychiatrist.

Such a localized delusion, particularly with contact-poor people as in both examples, is among other things linked with insufficient maturing during puberty. Most of the time, the environment suffers a lot under these delusions, often growing stealthily, and from the sudden outbursts when the patient starts to fight them.

The *liver* (*Jupiter*) is the organ that breaks down foreign proteins, and builds up body proteins. This organ forces matter into new forms. This compelling force may break down conceptions that have 'descended' into the subconscious, and reconstitute them into other conceptions. With respect to reality, strange visions and hallucinations arise.

The crossing of the threshold can lead to violent reactions, in which the often absurd hallucinations start playing a role. Commanding voices, or the influence of waves of electricity are experienced simultaneously as real and unreal. Real and unreal here means that the voices and so on are, in fact, heard and experienced, while at the same time the intelligence knows that they are not real. When this last foothold, too, has dropped away, then, according to common parlance, 'he's gone crazy!' (a hallucination is a mirror image in the astral body of an organ of the ether body. Because of the mirroring effect, consciousness of the organ's function arises. This mirroring disturbs normal soul life).

The nature of the hallucinations on the way inwards always has something to do with the person's biography. The content is related to moral problems that were experienced already in the first place. Someone with a fearful, compulsive character will have different hallucinations and delusions from someone who by nature enjoys life.

For the *heart type* (sun) – the person for whom the forces active in the circulation break through into consciousness – it is, particularly at the beginning, a remorseful conscience that plays a role. With the 'heart' we judge ourselves and our deeds differently from the way we do with our 'head'. When these pangs of conscience are pushed away, fears arise. Different from the lung type, these fears are undirected and general. It is a fear of life, which at the same time alternately is a fear of death. It is generally known that coronary infarctions and angina pectoris can cause acute, violent fear. For the patient who seemingly has a healthy circulation, this fear is more like something that is there outside daily activities. It is a mixture of pangs of conscience, self-reproach, and feelings of inadequacy, existing side by side with cordiality and sociability.

A typical example of this was the following: At a management course for senior executives, an older executive surprised his colleagues during the introductions with this comment at the end of his story: "And do you know why I am here? I am scared stiff of dying!" He was still fully active in a flourishing company he had himself built from scratch – a company that was well-known for its good social conditions. A few years later he died of a heart infarction.

This is characteristic of the heart type: active people, often with social talents and social sensitivity, but also experiencing many disappointments because the good-naturedness they radiate is frustrated again and again by bureaucracy or indifference. With the heart type it is also common that obstruction is met with bursts of anger, about which later they are sorry.

In the real psychosis, these phenomena can lead to madness.

Four organ types have been described here. It will have become clear that in reality there are many cases of mixtures of these types. For the anthroposophical physician it is important to recognize the organ in question because anthroposophical medicine will always treat the organ specifically, besides other measures. Nowadays one can quickly suppress the symptoms by means of the modern anti-depressive and anti-psychotic drugs, so that the patient does not notice his condition as long as he keeps taking his pills. But this, in essence, produces no cure. The threshold crossing remains a reality, the mirroring of organs in the consciousness has not changed. Only day consciousness has been cut off from knowing about the real situation. Being cut off does not apply solely to the depression or the delusion, obviously.

Someone who is 'under drugs' is not in possession of his full humanity. He is not allowed to drive a car, for instance. He may not take important, long-term decisions.

After the descent into the unconscious part of the astral body and the further descent into the ether body, where the ego is overpowered in the metabolism by organic processes, a third step may follow. Just as it happened in the Egyptian mysteries under supervision of the hierophant, modern man, too, can get caught in the forces of the *physical body* during his 'descent into hell' (as Jung calls it). This occurs in the case of deep psychosis, among others in schizophrenia. Then it is not only the etheric-organic process that is stressed and damaged, but also the physical organ. One is then caught up in damaged physical organs. The psychical life is limited to remnants of organic processes.

In summary, we can say that the path inward consists of three levels. At the first level the ego is caught in the lower part of the astral body (the region of desires, wishes, and longings); this is the level of the neurosis. At the second level the ego is caught in the ether body of the metabolic processes; this is the level of still reversible psychoses. At the third level the ego is caught in the damaged physical body; this is the level of the permanent psychosis, the sad end.

When a therapy has to be selected, one has to reckon with all three levels. For the first step the conversation and artistic therapy are the main thing. Still, here too, there will have to be treatment with potentized medicines in order to regulate the etheric processes and prevent a further descent. In the second phase, medicinal therapy is the main thing (but only with psycho-pharmaceutics if absolutely unavoidable) and artistic and conversational therapy play a helping role. Even in the last phase, attempts can be made to reactivate the physical organ by medicines, and the artistic therapy and conversation are continued.

If one has experienced how a mute, catatonic patient, with whom seemingly no contact whatsoever was possible, told later that he had not only heard everything that was spoken to him, but had also remembered it, and now wished to continue with it, one knows that the ego is always still accessible, and that patients suffer tremendously under a treatment that does not continue to regard them as fully human.

Modern psychosis is a kind of counter-image of the old Egyptian initiation, the difference being that the Egyptian initiation was conducted consciously by the hierophant, and the psychosis of today comes about involuntarily, and is not under the control of the ego. It is not too far-fetched to say: psychoses are 'failed initiations'! In an earlier chapter we discussed how the 'modern initiation', or path of development, can take its course. It is the same path, but is now experienced fully consciously and in a healthy manner.

I have been asked: 'But why would we want to go on this path? Let us keep our feet on the ground and be satisfied with the sense world. We are only too happy to have put this long period of superstition regarding a spiritual world behind us'. The answer can only be that times are changing fast, and that the constitution of western mankind has made the inward threshold 'unsafe' whether we like it or not. We are faced with the choice of either producing more psychopharmaceutics, drinking more alcohol, etc., or of acknowledging the causes and encouraging everyone to be responsible for his own spiritual health. Whoever is fully convinced of the latter can only:

— try to make others aware of what is going on;

— try to arouse a sense of responsibility in as many people as possible, so that they come to realize that something has to be *done*, and that one has to change one's habits and look after one's inner life;

— make a path of inner strengthening and development visible by one's own effort, however difficult this is.

Chapter Twelve
THE SHADOW ON THE PATH OUTWARDS

The path outwards was, as described in the previous chapter, common in the oldest cultures. All ancient, pre-Grecian cultures with a spiritualistic world outlook were based on the old forms of clairvoyance, which was accepted as a matter of course by the entire community. This clairvoyance was gradually lost. This was experienced as a withdrawal of the gods. The ancient Greeks spoke with nostalgia about the times when 'gods still sat at the same table with human beings'. When Homer started his *Illiad* with the words: "Sing me, O muse, of the wrath of Achilles . . . ", this was no poetic metaphor but a real 'prayer', directed at a higher being in order to invoke inspiration for the poet.

About 800 B.C. the 'twilight of the gods' took place. Thereafter, the old form of clairvoyance became atavistic and arose only in a few people as an exception. From Roman times, for instance, we know of the Sybils, immortalized by Michelangelo in the Sistine Chapel. They could give counsel in a sort of trance, in which they were in contact with the spirit world. For this, the Pythia ofDelphi needed intoxication with volcanic vapours, which rose from a crack in the ground.

In our times, the last remnants of these ancient powers live on some mediums, paragnostics, etc.

In the previous chapter it was stated that the present state of development makes the inward threshold 'unsafe'. This is the main public mental health problem. But at the same time, 'ego dilution' is taking place for many people, as a reaction, conscious or not, to this crossing of the inward threshold. This is a kind of escape 'to the other side'. One wishes to be free of this world, 'get high' in a world of intensive sense impressions, without contact with hard reality.

This 'ego dilution' is in our culture an enormous temptation. *Ecstasy* is experienced as an escape from depressive moods. This tendency occurs particularly among young people who are constitutionally not very 'well-grounded' anyway. For the experienced child psychiatrist and especially for the curative eurythmist, children with this constitution are recognizable at an early age, particularly by their way of walking. They walk on their toes, as if they do not want to touch the earth. In this phase, preventive therapy by means of curative eurythmy is still effective. After puberty this becomes more difficult because the young people then have an aversion to anything that ties them to regularity and responsibility. Any exercise, intellectual or physical, is soon dropped. A style of life is sought in which one can let oneself drift into situations that facilitate escape from the world. Later on we shall go into this further.

One of the foundations for an understanding of the neurotic and psychotic phenomena caused by this form of escapism is the relationship of macrocosm and microcosm. In man, the same creative forces are active as in the cosmos. Zodiac and planets are not arbitrary lumps of matter in a limitless void. They are expressions of the activities of the hierarchies – creative qualities, therefore.

Cosmic qualities are not just laws of nature operating blindly, but elemental beings active in a living way, behind which stand higher, hierarchical beings. Unprepared for entry into this world are those who by means of whatever manipulations breach the threshold of the sense-perceptible surface world, and are immersed in the reality behind those surfaces.

Apart from cases in which the crossing of the threshold takes place spontaneously, many kinds of manipulation are possible to force this crossing. The most well-known are: hyperventilation, starvation, extreme exhaustion, too much confusing information, alternation of threats and promises, extremely loud sound – perhaps accompanied by flashing light, drugs such as LSD and hashish, and, finally, socially accepted stimulants such as drinking alcohol in the West and smoking opium in the East. ('Social' drinking is what is meant here; it has in the first place the purpose of making one happy, relaxed, etc. This is not the same as alcoholism, as mentioned in the last chapter, which is a manifestation of the attempt to sink into stupor, with unconsciousness and damage of the physical organs as the ultimate consequence. For the East, the same distinction can be made between more or less accepted 'social' opium use and the destructive consequences of heroin addiction.)

These manipulations have always been popular means of escape from the stress of daily life through intoxication or ecstatic experience.

Ritual dance, such as that of the Dervishes, or the Balinese creese dance, or the ceremonial dances of Africa – war dances or initiation dances – all have the same function. The Scottish bagpipe, which once led men into battle, brought the warriors into a wild state of intoxication. It is always a matter of protracted repetition of the same movement, the same melody, or the same rhythm, which causes a mild degree of excarnation. This also explains the delight of the Viennese waltz. Without these effects, our discos would be empty.

It may be noted that variations of manipulations such as these are part of the methods of many of the *youth sects* that have caught attention in the last few years.

The unprepared crossing of the threshold outwards starts with feelings of bliss, of release from cares, and of liberation, which can increase to complete ecstasy. This first stage is a great temptation, and can in itself even lead to addiction, whether that involves alcohol or visits to the disco.

The creation of such conditions of excarnation is experienced as an antidote against the malaise experienced when going too far inward, as described in the previous chapter. That is why it is becoming a more and more serious problem for our western culture.

The degree of excarnation can in this first stage be limited; ecstasy is followed by a swing over to the opposite side: a period of depressive emotions because of too deep an incarnation in the 'hangover', accompanied by physical phenomena such as headache, sore muscles, nausea, etc. After 'stepping out', the return is experienced as all the more painful (with drying-out cures, these physical phenomena also occur). As is well known, however, this hangover can lead to a new longing for the means used to step out, and thus the circle of addiction is completed.

Excarnation can still go a step further. With a sudden shock, the person in question enters another world. In this world all sense impressions as we know them in the physical world are amplified a thousandfold. Colour, sound, and forms have an intensity that is unknown and unimaginable to ordinary consciousness.

This phenomenon of entering the other world with a shock was described by Rudolf Steiner in 1910 as something that occurred during initiation of the North-Germanic people. To this same phenomenon, but now in the way it occurs in our own time, the American researchers Conway and Siegelman devoted years of investigation, which they describe in their book *Snapping*.[1] 'Snapping' is the phenomenon of shock accompanying the transition from the first stage to the second. The consequences of this second stage are much more serious than those of the first. Whereas in the first the return to ordinary life was paid for with a more or less severe hangover, the return from the second stage is by no means guaranteed, and when it does take place, a substantial personality change has occurred.

These effects are the aim of brainwashing, as it was experienced by prisoners of war in Korea (and Vietnam) as well as in youth sects. Following long periods of deprivation of sleep, a protein-poor starvation diet, alternating threats and friendliness, endless repetition of movements and words in exotic rituals, a never-ending flood of 'information' through lectures and talk sessions, and finally total exhaustion, snapping occurs eventually, and the person in question has lost his ego experience. Taking its place is automatic action, programmed by the sect. What this can lead to was demonstrated in the news in a shocking way some years ago by the group-suicide of followers of the 'Jones Church'.

The most important condition is a total cutting off of all contacts with the earlier environment, which is painted as belonging to the devil and doomed, etc. The sect itself, on the other hand, is one's salvation. Those who want to know the shocking details about this should read the book *Snapping* or the book *Die Himmlischen Verführer*.[2]

In the U.S. it is estimated that some 300,000 young people are captives of semi-religious sects such as the Unification Church (Moonies), Children of God, Hare Krishna, Divine Light Mission, Forever Family, Church of Scientology, and the Jesus movement, to mention some of the more important ones. There are some additional ones of a somewhat different nature, aimed more at adults, such as the Transcendental-Meditation movement and the Baghwan movement. TM promises inner peace and strength, by way of its monotonously repeated word meditations, and the development of unusual abilities such as overcoming the force of gravity in hopping or flying. The Baghwan movement appeals to unsatisfied religious emotions; it involves total surrender to the guru Baghwan. Followers are radiant with bliss, on account of an unrestrained life style, also sexually.

So much, for now, about excarnation as a cultural phenomenon and as a commercially exploited 'liberation' for the unfortunates of our welfare society.

These same phenomena can also appear as individual neuroses and psychoses.

Neuroses, which are still reversible, become psychoses when 'egress' in the second stage leads to situations in which return to day consciousness has become impossible.

I only want to mention the occurrence of neuroses and psychoses here. In the second part of this book, a few syndromes will be dealt with in more detail.

The occurrence, particularly among young people, of periods of deep apathy, which in our time is a quite common phenomenon, I consider to be among the neuroses of the first stage. The persons concerned (mostly young) fall into a state of absolute inactivity, stay in bed or don't get up until the afternoon, to spend half the night preferably smoking hash in a group, or just sitting around on cushions on the floor. The mood is most congenial as long as nothing is demanded of them. A conversation is difficult, and always revolves around the same thing: 'Why should I be active? I am entirely happy this way. Why should I work? The world is bad enough as it is. Social security exists for people such as us; if it stops, well, I'll die – so what?'

Soon the consequences of one-sided and poor nutrition reinforce the neurosis. Conversations with these people serve little purpose; one does not meet their ego, and it is difficult to pull them out of their apathy by external means. Yet they crave real contact, and look for someone who can listen to their stories 'empathetically'. Only by way of a warm, positive approach it may happen that 'for your sake' they will go and do something.

Part Two

Chapter Thirteen

THERAPEUTIC THINKING IN ANTHROPOSOPHICAL PSYCHOTHERAPY

Every therapist has to deal with four 'organizations' in the human being, each of which works according to its own principles, but also interacts with the others. These are the four 'sheaths', or 'members' of the human being that have been discussed in previous chapters.

Of its own, the *physical* organization can change in only one direction when left by itself: it falls apart. Plants wilt. The body of an animal or of the human being decays as soon as it is no longer permeated by the activities of life. The physical organization is passive with respect to its configuration in space.

The organization of life, of the ether body, is a *time organization*, not spatial of its own, but active in the spatiality of the physical body. The etheric organization is the interplay, a composite, of hundreds of rhythms, each of which stimulates a certain process. Together they keep the entire organization going.

This rhythmic organization operates faultlessly for as long as there is no interference from the higher principles. In tissue cultures, in which these higher principles have been eliminated, there is unlimited continuity of life forms repeating themselves.

Any disturbance of the ether rhythms, whatever the cause, produces symptoms of illness. At first these are still purely functional and reversible, but, if persistent, they can cause deformations in the physical organism.

The etheric organization itself is based on *four different ether principles:*

1. The *form ether*, also called crystallization ether or *life ether*. The rhythms of this ether quality bring about the geometric ordering of matter in the crystalline grid structure. The form ether's activity is to make rigid. A good picture of this force is that of the 'Snow Queen' in the Andersen fairy-tale, who 'freezes' everything she touches.

2. The *chemical* or *sound ether* orders matter in the fluid state. The combinations and decompositions in endless series of chemical conversions and compounds characterize this ether activity in the metabolism. Disruption immediately and demonstrably creates chemical substances normally not occurring in the fluid organism. Biochemistry has been trying busily for years to unravel the secrets of these activities of the chemical ether.
3. The *light ether*, which one could also call the consciousness ether. In the rhythms of the light ether lives the consciousness. As such, these rhythms are the link with the next organization principle, the astral level. The main area of activity for the light ether is the nerve-sense system. The rhythms of the light ether organization are reflected in electrical phenomena, which can be measured in the electro-encephalogram (EEG).
4. The *warmth ether* penetrates the entire organism with its activity. It has its primary organ in the blood circulation, and is the medium through which the spiritual ego of man can come into contact with the living bodily nature. The warmth ether penetrates all previous ether qualities and consequently is the most important medium for therapy. Anthroposophical psychotherapy is centred on the ego (and not on teaching tricks to the astral body).

Disruption of the ether-rhythm organization is in the first instance caused by the *astral organization* – the carrier of our drives, emotions, and conceptions. This astral organization is an orderly composition of psychical qualities. While existing itself as a quality outside time and space, it influences the rhythmic organization of the ether body, and via the ether body also the physical body. Every emotion, every conception, every desire accelerates or decelerates certain rhythms. With violent psychical movements such rhythms can be disrupted or even destroyed. The latter then also results in anatomically demonstrable changes in the physical organs. Such anatomical changes, therefore, are always the finale, the fifth act in a long drama.

It is important to diagnose disturbances coming out of the astral organization at an early stage, in the first or second act, because they can then still be influenced at the psychotherapeutic level. The astral organization is the totality of our psychical world. If this astral or psychical organization is without the control of the ego, associative thinking or daydreaming occurs. In the emotional life, one is tossed back and forth between sympathy and antipathy. In the life of drives and desires, one is totally at the mercy of these forces.

The *animal* organism consists of the physical, etheric, and astral bodies. In the astral organization, the action and reaction patterns we call the 'instinct' of the animal species are fixed. The instinct is originally an astral structure that expresses itself in the forms of the physical body. In the animal, instinct and physical configuration go together. The physical instrument in space is *formed by the instinct*, and all action in time is *determined by the instinct*.

From a physiological point of view, however, man is born 'too early', and short of instinct. He must learn his most important action patterns (walking, speaking, thinking) *after* birth, by imitation of his environment. The human astral body is trained (conditioned) by education, and is therefore culture-dependent.

The astral body itself possesses seven main structures, which we call character structures. In *Phases* these have been described extensively as the 'basic orientations'. These basic orientations determine the way we react to stimuli and experiences from outside.

In the young person the basic orientation, as well as the etheric temperament, is determined by heredity. In approaching adulthood, this may change because the individuality brings its own temperamental structure and basic orientation, which often conflict with the hereditary structures. This is a central issue of adolescence.

The fourth and highest principle is the *ego* of the human being, his spiritual being, which is characterized by continuous development. In the first part of this book a distinction was made between a 'first' and a 'second' ego. Here, we refer to the second ego, which in essence is the higher ego of the human being, and accompanies the incarnation from the spiritual world. The higher ego is the carrier of our biographical leitmotiv, of our ultimate objective.

Ego development from birth till death is a continuation of previous development and the preparation for future development. The ego is forever 'becoming', full of aspiration, future-oriented. Wherever it is connected with the three lower principles in a healthy way it determines the course, the common thread, of life. This is how this life becomes a biography and not a coincidental accumulation of whatever happens to one.

Our ego reacts to external events, makes choices, determines priorities, according to life's aims in as far as they are more or less clearly in view. Through the ego, life and its aims acquire meaning. The ego takes account of 'karma', of the positive and negative results of previous development.[1]

The ego works in the *thinking* as intelligence, as the ability to order sense impressions meaningfully. This is where our task and our aim in life must become conscious. In the *feeling* the ego attenuates the violent motions of the astral body. The ego develops the emotional life by gradually replacing feelings caused exclusively by the body with feelings oriented to spiritual values, such as in the arts and in religion. The ego works in the *will* by modifying the impulse action patterns to actions aimed at a goal set by the ego.

The ego adjusts, curbs, promotes, and directs all 'natural' impulses coming out of the etheric-astral being, not as a hostile power, but as a loving educator.

Many modern psychotherapies are manifestly hostile to the ego. The ego is often regarded as the villain, who oppresses and tyrannizes. The uninhibited indulgence of the physical-astral being is supposed to have a purifying effect and to resolve the complexes caused by the ego.

That which often is meant by the ego is *not* the spirit-ego that is spoken of in this chapter, but a conglomeration of indurations, fixed patterns of the astral body, which, indeed, have a tyrannizing effect. How can these be best resolved? Certainly not by astral 'indulgence', but by activating the true *spiritual* ego, which can bring the fixed patterns into motion and into meaningful development. That is also what Jung calls the path to the 'self'.[2]

The ego works on the astral body in a way that brings order and gives direction. The astral body works on the etheric body by acceleration and deceleration, and can also be the cause of disruption of vital rhythms. The ether body, in turn, works on the physical body by keeping it in movement, building up and breaking down, preventing decomposition. In these four interactive principles the self-conscious, living human being manifests himself.

But there are also astral-etheric structures that do not have a direct physical correlation. A conception, a thought, an idea is a configuration of an astral-etheric nature that may or may not be structured by the ego.

Such an astral-etheric *Gestalt* is a *being*. This being belongs to the group of 'elemental beings' already mentioned in Chapter 2. Such forms, such beings, also work in the processes of nature, in the plant world, and in all rhythmic cosmic processes, such as day and night, summer and winter, etc. When the human being thinks a thought he creates at that moment an astral-etheric form, an elemental being, which lives for as long as the thought exists. Then the form is again dissolved, but a reflection of it is preserved in the mirror of memory (which in reality is the surface of the internal organs).[3] When we 'recover' an old thought or conception, we read the structure of this old form in the mirror of memory, but we have to think it again, that is, we have to *recreate* the astral-etheric form. Afterwards we can once more dissolve it by forgetting it if we want to.

This is the normal course of events. What is pathological is when conceptual forms are not only preserved as imprints in the memory mirror, but *continue to exist* as astral-etheric forms.

This occurs in the case of etheric disturbances and deformation of the etheric-physical organs. Then the memory forms are not at rest, not merely present as memory images, but they are active as conceptions working actively in the unconscious organic realm.

We can become possessed by such conceptual forms; Jung also discusses this. They have then become actual demons, which influence us in a disturbing way out of the unconscious.

We are then dealing with obsessions that continually come to the surface, interfering with the normal way the current conceptual life takes its course. Under different circumstances, these demonic forms can call forth fears, hallucinations, or compulsive actions.

It is understandable that once such demonic forms have been created, conversational therapy is no longer of much help. The demonic forms have moved just out of reach of the ego and have an independent existence. In the first place, the deformed organ that retains the conception must be treated medicinally. That means: etheric dysfunction or malformation has to be regulated by specific organ therapy, otherwise one compulsion is merely replaced by another. Only when the organ in question functions normally again can psychotherapy have any lasting effect, because it offers the ego the possibility again to work towards a meaningful future.

But demonic forms do not arise only from the interaction of conceptions and the memory mirror. They can also arise as a result of the isolation of certain *feelings*, which start to function as independent 'islands', and in this case as islands that prowl around in the psyche in a compulsive and disturbing fashion. Freud called these disturbing feelings 'complexes'. In reality these are demonic elemental beings, which we once created ourselves in our dreamy emotional life. Here, too, specific organ treatment must accompany psychotherapy.

Finally, out of the metabolic and will sphere, decisions and actions that are in themselves meaningful can release themselves from the normal stream of activities and acquire a fixed, immobile character. This is often useful because they are carried out automatically by the 'activity form', but often also disturbing because they may also appear at times when out of one's ego one would wish to act or react differently. Every behaviour therapy drives activity into our metabolic and will life, and thereby robs the ego of some of its freedom and the possibility to develop. Can one really consider it therapy when an old *Gestalt* is replaced by an equally demonic, new *Gestalt*, even if the latter is socially less bothersome?

It is evident that there is a difference between a thought process automating certain thought functions, emotional complexes, and activity patterns (i.e. turning them into fixed forms), and fixations brought about in these three areas by a shock process, although the dividing line between them is by no means a sharp one. In order to assure that learning processes avoid fixed forms as much as possible, Rudolf Steiner introduced a number of methodical and didactic principles for Waldorf education.[4] From these principles we can learn much that could be applied in anthroposophical psychotherapy. While education must have a prophylactic effect, treatment, unfortunately, can only have a therapeutic effect after the event.

One of the first principles of Waldorf education is not to *define*, but to *characterize*! Definitions are fixed forms that have an immobilizing effect on the ether body from outside; characterizations remain mobile. They are multi-dimensional, have an emotional content, and encourage the will to form new conceptions of its own. That is why during the first eight years the pupils' own descriptions of their experimentation and their artistic representations of (seemingly) abstract subject matter are emphasized in Waldorf schools. After class (grade) 8, the pupil can manage it to summarize afterwards in the form of a definition what has been characterized earlier. Because of the preceding process, 'ego filled' conceptions have been created, which can subsequently be handled freely.

For psychotherapy this means that a way has to be found to 'fill' the empty, abstract conceptions, which have no ego content but have been taken over from outside, with the qualities that are lacking – the person's own thought, feelings, and will. Rudolf Steiner called empty conceptions, feelings, and actions the three scourges of our culture: the *phrase*, the *convention*, and the *routine*.[5] In psychotherapy we have to bring phrase, convention, and routine into development again by linking them to the ego, so that free thoughts, warm feelings, and courageous will can be given a chance.

Besides people who become stuck in their own organic processes (the 'inward' or 'incarnation path') there are also people who shun the incarnation of the ego and seek a path outward (excarnating). This can occur already in young children, for constitutional reasons or as a result of shocks or severe neglect.

A certain group of such children we can call 'cosmic children' with a delayed incarnation process. This may include the still normal 'late bloomers', for whom the developmental age lags with respect to the calendar age, as well as those dreamy darlings who are really behind in their development.

A special category are the *autistic* children, who for many and various reasons do not bring their ego to bear, and as a result have a development that is determined by the astral body. For this reason all kinds of extremes, such as compulsions, phobias, and hallucinations come to the fore. In the autistic child one can see what the human being would be like if he really had no ego, which is what many psychological schools of thought maintain.

While autism occurs in young children, another expression of the tendency to avoid the incarnation process often occurs at age 19. This is the *crisis of adolescence*, in which the person's *own* soul-spirit being, carrying with it not only the old karma, but also the intentions for the course of this life, becomes conscious of having to live in a bodily instrument that for a large part has been formed and misformed by cultural norms in education, on the basis of inherited aptitudes. These inherited aptitudes and this education are, as said before, not entirely coincidental. For development occurs only as a result of overcoming resistance. The higher ego has before birth looked for resistance in a certain heredity and a certain educational pattern.

But the awakening ego – around 18 or 19 – has to give concrete form and content to this intention to overcome a certain resistance, and in circumstances in which ego-consciousness and life experience are still weak. Often this centres on the choice of vocation, or in confirming or rejecting a vocational training determined by others. This can lead to startling discoveries. An investigation in the Fifties concerning the employment of people five to ten years after they had received their diploma from a vocational school revealed that after 10 years only 20 per cent of them worked in the trade for which they had trained.

To an increasing extent there is an aversion to making choices. It is avoided by 'first having a look around India and Nepal' or, closer to home, by accepting irregular, temporary jobs. To this the problem of youth unemployment has been added in the last few years, which has dimmed any prospects of a meaningful future for many.

Shunning one's own development towards the future ('future-shock') can occur at any time in the biography, but particularly at times when a certain phase has ended and the problems of the new phase have not yet become visible. Such times are for instance the ages of 29 and 30, 42, and the period after 56. Retirement is for many such a shock that it has a disintegrating effect on life, followed by rapid deterioration of bodily health.

If anywhere, this is where ego-centred therapy is needed, even though the symptoms appear to point in the direction of an 'inward neurosis' because of secondary depressive conditions. Ego-therapy is conducted in the warmth of the meeting between client and therapist. In ego-therapy the latter must regard himself as 50 per cent of the therapeutic situation. He has to (temporarily) link his destiny to that of the client. Aloofness in conversations are for the client in this situation extremely frustrating, even if one has learned to listen empathetically.

Important symptoms are tiredness, often in disguised forms, headaches, and periods of lethargy. As soon as a future has been identified that can be accepted with warmth and enthusiasm, these symptoms disappear without specific treatment. To help the client find such a future, the therapist will have to forego a non-directive attitude and instead become creative together with the client in finding unusual solutions. The best approach is to listen carefully to the deepest longings, which may never yet have been expressed in words, but which, brought out into the open, can be discussed as a proposal ('why not . . . ?'). Often this prompts surprising activities. These are activities resulting from an ego-incarnation, directed at a future that is meaningful for the person in question.

The field of excarnating neuroses includes, among others, anorexia during puberty, pseudologia fantastica (starting with adolescence and sometimes continued throughout a life of deception), hyperventilation, and hysteria. A few of these will be discussed separately later on (see Chapters 16 and 17).

A final remark about two important schools of thought in psychotherapy, which have a special relation to the two 'escape routes' – the incarnating and the excarnating. We refer to to Freud and Adler, who have been mentioned before.

The big difference between the therapies of Freud and Adler is, in our view, that Freud looked for the personal past, the path inward, while Adler, in his attempt to make the life-plan conscious, and in his 'encouragement', looked for a meaningful image of the future. To those who knew Adler it was known that his secret lay in a warm interest in and compassion with the struggle of the patient, and a way of encouragement that did not come across like a technique, but as warmth flowing from the heart. In contrast there is Freud's aloofness of the professional therapist. Two people, two polar opposites in therapeutic approach, and perhaps also two kinds of patient, each of which should be treated in their own specific manner.

Recent developments in psychoanalysis, meanwhile, have abandoned the aloof spectator attitude and reintroduced the conversation. This also manifests itself outwardly in the physical set-up: the couch has gone, and one sits face to face again.

Chapter Fourteen
VIEWPOINTS FOR DIAGNOSIS AND THERAPY

We wish to distinguish three aspects of therapy:

a. Diagnosis
b. Choice of therapy
c. Method of therapy

a. Diagnosis

The basis for a responsible choice of therapy is a *differentiated diagnosis.* For anthroposophically oriented psychotherapy this means a diagnosis that makes the symptoms understandable by distinguishing disturbances in the function of the ego organization, of the astral body, of the ether body, and of the physical body respectively.

As long as the illness manifests itself between the ego organization and the astral body (put in another way: between spirit and soul), general psycho-hygienic measures, conversational therapy, and art therapy are indicated.

As soon as the psychical problem has caused a permanent disruption of the life processes (the ether body), medicinal treatment of the organic system is necessary besides general therapy. In the context of this book, this means medicinal treatment according to the viewpoints of anthroposophical medicine.[1]

This medicinal treatment is primary if the chronic disruption of the ether body has caused changes in the anatomy of the organs, such as infections or degeneration. Here, psychotherapy is effective only if first the organic processes have started to recover.

Such a differentiated diagnosis actually requires a full medical training, plus an equally full training in anthroposophical medicine. In case of the lightest forms of neurosis a psychologist trained in anthroposophical psychotherapy can select a therapy. He would do well, however, to seek an amicable form of co-operation with an anthroposophical physician, with whom he can discuss dubious cases, and to whom he can refer the client/patient. The differentiated diagnosis can then result from consultations.

b Choice of therapy

Possible choices of therapy may be: individual conversational therapy, participation in a number of group conversations, or a weekend- or residential course of a few weeks to three months. In addition, a form of *artistic therapy* will virtually always be indicated: curative eurythmy, speech, painting and clay modelling.[2] Certain study tasks, and even work in a garden or on a farm will for many be a necessary form of additional help.

Once the therapy has been selected, and a provisional plan has been made up, the selected form(s) of therapy have to be put into effect. In practice, there is a gradual transition from the first phase to the second. For the differentiated diagnosis an extensive anamnesis is required, which already of its own awakens for the client elements of biographic insight!

For these anamnestic conversations, considerable open-mindedness and empathetic contact is necessary on the part of the therapist. In listening to the anamnesis, the therapist distinguishes between the complaints and events, on the one hand, that are connected with the life situation, and reveal something about the karmic situation of the client, and, on the other hand, complaints and events that are in the realm of the client's own choices and decisions, which point at his objectives.

If the topic of suffering becomes a matter of discussion, one can speak about the necessity for acceptance of one's karmic past, which forms the starting point for this life. That includes heredity, the conditions of the upbringing and parental home, school chums, and all significant events up to age 20. They have been 'arranged' by the higher ego. Having a dominating father or mother is not an external misfortune, but has been sought out by us in order to heal old karma by overcoming resistance, and thus to realize development towards the future. It can begin to dawn on us that 'I *am* my destiny' – that is, 'it belongs to me in the same way that my body and my self-consciousness belong to me. There is no sense in fighting it, for this would be a fight against myself. I will have to accept "how-I-am-now" as the starting point of a path of development. It is like taking over a store as a going concern; at the start, following the take-over, there are assets and liabilities. There is no point in denying the liabilities. The fact that I have been born signifies that my higher ego has taken over the business, with its assets and liabilities. It makes sense only to ask how, with the existing assets, one can go about paying off the liabilities along the way. One finds out that old liabilities are overcome, while at the same time new ones are formed.

This realization, that there is a continuous process of development, in which the present is part of a long road with an ever-receding horizon, can be the first result of the anamnestic phase, which, therefore, *already contains an element of therapy.*

A first requirement is to conquer self-pity. This is coupled with a first view of the future, at first only in the near term – days and weeks – and gradually leading to the discovery of the leitmotiv that has worked in the biography until then, and will be a companion until the last breath. Although the leitmotiv itself does not change, progress on the path of development can be recognized by the fact that the same problem always returns at a higher level. If the leitmotiv is that of overcoming arrogance, for instance, this character trait, when only barely conquered at the social level, will have to be overcome again at the level of spiritual striving. As the saying goes: 'A fox loses his hair, but not his tricks'. Again and again we will run into our own 'tricks' on our life's path. The degree to which we are able to transform these tricks to positive objectives determines the starting point for the next life. We ourselves have it in hand!

c Method of therapy

Ideally, three phases can be distinguished in the method of anthroposophically oriented psychotherapy: firstly, the *diagnostic phase* – the past; secondly, the *development phase* – the present; and thirdly, the *consolidation phase* – the future.

The *first* phase, the *diagnostic*, has been described above. What should be added is that differentiated diagnosis, which goes further than a general designation, such as 'compulsive neurosis', includes a number of clearly distinguishable elements:

— The biography until now, first of all chronologically.

— In the biography one then looks for the mileposts and turning points, which lend a dramatic element to the chronological biography.

— Correspondingly, areas of conflict are made conscious and are named.

— An initial exploration of conflict qualities can be undertaken (see for instance Chapter 8 about the doubles). This makes the depth of conflict visible and real, and provides an indication for the prognosis.

— In this first phase, certain episodes or problem areas can be examined in more depth by empathetic questioning, or they can deliberately be left alone for the time being.

During this entire process, the therapist will try to find an answer to the following question: *Where* exactly do these conflicts, ecstasies, fears, etc., manifest themselves? The following possibilities can be considered:

– At the ego level; what is meant here is the level of the consciously striving human being.

– At the astral level of the animalistic human being with his desires, envies, lust for power, need for being cherished.

– At the etheric level of the life processes with its many organic rhythms, such as sugar metabolism, blood pressure variations, temperature curve, etc. Also in the vegetative processes of organs such as liver, kidney, lungs, spleen, heart, and the like. Disturbances in these vegetative rhythms are reflected in the consciousness as moods such as fears, compulsions, depressions, and hallucinations.

–At the physical level, in which protracted disturbances eventually lead to anatomical deformations. These are more difficult to bring into motion again. We are dealing here with either partial, very stubborn disturbances in a few organs, or with 'psychiatric residual conditions' from 'extinguished' schizophrenics, from cases of severe multiple sclerosis and from Parkinsonisms. We may also be dealing with so-called 'defect-cured' patients who knew them in the early days after a treated lues cerebri.

Anatomic changes are always the last act in the drama. Since the brain is one of the central organs, brain damage also belongs in this category. The anthroposophically oriented psychotherapist is careful to avoid the all-too-tempting projection of psychical disturbances to the central nervous system.

We now come to the *second* phase. The method of the *development phase*, understandably, includes a great variety of possibilities. For the choice of sequence in the treatment the important rule of thumb is: 'Tackle the solvable problems first'. The development phase of the therapy has as its objective, after all, to get a blocked, inhibited, or derailed development going again. In the diagnostic phase, a large number of problems have come to the surface. Some of these are tricky, but not deep-rooted. Others are fundamental, vital problems, which will probably have a determining effect on the development for years. These core problems one should not tackle head-on right away. It is better to make a circling movement and to deal first with those problems for which there is a reasonable chance that noticeable results can be obtained relatively soon. This results in confidence in the therapy and encourages the client to accept further suggestions with respect to artistic therapy and other tasks.

The right choice of initial approach often is the determining factor in the subsequent development of the therapeutic process. One should be on guard, however, against superficial methods designed to give quick results. The first therapeutic step, too, must serve the conscious ego development of the client, and not his robotizing by means of, for instance, successful behavioural therapy or suggestive treatment.

(In Chapter 11, specific therapy for organic neuroses and psychoses has already been discussed.)

In support of the development phase, artistic therapy will preferably be included (provided the possibility exists). Artistic therapists should in the course of their training have gained sufficient insight into what their art can achieve to be able to be a consultation partner for a psychotherapist. The art therapist will have to be able to translate the diagnosis of the psychiatrist or psychologist into the possibilities of his artistic specialty. Many things the art therapist notices during the painting, eurythmy, or speech session will provide indications for the psychotherapist as to the approach his own therapy may take.

Special *exercises for the will* also belong to the arsenal of psychotherapy. These can consist of quite simple tasks, such as looking after a plant at a set time twice a day, or they can be complex assignments, worked out between the therapist and the client. These kinds of exercises further the ability of the client to gain a better grip on his own life.

Also useful are *observation exercises*, through which the patient begins to build a new relation to his environment. The assignments can, to begin with, be quite simple, such as: 'Try to notice the trees on the right and left side of the road on your way to the bus stop every day'. Later, the aim of the exercise may be, for instance, to observe the characteristic differences between a birch, an oak, and a lime tree. Also very effective in awakening consciousness can be questions such as: 'Can you describe what kind of bush is growing in the garden of such and such a house, which for years you have passed twice a day? Go and really take a look, and describe it to me during the next visit'. In this area, too, endless variations are possible, dependent on the range of experience of both client and therapist.

There is no fixed technique for anthroposophical psychotherapy that can be learned from someone else. Each therapist must discover his own way as to the form of therapy he wants to use, and learn to master it. That which one person achieves through enthusiasm for nature, another achieves with a discussion about fairy-tales, or situational play. The therapist uses his own 'instrument' and field of interest, and adapts to the potential of the client.

Another kind of task can be the practice of positivity. One can, for instance, ask the client to buy an ordinary notebook and to describe each evening a positive event of the day in no more than half a page or so. The client is not allowed to go to bed without having written something, even the simplest thing. He brings the notebook to each session and the content is then discussed.

In addition, one encourages the client not only to carry out assignments, but also self-imposed tasks, and to persevere in these no matter how simple they are. Self-imposed tasks work out of the ego on the ether body, and bring it into movement – notwithstanding an existing condition of depression, fear, or compulsion. As a result, 'hard spots' that can lead to compulsion are dissolved again.

Under certain circumstances it may be quite meaningful to work with images. These could be derived from fairy-tales, stories, or legends (for instance, the Parcival epic) with a theme that is relevant and recognizable to the client. The experience of such active images can also have a loosening effect on the ether body.

The third phase is the *consolidation phase*, which results in finding a new life-style.

Once the client is well on the way, and is following artistic courses (for instance), once he has been able to resume his life, or to find a new direction, and once he has gained growing self-confidence and self-acceptance, then the last phase of the therapy begins. The client has to be prepared for continuing independently on his own. A new life-style has to be found.

It can be meaningful (depending on the client's inclinations) to start a study of, for example, the course of human life, or about religious or historic literature, or a 'Goethean' nature study of plants or animals.[3] As a result, new fields of interest open up.

The new life-style will also require that a new life rhythm be found. To be involved in day-, week-, month-, and year rhythms has an order- creating effect on one's own rhythms. Regularity in one's work, and regular times of relaxation, nutrition, and social life is like restful breathing.

Finally it is of importance that new, permanent tasks are found, new objectives, which can go to the extent of finding a more meaningful vocation for the client.

In the consolidation phase, tasks are initially set by the therapist, but can later be replaced by tasks chosen by the client himself. In certain cases a beginning can be made after a short while to learn to work with meditation – that is, an intensive, regular immersion in the content and sound of a text or verse. Various kinds of meditation may be suitable. Particularly effective are meditations for going to sleep and awakening.

Chapter Fifteen
THERAPEUTIC TREATMENT FOR DISTURBANCES IN SOUL DEVELOPMENT

In Chapter 10 the three soul qualities – sentient soul, intellectual-mind soul, and consciousness soul – have been considered. In this chapter, a few relevant pedagogical and therapeutic viewpoints are brought into discussion.

The transformation of the body-bound astral *body* to sentient *soul* took place for humanity as a whole in the Egyptian-Chaldean culture period (from about 3000 B.C. to about 700 B.C.). It was conducted by high hierarchies in the venus sphere. It was their task to permeate the astral body with images by means of sacral art, and with developmental processes by means of temple rituals. These ennobled and humanized the astral body, while mars forces directed it to the world. This made the sense impression into observation, which could *continue* to live in the soul as an experience full of feeling even when the sense impression itself was no longer there. In other words, the outer world was made into an inner experience permeated with feeling.

In this phase, man acquired a continuous inner experience. The older, original Persian and Indian cultures did not yet have this continuity of inner life. They lived in direct beholding, and subsequent disappearance, of the content of the experience. This is also the reason why in cultic texts and mythological stories events and descriptions of personalities were repeated again and again.

Modern man has to develop his individual sentient soul in a culture that is already two stages further in its development. As a result, the child takes over the forms and content of the sentient soul in imitation of forms that have already been permeated by intellectual- and consciousness soul elements.

From age 3 on, the child starts to develop a continuous inner world.

It is of importance, and consequently a determining factor in early childhood education, that the child over 3 is offered forms and content that still have the pure sentient soul quality. This can occur by means of fairy-tales, which can become part of the toddler's inner life by way of puppets, story-telling, and play. All activities – painting, drawing, acting, listening to or making music, making things, and the child's own creative play – have to remain pure *experience*, without any *explanation of the meaning* from the intellectual soul, or moral interpretations from the consciousness soul. (We referred earlier to morality as an element of the consciousness soul.)

This principle of early childhood education is at the same time the principle of therapy in cases where, because of aptitude or education, the sentient soul is underdeveloped. The patient then complains of inner emptiness, about lack of inner warmth and enthusiasm, about being out of touch with the world and with people. The therapeutic conversation should then not be concerned with intellectual explanations or emphasizing the morality of a situation. Don't say too much. Instead, read a fairy-tale to the client, or a simple story, or a parable from the Bible. Let the pictures speak for themselves without explanation, or let the client draw or paint an image from what has been read.

Let the patients do eurythmy and curative eurythmy in groups, and instruct them to recall the images that have been taken in, or the activities of the day, before going to sleep. Enrich the inner life with reading assignments and with observations in nature – not explaining, only descriptive: What have you seen, what did you like?

Avoid emotional outbursts and violent confrontations in group conversations. *These reinforce the bondage of the astral body in the bodily nature*, as encounter groups and such do. Avoid also giving voice to judgments about others or about oneself. This leads too rapidly to a perverted consciousness-soul development, without real moral deepening, which is gained only by way of sacrifice and love.

The underdeveloped sentient soul is a fact of life in our intellectual, materialistic culture. With neuroses this phenomenon shows itself in an enhanced form. This is the reason that all social-hygienic activities must in the first place have the objective of catching up on what has lacked during toddler age. The sun-self has to be strengthened for all of us.

Secondly, we have to be concerned with the developmental problems of the intellectual soul. The intellectual soul first started to develop in ancient Greece under the influence of the Jupiter-Zeus culture. The development of the forces of feeling (mind soul) did not yet play a large role. Firstly, the colourful world of the young sentient soul lived in the middle, in the sun-self, which was nurtured by mythology. Secondly, the awakening mind soul was still being experienced in the image of the mercurial Hermes forces, which worked in a chaotic-dionysian way from below. In the contrast of the apollonian and the dionysian elements we recognize the image of the beginning intellectual-mind soul development.

The ancient Greeks still had to learn to control the chaotic organic ether forces. Greek drama, with its catharsis, played an important role in this.

In art, too, we find a good picture of Greek soul development: the Greeks experienced themselves as chariot drivers, who had to control their teams of horses.

As said before, this development was still conducted through inspiration from the jupiter world. Only in Roman times did the mercury mysteries spread over Europe and the conquest over the metabolic forces by the human sun-being was celebrated in the Mithras mysteries.

The foundations for the intellectual-mind forces in *individual* development are laid between age 7 and 14. Pedagogy has to reckon with this. The transition from 'experienced' image to 'understood' image has to take place cautiously and has to be tied in with a permeation of the forces of feeling by etheric sun forces. Otherwise there is a danger that the mind soul remains underdeveloped. This underdevelopment of the mind soul is, like the empty sentient soul, a cultural symptom of today.

The mind soul that has not been permeated with sun forces expresses itself in social convention and bourgeois cosiness. This is what young people protested against after 1950, but that protest also showed the other side of the mercurial life forces: chaotic protest, and a variety of solutions that rapidly succeed one another. Mercury is not constant!

Therapy for the problems of the intellectual soul must be sought in learning to think for oneself, which has to replace the kind of thinking shown in mirror-like recall, for which students are now conditioned by programmed subject matter and multiple-choice questions.

Among the complaints of their elders, one could mention in this connection: lack of originality in a conversation or at work; acting out of routine, outside the soul, as it were; passivity in the use of spare time; the feeling of being a nothing and being useless.

Here, too, therapy has to take the middle as its starting point. The client should be encouraged to occupy himself thinking about a new subject area, which is not related to anything he remembers from school – for instance, starting a therapeutic group project with an intensive course in observational astronomy or phenomenological nature observation. This overcomes laziness in thinking, and the participant discovers that he can think for himself.

The next step could be participation in a study group with a number of patients in a therapeutic centre.

The mind soul is the foundation for social life, and only there can it be completely developed. Disturbances in social abilities, loneliness, feeling rejected, or getting carried away in social activities can be remedied only in practice. This is a field of action for therapy in groups, particularly in the case of eurythmy. Situational play, with defined tasks and evaluation, offers unlimited scope for practice. The unstructured meeting in an emotional atmosphere must be avoided.

The consciousness soul is the first soul force that has to be developed by human beings themselves, without help from the hierarchical world. On the contrary, humanity will have to offer these forces to the hierarchies as a contribution to evolution, which, in the next step, must lead to the jupiter phase of human evolution.[1]

This means that the consciousness soul has to bridge the enormous gap between the far-off saturnian spirit world and the nearby moon-world activity. The middle, the sun-self, will have to develop extra forces for this. But whereas in previous developments the hierarchical world came to man's aid and helped to direct the extremes towards the middle, man must now take his own measures to this end. These measures consist of creating social institutions that can keep the three forces of Saturn, Sun, and Moon in balance in a meaningful way. We have referred before to this background to the threefold social organism; social institutions, social arrangements have to help provide the opportunity for the spiritual life, social life, and economic work life each to make its own contribution.

The danger attending the development of the consciousness soul is that the soul forces may *fall apart*. This means, on the one hand, to be pulled away in luciferic areas of spiritual life that are estranged from the world – such as those being offered in sects that make old spirituality available to modern mankind – and, on the other hand, to become imprisoned in the moon processes of the physical body. The latter may express itself in uninhibited sexuality or in glorifying the physical superman in competitive sports.

The saturn forces, acting 'vertically' from one world midnight to the next, produce a one-sided experience of one's own egoistic personality. Hunger for power can be the result of this. The moon processes, acting 'horizontally' in the stream of generations, tie man to his inherited instrument, and promote materialism and living in the flow of the forces of heredity.

The middle, the sun-self, has to practice unselfishness, tolerance, and positivity towards others in order to maintain itself. Otherwise the circulation processes harden, and many forms of heart infarcts and artereosclerosis can arise. Even if it does not go quite that far, one can notice a stiffening of the feeling life in the psyche, which manifests itself in anxiety over the inability to experience real enthusiasm and to take the interest of others to heart. One then feels as if tied into a stiff corset that makes it impossible to express one's feelings. This often occurs in relational problems (marriage, friendships, or working together). It is here where the therapeutic conversation and the guided group discussion are useful forms of therapy. In addition, artistic therapy in many forms is always a foundation for any therapy in this area by virtue of its reinforcement of the sun-self.

The sun-self is the correlating force that prevents the distant spirituality of Saturn from becoming estranged from the world, and directs it towards clarification of the tasks here on earth. The same force raises the moon forces from the sphere of procreation, and humanizes this sphere so that soul can meet soul, and spiritual love can arise.

In human evolution we are only at the beginning of the development of the consciousness soul. The new country we, mankind, have entered is a region not without its risks and dangers. The unifying force of the intellectual-mind soul – piety – is more and more lacking, and the new unifying force – *the moral power of judgement by the heart* – is still weak.

The goal of the modern path of development is to develop this moral power of judgement. A modern spiritual psychotherapy has to aim for the development of this power.

Chapter Sixteen
THE HYSTERIC CONSTITUTION

The example of hysteria demonstrates how closely the path outward during the night and the path inward into one's own organism during the day are related. They are like the scales of a balance, with a stable, unmoving fulcrum in the middle.

Man is a being of the middle. His normal day consciousness is stable only when there is a balance between the loss of consciousness when falling asleep on the one hand, and 'imprisonment of consciousness' when awakening on the other. With practice, however, the human being can expand his consciousness in both directions, but he then crosses boundaries that can not be breached with present normal day-consciousness. This has already been discussed from different points of view.

Man today could stick to normal day-consciousness, in which he can construct his sense-based world view, if it were not for the fact that the 'downward' and 'upward' thresholds are no longer secure and let through experiences that this current day-consciousness does not know how to handle.

In hysteria, the stable middle sphere is being threatened by changes in consciousness that have to do with an irregularity in the ex- and incarnation of going to sleep and awakening. At the basis of hysteria lies a constitution* in which the functional, etheric-astral boundaries of the organs (which form, as it were, the 'skin' of these organs) are permeable – and in two directions. Firstly, internal organic qualities (etherically: organ functions) are admitted into day consciousness through the memory mirror, and cause 'abnormal' experiences there.

Secondly, the astral body, which determines the quality of any organ, seeps into the environment and unconsciously observes it.

Normal observation occurs by means of the astral and the etheric

* The word constitution is used here in a different sense from that in previous chapters. What is meant here is not only the *physical* constitution, but also the way all members of the human being interpenetrate and interconnect.

body of the *sense organs* suited for it. We have learned to recognize and to order the information about the world thus received, and to make this information an inward experience in the form of conceptual images. Our education has taught us to handle conceptions and mental pictures. They are all concerned with information that is obtained by looking *at* the world from outside, and *at* our own body, too. What occurs in hysteria is an *abnormal sense perception* by means of organs not suited for the task. These perceptions are then translated by the consciousness into 'organic language' of the related organ.

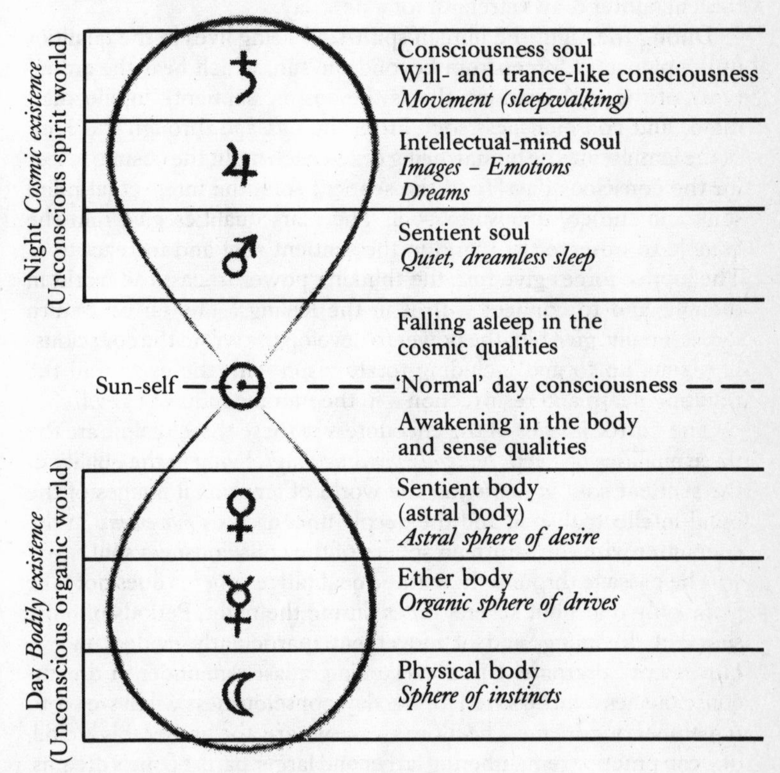

Path of the spirit-soul being through night and day

When going to sleep, the ability to move disappears first. Then the ability to remain in touch with the world by means of various senses disappears, and finally day-consciousness itself.

The subsequent state of sleep has several qualities:

1. Peaceful, dreamless sleep
2. Dreaming
3. Movement in a trancelike consciousness while asleep (from eye movements and talking aloud to sleepwalking)

When in the drawing on page 170 these three conditions are drawn as passing through three spatially separate layers, then this is meant only as a schematic representation. In spiritual reality, spatial separation does not exist, only a qualitative separation. The soul-spirit being of man unites itself with the cosmic soul-spirit qualities, and from this encounter draws strength for a new day.

During the night the human spirit-soul being lives in the qualities of the planetary forces from beyond the sun, which bear the archetypes of the soul qualities; this is the cosmic sentient-, intellectual-mind- and consciousness soul. From the passage through this loop of the lemniscate the human being draws each night the cosmic forces for the conscious day life of the sentient soul, the intellectual-mind soul, and the consciousness soul. The mars qualities give him the 'punch' to observe the world in the sentient soul and to react to it. The jupiter forces give him the thinking power to cast the world in thought and to connect with it in the feelings. The far-off Saturn forces, finally, give him the power to develop the will in the consciousness soul, up to and including total unison with the earth and the resulting death and resurrection – in the moral conquest of evil.

The mirror images of the encounters in these three realms are the three qualities of sleep: *peaceful unconscious sleep*, living in the quality of the sentient soul; *dreaming*, in the world of emotional images of the mind-intellectual soul; and the deeply unconscious *movements* in the encounter with the saturnian sphere of the consciousness soul.[1]

The passage through these three qualitative spheres does not take place only once, but several times during the night. Periods of quiet sleep, of dreaming, and of movement (particularly evident in eye movement) alternate. Upon awakening, a last remainder of dream-consciousness can be saved for the day-consciousness when we try to remember our dream. The more awake we are, the harder this is. Still, one can practice remembering larger and larger parts of one's dreams.

At awakening, the conscious ego enters the bodily nature of the organic world with the soul qualities mentioned. If the conscious ego were to enter this world unprotected, it would meet with the qualities of the astral, etheric, and physical body in their interaction in the organic processes. These processes are, as has been mentioned before, compulsive. They can break down and build up substances. With the same compulsive power they would meet and overpower the soul world of sentient-, intellectual-mind-, and consciousness soul. Moreover, these soul qualities would then come in contact, unprepared, with the unconscious astral world that includes the memories (complexes), emotions, and invasions Jung has described phenomenologically.[2]

The protective power within us, called the lesser guardian of the threshold (see Chapter 8*g*), directs the soul forces at the outer world immediately upon awakening. In the twentieth century, however, this inward threshold is getting lower and lower. Parts of the lower world are admitted into the consciousness without preparation, with the results mentioned before, such as all kinds of disturbing inner experiences.

The first quality to appear is the sphere of unconscious astral *desires*, which in the venus quality unfold their positive organic activity. The second quality is that of the etheric drives, such as hunger, thirst, vital urge, etc., which are mirrored in the soul and drag it through break-down, conversion, and reconstitution processes, on and on (mercury quality). Finally, the spirit-soul comes in contact with the *instincts* tied to the physical organism, which almost entirely determine the action patterns of the animal world. To this belongs everything related to procreation, nest building, etc.

Upon awakening in the morning in a hysteric constitution, the higher soul forces of sentient-, intellectual-mind-, and consciousness soul enter the organism. In the normal constitution they are contained by the body skin and by the inner 'skins' of the organs, but in the hysteric constitution they pop through the skin, as it were, into the outside world.

Since this occurs partially, through certain organs only, there is a partial loss of consciousness and a partial semi-conscious perception of unusual qualities – unusual because now one does not look *at* the world, but observes from inside *in* the activities.

This can bring about sensitive and artistic perception of moods in nature, or intuitive experience of the needs of another human being – for instance when helping someone who is ill. It can even result in perceiving everything that can arouse emotions, since the unconscious desires, drives, and instincts of the organs are partially free to express themselves. Normally only a filtered, attenuated effect of these desires, drives and instincts enters day-consciousness, and we have learned to handle them. With the hysteric constitution, however, they bypass day-consciousness and work directly in the actions.

The hysteric constitution is characterized by a numbe of other manifestations. One of them is caused by the relation between the day- and the night world.

Because of the interrelation of the passage of the soul through the worlds of day and night, as drawn in the lemniscate, a disturbance in day-consciousness brings about a disturbance in the night-consciousness as well. The direct, over-intensive contact with the world causes a weakening of the capacity for nightly contact with the cosmic soul qualities. That is why someone with a hysteric constitution enters the day with weakened soul forces.

Equally characteristic of the hysteric constitution, and generally known, is the fact that it is often judged negatively. This can be explained as follows:

The sentient soul in particular, but also the intellectual soul and the consciousness soul, are part of the animalistic astral body raised from the animal level into the human soul world, first in childhood through culture and later by the ego. In the animal, the organic instincts, drives and desires work in a direct way. In man they work as well, but they have been partially withdrawn from the animalistic sphere and are metamorphosed to human soul forces. In the hysteric constitution, however, this process is continuously short-circuited, and as a result the formation of human soul qualities is omitted. The hysteric constitution reacts *partially* (!) to situations on the basis of instinct, drives, and desires, while in a healthy person these 'primitive' reactions are humanized to inner soul qualities.

In the previous chapters it has been pointed out already that the path inward always means a return in one's own individual time, to the past. This partial way inward (subsequently seeping out into the environment) also means a return in time. This explains the regressive reactions of the hysteric. A regressive and infantile condition, co-existing with often intelligent and social behaviour in the present, can be a contributory reason for the negative judgement of the hysteric constitution by the environment.

We now wish to deal with a number of hysteric symptomatic areas that relate to the degree in which the outflow into the environment occurs. Once more we visualize the schema of the lemniscate for day and night (see page 171).

If the symptoms manifest themselves primarily in the first layer below the middle, the astral body, as the mirror image of the sentient soul in the upper loop, plays the main role. The symptoms then are in the first place pathological *changes of consciousness*, that is, a lowered consciousness in specific areas or even loss of consciousness of the total person.

The former manifests itself in specific loss of memory or in the inability to experience one's own actions in specific areas. The latter manifests itself in fainting. Since there is always an unconscious experience of astral configurations outside, besides the lowering of consciousness, the astral body directs its desires at emotional situations. That is why fainting always occurs wherever it can arouse emotion. So it takes place in company, or on the street at a busy corner, while the same person can drive a car without ever fainting. The hysteric person gladly suffers negative reactions from the environment as long as emotions are aroused. To be sure, emotions are in reality astral-etheric forms created by ourselves. Jung calls them 'demons', and this seems to us an apt designation. The emotional 'demons' feed on emotions in the environment. The more they are fed, the stronger and the more demanding they become.

The second layer includes the activities of the ether body in the mercurial sphere, the counter-image of the intellectual-mind soul, which develops in the jupiter sphere.

The ether body always expresses itself in pictures – mental pictures in the intellectual soul and 'organ pictures' in the ether bodies of the organs. Here the so-called body-schema, the picture of ourself that is unconsciously within us, is at work. In this realm, the emotions always participate from out of the astral sphere. The experience of the organs is translated in the language of the inner sense organs – sense of touch, sense of life, sense of motion, and sense of balance – while smell and taste often become involved as well.

This means that the hysteric constitution always gives rise to all kinds of organic experiences: numbness – for instance of the throat, or of the fingers or the hands, and so forth – or over-sensitivity in certain areas. The sense of life gives experiences such as nausea, vague intestinal cramps, or unpleasant sensations in certain areas of the body. The sense of motion gives feelings of powerlessness, or, on the other hand, of not being able to experience fatigue. The sense of balance gives feelings of dizziness and unsteadiness in walking or standing. The picture-forming activity occurs in the mercury sphere. Here the fantasy runs wild and becomes untruthful, resulting in the ability always to come up with a good story, made up on the spur of the moment (every sales person has to be a little bit hysterical!)

The third layer, finally, is that of instinctive reactions linked with the physical body. They are the counter-image of the development of the consciousness soul in the saturn sphere, where moral will-power is developed. Instead, basic instinctive behaviour, outside the ordinary consciousness, occurs. This takes place in the moon sphere, in which, among others, the reproductive organs play a role. When the problem has gone this far, sexual problems always arise, in the form of frigidity and insensitivity, as well as hypersexuality with insatiable needs, which are on the animalistic level (without a soul component). Since more severe hysteria always includes these sexual problems, the common view is that hysteria is connected with sexuality, and in particular with female sexuality. In order to show how one-sided this view is, we will discuss a case of male hysteria later on.

Therapy in cases of hysteria has to take place at several levels.

The first is the *social level.* Hysterics make sure they are a social problem for their environment. Still, less severe hysteria has its positive side. The hysteric constitution is suitable for the care-providing occupations such as nursing, child care, or care of the aged, and also in occupations in which one is dealing with the public, such as that of receptionist. In all of these situations, the hysteric can have a beneficial influence because of his sensitivity. Men especially are often successful in commercial functions.

It is of importance immediately to try to change the social conditions of the hysteric patient in such a way that the hysteria can work positively. If that is successful, it becomes apparent that the hysterical personality is capable of making great sacrifices.

The second level is the *general constitutional level,* for which medicinal treatment is called for. In anthroposophical medicine the ego organization is treated with mineral medicines, especially metals, while the astral organization is treated with plant medicines, and the etheric with medicines of animal origin. The physical organism is treated by means of human transplantation. Of this transplantation therapy, blood transfusion is the most well known example.

For hysteria, plant-based therapy is generally preferred. In most cases this is Bryophyllum in low potencies. In addition, a specific organ therapy will have to be carried out. Each organ astrality has its own (plant-based) medicines. One can also select a mineral as a general basis for the medicinal therapy. One then works on the astral body via the ego organization. Antimony (Stibium) in various potencies is often used in that case, since in its activity antimony brings together the qualities of the planets below the sun, and since regulating these three qualities is always necessary.[3]

The hysteric person 'seeps'. He has a moist skin with mostly cold, clammy hands, or, on the other hand, warm, moist hands. This 'seeping' can be treated through the warmth organization. Bath therapy,[4] curative eurythmy, and also healthy physical exercise are indicated.

A third level is that of *psychotherapy*, mentioned here deliberately in third place. The hysteric patient will always try to involve the psychotherapist in his regressive egocentric world, and when the therapist resists, to pull out all stops to force him to become a participant in this world. This may, for example, be a dramatic nocturnal suicide attempt, but with a built-in safety margin.

Rudolf Steiner, in his curative education course,[5] draws attention to the incredible cunning of the astral body, compared to which the ego is only a babe. The hysterical person has many tricks up his sleeve. When one symptom doesn't succeed in satisfying the desires, then others are at the ready to take its place. Thus a girl with a hysterically paralyzed arm said: "When my arm is better, I'll surely get migraines."

What counts in psychotherapy is the strengthening of all ego functions, and at the same time the forces of sentient-, intellectual-, and consciousness soul. This is achieved, for instance, with observation exercises (strengthening of the sentient soul) with the aid of therapeutic painting, drawing, and clay modelling. Awakening an interest for new areas of knowledge, through courses, or specific reading assignments, can enrich the intellectual soul, while taking on tasks in a social environment brings the mind soul in development.

The strengthening of the consciousness soul is the most difficult. This can be brought about by developing moral judgement in one's actions. Here it becomes apparent how much of an effort it is for the hysteric person to be really honest with himself and with his environment.

Our considerations of the ego functions can be illustrated with a case of male hysteria. It was 1939, during the mobilization for the Second World War. An army sergeant was admitted to hospital in a severely hysterical state of stupor. He lay in bed in the fetal position, his thumb in his mouth, not speaking, but only making baby sounds. At first it was impossible to establish any contact with him. After a while, when contact did become possible, the following life circumstances were revealed: The patient was by profession a teacher in a small, remote village, about 30 years of age, and unmarried. In the village he was regarded as an unrecognized genius. Actually, he was a sculptor, but was not recognized, and now he had to be a teacher, which was below his spiritual, artistic standing. In his spare time he was mysteriously busy working on a big sculpture, which no one was ever allowed to see. In a number of conversations much of this was exposed, and it became apparent that the sculpture did not exist at all, and never had. He finally admitted that once in his life he had tried to model a little rabbit. Suddenly called up into military service as a sergeant, his entire world of illusions had collapsed and he had fled into infantile regression. Therapy later on was aimed at gradually encouraging him to find a real orientation in life based on the ego.

Finding a real orientation in life is always a life-long struggle for every hysteric constitution, but every advance is a real gain, despite the fact that the hysteria patient can be the despair of the psychotherapist.

A final remark: Analytic psychotherapeutic treatment of the hysteric patient does by itself solve little, and often has the result that symptoms are shifted. Hysteria is primarily a constitutional phenomenon, and must be approached as such.

Hysteria as a phenomenon of our time

When considering hysteria one has to keep in mind the difference between, for example, the astral *body* (which Rudolf Steiner also called the sentient body) and the sentient *soul.* This has been mentioned before. The sentient body allows us to see the totality; the sentient soul is the reason that we thereby *experience* something (for instance, beauty, satisfaction).

In the morning, upon awakening, the sentient *soul* joins the astral *body,* making a connection with the impressions the latter received from the outer world. These same soul forces, which at night are renewed in the mars sphere, are directed at the outer world via the sentient body (astral body) during the day, and in the outer world they experience delight and suffering, joy and sorrow, beauty and ugliness. It is the venus force of the astral body that makes possible the sense impressions and offers them to the sentient soul.

This process is disturbed in the hysteric constitution because the astral body also offers impressions from the unconscious organic perceptions, for which the sentient soul is not prepared. To make this process conscious, and to learn gradually to handle unconscious organic processes by means of an inner training is ultimately the only effective, long-term cure for hysteric behaviour and being subjected to unconscious organic processes. The constitution itself is so deep-rooted that it can only be partly changed. The hysteric constitution has to learn to cope with itself from the centre, and to exploit the advantages it has because of its special condition. These can contribute to a meaningful biography, with special opportunities.

Thus, hysteria provides a picture of the battle of our time, the battle for the 'middle'. At the present, the 'middle' threatens to slip down into the organic processes. One can hold fast to the middle by taking a step outwards by means of the spiritualization of the sentient soul. Normally the latter is the bearer of the sense impressions and of the experience following these (sense impression: red, rose; soul perception: pleasant, beautiful).

For the preservation of the middle it is necessary to go a step further by intensifying the observation, and to begin to 'see' the archetype in the observation of the plant or stone. This is the path of Goethe in phenomenology. As a therapy for the time phenomenon of penetrating too deeply into the unconscious organic forces, the 'surfaces' of the sense world have to be penetrated, and the spiritual reality behind these surfaces has to be experienced consciously. One then enters the sphere of the cosmic sentient soul, which in fact is the world of the *spirit-self as a cosmic sphere*, from which each night we are given the strength to live consciously in the individual sense world for another day. One has to transform one's own sentient soul to the individual spirit-self. This comes about as a result of the ego's efforts in working on the spiritualization of the sentient soul. The hysterical constitution, on the one hand, presents an enormous obstacle to this process because the abnormal perceptions in the organic sphere and in the astral outer world are confusing. On the other hand, when the ego is strong enough, the hysteric constitution, because of its openness, is a help in coming to an intensive experience of the spiritual reality behind the sense world. *The hysterical constitution already lives in this reality, but can not interpret it.* To make conscious what is already present is a first step on the path of inner development to *spirit self*, by way of imaginative capabilities.

Similarly, the hallucinatory images of psychosis, which come out of the mercurial sphere of the ether body, must be transformed to *life spirit.* On the path of development that transforms the ether body to intellectual-mind soul and subsequently to life spirit, one passes through the emotional images the drives project into the consciousness. These have the same dramatic quality as dream images, but they have to be mastered and guided by the ego. This gives them an inspirational character, which opens the way to life spirit.

The most deep-rooted psychoses, finally, get stuck in the instinctive sphere of the physical body. This is also evident in hysteric stupor, with its regression to the infant stage. The ego must eventually transform the instincts, which have been given us by the highest hierarchies, to individual intuitions. These then gradually take the place of instinctive action, and thus realize *spirit man* in the distant future.[6]

What is important on this path of human development is to hold fast to the middle. The middle is the rhythmic world of breathing in and out, of contraction and relaxation, of day and night. 'Breathing in and out', the path of development goes through steps inward and outward, always seeking a balance.

Chapter Seventeen
ESCAPE ROUTES

Anorexia, psychopathic behaviour, addiction

In Chapter 12 we spoke about the phenomenon of 'escape' of the ego from the path of incarnation. We shall now discuss three common 'escape routes' that have to do with the unconscious rejection of 'earth-ripening', as Rudolf Steiner called puberty.

— The withdrawal back through the gate of birth, as it manifests itself in *anorexia nervosa*;

— Escape into pseudo-adulthood, into the aggression of *psychopathic behaviour*, or in extreme educational difficulties;

— Escape into ecstasy, into excarnation with the aid of alcohol and drugs, leading to *addiction*; an excarnation that in the final stage leads to forgetting one is incarnated on this earth with all the resistance it offers.

All three forms eventually lead to self-destruction. they are in essence aspects of the spiritual nihilism that pervades the culture of the consciousness soul.

In consciousness soul development, the good has to be done in the confrontation with evil. As such we are dealing with typically modern syndromes here. Those who, for whatever reason, have to go on these paths are the first casualties in the advance skirmishes over the development of the consciousness soul.

General viewpoints

Our point of departure is the viewpoint developed by Rudolf Steiner in relation to the *path of incarnation of man*, already touched on in Chapter 9, and dealt with in the lectures by Rudolf Steiner held in The Hague, on the occasion of the foundation of the Anthroposophical Society in the Netherlands, 18 November 1923. In these lectures Rudolf Steiner describes the path of the human spirit between two incarnations: after death the planetary spheres are traversed from Moon to Saturn, and back from Saturn to the Moon sphere.[1]

About the passage through the planetary sphere the following should be noted here:

1. The entry in each subsequent planet sphere represents an extension of the human ego, which comes into contact with a new quality penetrating it through and through. Each expansion also signifies a further dilution of the ego and a further rarification of ego-consciousness. Only those individualities who on earth already have been in contact with spiritual conceptions can maintain their ego-consciousness after death. Others pass through these spheres in a state of sleep.

2. The planet spheres, which are often thought of and depicted as concentric spheres, are in reality not spatially separated from each other, but interpenetrate; each subsequent sphere includes all previous ones. It is more a matter of a qualitative distinction of principles. The ego attains maturity at a certain moment to experience these principles. In the spiritual world one done not *confront* the planet qualities (which are in reality high hierarchical beings), but one stands *within* them and experiences their activity *within* oneself, just as here on earth we experience feelings such as joy and sorrow and the like within ourselves, and are able to distinguish them qualitatively.

When after death one has lived for three days in the ether body, which is the carrier of the memory pictures, and one has experienced these pictures around oneself as the 'life tableau', one withdraws from the ether body. And just as the physical body, when it has been abandoned, gradually dissolves in the earthly elements, so the abandoned ether body dissolves in the surrounding ether world. Only those ether forms (thoughts, feelings, impulses of will) that have been formed by abstract materialistic conceptions, feelings and will impulses, and are foreign to the cosmic ether world, do *not* dissolve. Just as synthetic plastics are refused by the earth and are not decomposed, so the thought forms foreign to the cosmos are refused. They remain behind in the ether world undigested.

Thoughts, feelings, and will impulses, however, are, as mentioned before, etheric-astral beings created by man. They retain a connection with their creator, also after death. These elemental beings, created by ourselves, we meet again during incarnation in the next life if they are not dissolved. They attach themselves to us as disturbing experiences. They represent one of the aspects of the double, as described in Chapter 8.

After release of the ether body, man relives his life once more in the astral world below the moon. He experiences what effects his words and deeds have had on others. After this period of kamaloka, further release from the earthly incarnation begins with discarding those specific abilities one had received at the beginning of the incarnation on the descent to earth. But one does not return exactly the same as what one had been given. Here the parable of the master who gave his servants each one talent to work with during his absence applies. Only the servant who returned his talent with interest, augmented in other words, could find favour with the master! Our moral deeds, warm and noble feelings, and spiritual thoughts are the interest we return to the higher hierarchies as the fruit of our earthly striving.

On the way through the spheres of Moon, Mercury, Venus, Sun, Mars, Jupiter, and Saturn we discard soul qualities. This process of discarding already begins during life, however. From the moment of birth we already start to die, and in the second half of life the process of dying increases. In the first half of life, the life processes still predominate – those we have received during the contraction towards incarnation. In the first place they work in the *body*. Because of the *dying* processes, however, we discover a *spiritual* life in the release from earth.

It has already been pointed out, and we repeat it here emphatically: The passage through the spheres is not a path through separate areas, but an 'expansion and dilution' of the soul-spirit being of man. This slow expansion, followed by the contraction of incarnation, is like a great cosmic heart beat: first the diastole, the expansion into the saturn sphere – to the boundary of the soul qualities – then the systole, contraction into the body on earth.

We can try to designate the incarnating and excarnating planet qualities by means of earthly concepts. These concepts are not meant as definitions, but as an entrance to the understanding of qualitative soul realms, in which one can immerse oneself by study, by entering into them artistically, and by deliberate action (for instance eurythmy). Then these qualities become more and more meaningful and start to come alive for us. (For a detailed characterization of the seven planetary qualities we refer to Chapter 9 in Part I of this book.)

When we give a schematic overview of incarnation and excarnation it is in order to give the reader an initial impression of the qualities working in us. These stay unconscious as long as they are active in a healthy way – in balance, therefore. They are the cause of specific syndromes as soon as they go out of balance and work in a one-sided way – too strongly, or too weakly.

At the most distant point between two incarnations, called by Rudolf Steiner the 'world midnight hour', at the boundary of the saturn sphere, the ego has discarded all earthly soul qualities, and, with the help of the hierarchies, it has transformed these into capacities for the next life in the course of the incarnation. Just as the plant ends the cycle of the year by forming the seed, which is the starting point for a new year's cycle, so does the ego carry within itself the seed for a subsequent life while it dwells in the realm of the world midnight hour.

With the contraction on the way to a new incarnation, this seed, carrier of the individual karma, gives the ego the possibility to form a specific astral-soul-body for the coming life while passing through the planetary spheres. The world midnight hour is to some extent the counter-image to the middle of earthly life. This important moment, at approximately age 35, has been experienced by great poets as a turning point. Dante, in the *Devine Comedy*, and Goethe, in *Faust*, start their dramatic course of events at the moment the incarnation force expires and a new impulse has to be found for the second, excarnating half of life. Dante experienced himself lost in a dark forest. Faust is desperate, and even wants to put an end to his life. A new resolve is needed for a meaningful second half of life. Similarly, a new resolve of the ego is also needed in the world midnight hour to begin a new incarnation.

What occurs then is the following: At the moment the ego stands alone as a spirit-being, Lucifer approaches him and tells him he does not have to go back – that in the stage of development he is in he can remain in Lucifer's kingdom as a spirit-being. No one would be able to resist this temptation, if the higher hierarchies did not at that moment make visible for the human ego the form (*Gestalt*) man will one day have to attain.

The ego then carries the memory of this cosmic man with it as a 'spirit seed'. From the discrepancy between this cosmic man and the ego's own individuality, the resolve of the ego arises to seek a new incarnation in order to come a step closer to the idea through arduous struggle.

A reflection of the encounter with the cosmic ideal of humanity is recognizeable in the path of the northern mysteries in the encounter with the Greater Guardian. The memory of this moment also lit up in the poet Schiller when he declared that in each human being lives the ideal man; to resemble this ideal man more and more is life's highest task.

The spirit seed, which is like a 'creative memory seed', is carried by the ego on the way to incarnation. This creative principle co-operates in the formation of the embryo as well as heredity, and has an influence on the struggle our biography represents as a 'time form'. It works in our *will* as a creative power on the path of life. Inwardly we can connect with this power until age 28.

If the decision to incarnate again, which is taken during the world midnight hour, is for karmic reasons not 'whole-hearted', and the human being continues to hold back from the incarnation, all kinds of disturbances can arise when adulthood approaches. In the following a number of such incarnation disturbances will be described.

♄	Saturn: *remembrance* Spirit seed down to the *dead* image of the *skeleton*	Saturn: *self-sacrifice* Resurrection in spirit development
♃	Jupiter: *thinking* Plastic formation of the organs in beauty	Jupiter: *ensoulment* Gesture as means of expression
♂	Mars: *speech* Drive	Mars: *ordering* Musical laws Harmony - Disharmony
☉	Sun: *warm-heartedness* Affirmation of incarnation	Sun: *striving* Spiritual striving in affirmation of excarnation
♀	Venus: *care* Enveloping Internal cell nutrition	Venus: *discrimination* Selective friendships (Selective excretion)
☿	Mercury: *mobility* Flowing activity Random	Mercury: *personal encounter* (Specific hormone functions)
☽	Moon: *conservatism* Cell division – Sexuality	Moon: *intelligence* (Differentiation of central nervous system)

♁

Starting at birth — Earth: *resistance* Leads to *experience* — Working on to age 28

In the diagram above, the planetary qualities the human being passes through between two incarnations – once 'breathing out' and once 'breathing in' – are once more characterized in a few words (a more detailed characterization is to be found in Chapter 9). From this diagram it can be seen that the descending curve represents existence before birth, but carries through into life; the ascending curve represents existence after death, but already starts at birth, and begins to predominate in the second half of life.

On this path of in- and excarnation, our current materialistic culture presents a great obstacle. Materialism wishes to acknowledge only the lowest stage – life on earth. More and more souls lack the strength to overcome this extra resistance to come to a) a full incarnation, and, b) realization of spiritual existence.

Anorexia nervosa

More and more since the break-through of materialism in the middle of the last century we meet the syndrome of *anorexia nervosa*, classified as one of the psychosomatic illnesses. Only a few cases have been reported from before 1850, but subsequently it has become more and more commonly known, particularly in the last few decades. Just about everyone knows of a case among acquaintances, or has at least heard about it.

This illness occurs less frequently among boys; it is a typical illness of *female* puberty.

Usually, these girls develop without any noticeable problems until age 12. At the first sign of puberty, a psychical change already takes place. This change manifests itself in illusionary experiences of the body, which is felt to be too fat and too heavy. These illusionary experiences provide the motive for weight-reducing cures.

The first symptom of illness is usually physical. After the first menstrual periods have started, they suddenly stop. Inner restlessness arises, which expresses itself in random activity without a set goal and in refusal of food. The combination of restlessness and the refusal to eat subsequently leads to severe weight loss, and a return to a child-like appearance. Everything is soon centred on food. Food is refused, or is at certain other moments gulped down, often stealthily at night, only to be thrown up again. Literature consists particularly of cook books. Often, delicacies are prepared for others with a lot of fuss, of which the patient does not want to eat anything.

With increasing thinness, the skin becomes dry and cold. Hands and feet look blue and feel woody. One would expect these patients to fell ill, but, to the contrary, they have no feelings of illness at all. They walk and run long distances because they want to get rid of what they have eaten. They also take laxatives on the sly. When this is prohibited, they know how to get hold of these with the cunning of a heroin user getting his fix.

The hormone balance becomes disturbed, and as a result of vomiting and laxatives there may be a salt deficiency. Otherwise, these patients rarely suffer from acute infection diseases. The climax of the illness occurs between age 13 and 18, but partial symptoms can continue long after. If patients drop below a critical body weight despite all precautions they have to be hospitalized, since otherwise they may starve themselves to death.

Current psychological thinking has sought the cause of this illness in family circumstances (dominating mother, weak father, or vice-versa; too much pressure to do well during childhood, etc.). This has not provided much to base a therapy on, while often it has led to feelings of guilt on the part of the parents – mostly without cause, while moreover such guilt feelings have negative effects. In addition, there is some recognition of the viewpoint that the illness involves a shrinking back from existence, and accordingly anorexia nervosa is seen as a crisis of maturation. From this viewpoint an individual therapy seems possible.

If one looks at the current syndrome in the light of the consideration presented earlier in this book, one will wish to look much deeper: at the *patient's own* will to incarnate.

If once again we look at the diagram on page 185 it can be noted that at the moment the incarnation has arrived at the point of a deeper connection with earthly reality, there is a shrinking back, followed by a step-by-step withdrawal from the direction of incarnation.

In his pedagogical lectures, Rudolf Steiner always spoke of puberty as the 'earth-ripening'. It is the moment when, with one's soul being, one comes to a real confrontation with the earth via the astral body. At the onset of the earth-ripening the anorexia patient draws back, step by step. Each subsequent step adds further symptoms to the syndrome. How is this to be understood?

In the first 14 years the basis has been laid for the different functions, but they have not yet been tested with regard to their resilience in adult life. At 12, the incarnation has proceeded far enough for the moon sphere to become active in the body and for menstruation to begin.

That is the moment withdrawal starts. Menstruation stops (withdrawal from *Moon*). The inner psychical mobility of the child disappears, and taking its place are rigid *idées fixes* and actions that often make little sense, perhaps even aiming at self-destruction, (*Mercury*). there is an aversion to taking food; all food is experienced as a heavy lump in the stomach. But particularly inner cell nutrition declines. Tissue becomes tough and hard, and the skin becomes flaky (*Venus*).

The sunny warm-heartedness of the child disappears in surly, defensive behaviour, camouflaged by a lot of rapid talk, without regard of the other. The circulation is insufficient, the skin of the extremities blue and cold (*Sun*). Motivation and speech impersonal, random, rambling, aimless, and repetitive, restricted to a few mannerisms and patterns (*Mars*). The plasticity of the body disappears, and the children are literally all 'skin and bones'. The face becomes a skull-like mask, the expression stiff (*Jupiter*). And finally all actions are oriented towards death, without the patients' being conscious of what they are doing. Until the end they deny anything is the matter at all (*Saturn*).

When it has been understood how these matters are related, the danger of this illness is clear. One then knows that the only possible therapy can be to encourage the patient to learn to accept the fact of becoming adult, and to accept the consequence, which means *living with the resistance.* The therapy, therefore, will be aimed at a strengthening of the will to incarnation, and a step-by-step recovery of the incarnating qualities. This is reinforced particularly by means of curative eurythmy, and also by metal therapy.

The incarnating qualities, however, will not be accepted in the long term if a relation is not found also to the excarnating qualities, which are at the right-hand side of the diagram. The intellect must be directed at a renewed interest in reading – for instance of biographies, which can later be discussed with the therapist. If the patient can not be persuaded to read, then the therapist will have to do the telling, briefly at first, for the attention span is short. Discussions about nature and about fellow human beings will also have to stimulate the interest. The first thing, indeed, is to rekindle the interest (*Moon*).

The second thing is to cautiously practice encounters with others in conversation, on walks, while playing music, etc. (*Mercury*).

The third step is to learn to form friendships selectively, and to give each friendship its own character. Warm friendships are particularly important. Should a patient really fall in love, it would be considered a step forward. However, she is not likely to fall really in love in such a way that it changes the whole world for her. At most, it will take the form of a somewhat forced affection, without much warmth (*Venus*).

Then comes the development of the spiritual *Sun* qualities, being full of enthusiasm for something that is not egoistic or egocentric. This is most difficult, for anorexia patients are extremely egocentric. It is the most difficult, but also the central element of the therapy.

The *Mars* qualities have to be fought for in finding order in the objectives that are set. Random activity will again and again get the upper hand. It is important to practice playing an instrument, to learn to draw and paint carefully. Getting results is decidedly important. If a few of these qualities have been mastered, the expression of the patient's own being changes spontaneously with it.

For the practice of the ensouled gesture, eurythmy and curative eurythmy have no equal. From the beginning, curative eurythmy will be needed, followed by eurythmy in groups, where the ensouled movement is practiced together with others (Jupiter)

Finally, the death wish, which unconsciously permeates anorexia, will have to be transformed to the will to live and the aspiration to take on tasks in which a sacrifice can be made. (*Saturn*). When the anorexia patient can really make a sacrifice (that is, not a compulsive and forced activity directed at others in order to camouflage the patient's own lack of participation), the patient is well on the way to recovery. Then there is a chance that *life can be accepted.* The latter is what the therapy aims at.

Why does anorexia drive parents and therapists to despair? It is because acceptance of life is what is being rejected, for deep karmic reasons. What that karma is the therapist can only suspect when he has met the ego of the patient. Every kind of speculation has to be foregone. Only a deep sense of compassion, and true love for the human being in the patient are of help.

Anorexia patients demand an enormous commitment. A number of years out of one's life may have to be sacrificed to make it possible to accompany another human being who shrinks back from adulthood in the consciousness-soul period. This highest saturnian quality, of positive acceptance of life in sacrifice for another, has to be *lived through* before it can be kindled in the patient. One has to gain credibility through one's own sacrifice for the child!

The therapy for a severe anorexia requires that another person be present permanently, who will set aside other life goals for at least a number of years, Because this is so rarely possible, there are many partial, half-cures. In later years relapses keep occurring, with compulsive behaviour and difficult human relations.

Many young people complain that because of unemployment they have no prospects of a meaningful life's task, and rightly so. But this is where there would be such a meaningful task: to share with such a patient joys and sorrows for a number of years as an example of the acceptance of life.

In the case of boys with anorexia, the same thing, in principle, applies.

Psychopathic behaviour

We now come to the mirror image of anorexia as a typical illness of girls: *psychopathic behaviour* in boys.

Rudolf Steiner once said that if one were to take the average of the degree of incarnation for humanity, women would be above average, and men below. In other words, women do not incarnate all the way, while men incarnate too deeply. The result is audible during puberty: boys' voices drop an octave.

With girls, the disturbance of the incarnation process takes the form of shrinking back from the earth-ripening (going back to before birth, 'dying' back through the gate of birth, as it were). In the case of boys, it can be a question of *skipping* the acceptance of the resistance the earth-ripening implies, and breaking into adulthood *too early*. The intermediate step of adolescence is then lacking, as well as the corrective effect of job experience.

Again, we will systematically follow the path of excarnation that is sought too early, and examine how the planetary characteristics appear in caricature as soon as the resistance of life experience is bypassed. For the excarnating forces are the metamorphosis of the incarnating forces, which have gone through the resistance that gives life meaning and are already on the way to transformation for a subsequent life. In other words, one starts dying the moment one is born. This dying process becomes stronger with age. What occurs with the youngsters under discussion here is the tragedy of *not experiencing this metamorphosis*, which has the result that the incarnating qualities start working negatively.

What does the phenomenon called psychopathetic behaviour look like from the outside?

Boys of 16 and over, sometimes still in school, but more often not, without regular work (by choice or not), look for an escape from boredom. Every situation in which there is a chance of experiencing something emotional is what they look for, or, if need be, what they create. Groups, or gangs, are formed, in which together they make a lot of noise with motor-cycles and cars, or look for places where fights take place or can be provoked. Acting tough, appearing 'macho' in dress and behaviour, getting fixed with girls, given over to unbridled sexuality, alcohol, drugs, and loud music, and 'against' everything that that comes along, either following the example of others or that of the media. From the 'angry young men' and the 'young Turks' of the turn of the century to the 'Hell's Angels' of our time they present the same picture; only the objectives and the violence of their reactions have shifted.

From a physical point of view, it is a group that is particularly well incarnated: healthy, strong, incredibly clever with engines and electronics, alert, intelligent. But on the other hand, they are emotionally unstable, alternately apathetic and hyperactive, alternately idealistic and disillusioned, looking for and finding scapegoats for their own misery everywhere. They are presumptuous, and talking tough, but in a confidential conversation one bundle of misery.

One gets the impression one is dealing with individualities that are a cut above the average, impatient to enter life, but lacking restraint, and fearful of the kind of resistance that gives *meaning* to this incarnation on earth. That is why words such as 'pointless' and 'useless' are repeatedly used in conversations. They imply the unsuccessful search for values and meaning, even if that is never admitted.

We are confronted with the phenomenon in many forms – from urban 'gangs', which spring up wherever there is an opportunity to fight the authorities, to ruthless terrorists, who do not shrink back from the systematically planned murder. The connection with political objectives gives an appearance of legitimacy to this life-style. Many political terrorists were intelligent students, such as many of the members of the Baader-Meinhof group. The Red Brigade in Italy and the IRA in Ireland also have to be seen in this light.

The difference with normal, courageous freedom fighters lies in the subtle distinction between real sacrifice for an ideal, and fanaticism of people with essentially weak egos, who are slaves of their own fanaticism. Within larger groupings there are numerous shadings between these two extremes, of course. The real idealists, however, tend to be shouted down by the 'sick' fanatics in the long run, so it is the latter who are left in the end.

If one witnessed the student rising of the late Sixties from close by, one could recognize both groups operating there too. In the Seventies they disbanded, however.

If now we turn to our diagram, we notice the following:

The *moon forces* appear early: sexual maturity comes early, and for boys an early development of the intelligence is in evidence as well. The latter expresses itself in sophistic, pseudo-philosophical argumentation, the vocabularly mostly derived from and based on Marxist and neo-marxist jargon. It does not go much further than the vocabulary, however.

We shall see that all of the qualities on the incarnating development curve appear in a perverted form, and that all of the qualities on the excarnating curve come too early and are coarsened. Thus, the moon function is developed early, with uninhibited sexuality. Intelligence is there, but not oriented to thinking for oneself. Instead it seeks to simply take over a mirror image of what is current in the environment or in the media.

The *mercury function* of incarnation takes the form of alternating between apathy and sudden burst of activity. Real human encounters are lacking. Pseudo-encounters take their place in the formation of gangs.

The *venus forces* are generally weak, and sometimes manifest themselves in infantile forms, such as holding on to mascots and the like. They also show up in the care of items such as motorbikes. Nutritional drives are well developed. The excarnating venus forces in the psychical realm – selection of friendships – have been perverted to a form in which holding on to a group relationship is all that is left, often in the manner of a drowning person clutching at a lifebuoy.

The *sun quality* of incarnation is present physically in the form of overabundant life forces. But the excarnating sun forces – the will to live spiritually – is underdeveloped and expresses itself only in protest actions dictated by the fashion of the day. These can change rapidly, just like fashion. And although on serious examination the subject of every protest has a basis of legitimacy, the purpose of participation in mass protests is actually to satisfy emotional needs, which covers up the inner discomfort caused by the weakness of the sun forces.

The *mars function* is particularly strongly developed in incarnation. The excarnation function is without ego control, however. The ordering of life, of the immediate environment, and of the future, falls short all the time and is replaced by an order based on the alternation between sympathy and antipathy.

The physical *jupiter forces* are well-developed in the bodily configuration, visible in the musculature and in balanced growth. The excarnating qualities, ideally expressed in the ensouled gesture and in the individualization of the voice, are caricaturized in the movement patterns of the group: walking, moving your arms, getting on your bike in a certain way, etc. This also shows in the sudden change from hanging around aimlessly to arbitrary aggression against a passer-by, preferably with the whole group participating.

The *saturn function*, finally, is characterized by an accelerated incarnation drive on the one hand, and the inability to bring conscious sacrifices on the other. Instead of individual sacrifice, there is the death wish of the group (a death wish without resurrection), constantly provoking danger, going to the very limit.

So much for development related to boys. Just as a small percentage of boys goes the way of anorexia, a small percentage of girls goes the same route as the boys. This expresses itself in hyper-individualistic behaviour, which is not a symptom of strength, but of extreme vulnerability in the guise of indifference, willfulness, or provocative impudence (perverse mars function). One has to distinguish these few from girls that are allowed to join the boys, but only for purposes of show or sex, and not as individuals. The cynical practice in the group of exchange 'after use' is a symptom of these impersonal relationships.

Psychopathic behaviour in adolescence can also occur *partially*, and manifest itself particulary with respect to a single planetary quality only. The picture of the playboy (and the playgirl), for example, arises from the non-metamorphosis of the *moon forces*.

With the non-metamorphosis of the *mercury quality* one gets the perpetual fraud artist. Here the activity of mercury is not supported by a moral ego development.

With an underdeveloped *venus force*, one sees Don Juan, the tragic figure who cannot find any real connection. To some degree we find this with often-divorced men and women, or with the lonely vagrant who cannot find a home base anywhere.

Undeveloped *mars forces* give a picture that at a distance resembles a choleric temperament, but in fact results from the inability to bring order into life, so that there is a constant atmosphere of chaos around this person, which once in a while is interrupted by furious attempts at creating order.

Undeveloped *jupiter forces* result in chaos and weakness in independent thought. As a result there is the tendency to look for support from an authority, for instance in a sect or in an authoritarian political movement. Frequent change of authority, yet total conviction of the rightness of each last one is common.

Immature *saturn qualities* lead to extreme egoism, more out of fear than out of deliberate choice. What comes to the fore here is the inability to make any sort of sacrifice or to accept renewal, living in a narrow circle with a materialistic orientation.

In all these cases there is a shortage of sun-force, of happy, warm positivity towards life, directed at human interaction.

The above is a description of psychopathic behaviour from the viewpoint of individual development. Most descriptions are from sociological or from pedagogical viewpoints. What is pointed out then is that deviant behaviour is caused by emotional and also material neglect because of broken families, unemployment, etc.

In most cases, one can, in fact, recognize a number of these factors, but are they the causes? How is it that for every youngster with extreme deviant behaviour there are hundreds of others with the same negative factors in their anamnesis who do not fall into psychopathic behaviour? Moreover, extreme deviant behaviour is found as well in youngsters who have grown up in the sociologically and pedagogically most favourable circumstances.

Besides the external factors there always has to be an internal factor that determines the reaction. Those that have to educate these young people – boys as well as girls – in institutions of child welfare agencies also point at these internal factors.

In the first place, however, it is worth noting that under the designation of 'maladjusted' there are birds of many feathers. A portion has mildly neurotic aberrations and belong to the MBD (minimal brain damage) children. These can not keep order in their environment and panic constantly, since the bodily instrument, the central nervous system, is damaged.

In the second place, those who are 'maladjusted' differ from those who form gangs described earlier in that they have not been able to cope in life, and ended up in the child welfare system, where they gradually got themselves classified as educationally hopeless, while the first group has at least been through the primary and in most cases part of the secondary educations system. Their problems start with and after puberty with the necessity of attaining adulthood. With *this* adulthood in *this* twentieth century, in a society that struggles with the transition from an intellectual-soul culture to a consciousness-soul culture, they cannot cope. Out of weakness they have to skip the process of becoming adults, the process of earth-ripening, and escape in a pseudo-adulthood, as has been described.

This is a problem particularly for boys, perhaps also because for some girls prostitution provides an escape, which covers up the fear of undertaking the laborious journey to adulthood.

All of these phenomena have in the last few decades become linked with the problem of drugs, and the associated phenomenon of addiction. This is the subject of the next part of this chapter.

A differentiated diagnosis of the developmental disturbances described above is of importance for medicinal therapy as well as for curative eurythmy, which are the two therapies that have to form the basis for further socio-therapeutic measures.

Addiction

A third disturbance of adolescence and subsequent years is found in the group that falls into addiction.

In the chapter about first and second man within us (Chapter 5) it was pointed out that the higher ego of man does not incarnate, but stays behind in the sun sphere. What we call our ego here on earth is only a reflection of the higher ego, but indeed an active reflection, in the ego organization, the warmth organization of our body. The warmth organization, like warmth itself, is a boundary phenomenon. Warmth is both spiritual and physical. Each intervention of the spirit into matter occurs through warmth, and so it is within the human organization.

The influence of the higher ego, of second man within us, which carries within it the intentions for this incarnation, is especially strong at those moments when the 'lunar node' has returned to the position the zodiac had at birth – each time after 18 years and 7 months. As has been described in Chapter 5, at that moment the 'gate of birth' is momentarily open again. This constellation should not be seen as one single moment, but as a phase in which first there is an increase and then a decrease in the special influence of the higher ego, renewing the activity of the impulse for the future. The first moon node, therefore, occurs at about age 19, the subsequent ones at 37 and 56, and in old age once more at about 75. These points are critical in the biography. Especially the first, but also the second (shortly after the mid-point in life) is determining for the realization of future karma.

As with anorexia, and with psychopathic behaviour, a specific failure of the incarnation is possible here too, which again can only be overcome through the greatest power of sacrifice of fellow human beings.

There is a group of young people who at first pass through puberty in the normal way, often even maturing somewhat early, but who do not, some time between 17 and 23, get hold of their own future. Ego-consciousness as a toddler, and the ego experiences at age 10 have been unexceptional. Both were still carried by the ego impulse that had entered at birth through the 'moon gate'. With the third ego impulse, when the actual ego realization takes place, this impulse falls short. It has to be renewed by the birth of second man within, otherwise it is only the expiring forces of old karma that are active. Rudolf Steiner describes this process in a verse, in which he summarizes a lecture in London, 2 September 1923. In translation, this verse is as follows:

> I gaze into the Darkness.
> In it there arises Light –
> Living Light!
> Who is this Light in the Darkness?
> It is myself in my reality.

This reality of the 'I'
Does not enter into my earthly life.
I am but a picture of it.
But I shall find it again
When with good will for the Spirit
I shall have passed through the Gate of Death.[2]

Of particular importance are the words "with good will for the spirit". One can have the feeling that this good will for the spirit is always a central condition for the break-through of second man at the moon nodes: any hesitation in the activation of second man, in the willingness to meet second man, and life becomes meaningless and lacks a sense of future.

The birth impulse works through to age 28, and in a certain sense still has an after-effect till age 35. But by then the capital resouces that had been brought in have been fully used up. Without a new ego impulse the human being can only fall back on repetition and gradually extinguishes.

The available capital resources themselves, however, may be scarcely sufficient to carry development through puberty to begin with. What may happen then is that an external prop is sought, for instance in alcohol use, hashish, pep-pills, and finally heroin. Particularly when obstacles exist also in the external circumstances, such as living in a broken home, serious neglect because of alcoholism in the environment, and lack of trust in relations with older people as well as contemporaries, the incarnation forces sometimes fall short. The meeting with the higher ego can, therefore, often fail to take place in adolescence. The inner void resulting from this strongly resembles the experience of those who as a result of incarnation weakness have already lost touch with their ego impulse before puberty.

For those who for one reason or another do not find their second individuality, life becomes uninteresting. The only thing left is to find a way in which earth resistance can be made to disappear. Consciousness then wanders in a realm of shadows, where pain and duty have vanished and make room for a vague sense of wellbeing. This condition is achieved by means of alcohol and the many drugs. What these have in common is that they provide a condition of pseudo-happiness, although of limited duration. They do this by changing the relationship between the astral body and the ether body.

The astral body enters a luciferic realm of arrogance, of pseudo-peace, or of bliss. The ether body, no longer impelled by the astral body, links up more strongly with the physical body, which leads to functional deformations. These are experienced as the hangover upon return of the astral body, which, after all, is the carrier of consciousness. This hangover experience provides the motive to look for a new excarnation of the astral body, which results in a still more severe disturbance of the ether body. This is the mechanism that causes *addiction.*

Every addictive substance leads to slow suicide, and heroin even to fairly quick suicide. To 'moderate' drinkers or 'users' this may sound like an exaggeration. They think they are in full control, and that they can stop at any time. But even if they succeed in stopping, the damage already done is much greater than is commonly thought.

This damage occurs on the one hand in the physical-etheric life sphere, and on the other hand in the inability of the higher ego to provide guidance in life. When the astral body withdraws from the physical-etheric organization, the ego no longer has the contact point from which to manifest itself in the sentient-, intellectual-, and consciousness soul. The higher ego is, as it were, thrown back, and with it the possibility of a meaningful individual future. Through every addiction substance, the human being loses some of the potential to give meaning to his incarnation!

There has always been addiction to narcotic substances. But one cannot ignore the fact that in the past 25 years the worldwide drug trade, which involves fortunes, shows that the phenomenon has been internationalized and has intensified.

The most common drugs can be divided into four categories:

— Opium and opium derivitives;
— alcohol and cannabis products;
— LDS (ergot), psilocybine (mushroom), and mescaline (cactus);
— cocaine and the wekamines (pep-pills).

Opium and its derivatives come from the Far East. Opium gives the user a world of dreams, which are experienced in solitude. The opium user loses weight and 'wastes away'. The ether- or life forces are extinguished, and the astral body is drawn out of the physical-etheric organization and experiences an egoless dream consciousness of its own.

There are a number of opium derivatives with specific effects, such as morphine (pain killer), codeine (relief of cough), and heroin, which is the most dangerous of all opium derivatives, notorious for its almost immediate addictive effect.

Alcohol is a stimulant well known throughout the history of European culture. In antiquity (Hebrew and Greek), alcohol still had a sacramental function. In intoxication the divine was still experienced, at a time when the soul was already closed to the spirit – in the period following the 'twilight of the gods', therefore. In the hangover afterwards, a firmer connection with the physical body was experienced. In the latest Greek mysteries (for instance Eleusis) it was particularly this hangover that was important. Mankind was still on the way to deeper incarnation and a stronger bond between the ether body and the physical body, which was promoted by the use of alcohol.

In our time, we are incarnated too deeply, and have to learn to breach the boundaries that lead back to the spirit. On this path, alcohol is an immediate enemy; we have pointed this out before. Still, it is understandable that many who experience the uneasiness of breaking through the inward boundary look to alcohol to help them escape the uneasiness, the self-reproach and the depression by means of a light degree of intoxication.

With the *cannabis* products something similar happens. Smoked as *hashish* or as *marijuana*, these substances cause a state of intoxication in which sense perceptions are enhanced, and bring about a state that is called 'being high'. Here the astral body is lifted out of the physical-etheric organization, and experiences the boundaries of the elemental world in a semi-conscious way.

In a moment we shall return to the question of whether these substances are injurious or not.

LSD (a synthetic substance based on a component of ergot), *mescaline* made from a Mexican cactus), and *psilocybine* (made from a mushroom) belong to the category of hallucinogens. They cause a condition in which ecstasy and hallucinations occur. Experienced in what appears as a state of wakefulness, the experiences can be recounted afterwards. LSD was particularly in vogue a few decades ago in the investigation of hidden psychical phenomena. Mescaline and psylocybine are well known as a result of descriptions by many western researchers. They wee used at one time by Mexican indians to attain an 'expanded consciousness', and they once had a sacred function.

We know the most about LSD, partially because it was used at one time in the treatment of neurosis – in the hope that LSD hallucinations would reveal more about the subconscious than dream analysis could. (This kind of treatment is now rarely used anymore.)

The LSD experience is an illustration of the crossing of the outward threshold, but without the necessary preparation. This means there is no telling in which region of the elemental world the user will end up. 'Good' and 'bad trips' can occur, without the user having much influence on it. Everything that has been said about the way into the elemental world applies here (see for instance Chapter 3). The entry into this world is experienced *in* the psyche – colours, forms, images, one after the other, good or horrifying, but a hundred times as intense as ordinary sense impressions; this is typical of entering the elemental world.

Cocaine occupies a special position. It produces an abnormal (apparent) enhancement of consciousness and intensification of all observations.

Many contradictory 'scientific' statements have been made about the harmfulness of alcohol and drugs. The experience from my own practice is this: With real primary addiction (i.e., the addiction resulting from one's biography), the failure to find a perspective on and confidence in the future, i.e., to find the higher ego, comes *first*, and only *later* the escape into intoxication. Smoking up or LSD can then reinforce the failure of the ego. I know of two recent cases of youngsters who fell into an acute and long-term psychosis following LSD use.

Furthermore, there are always functional disturbances of the ether body, which in the long run cause damage right down to the physical organs – in the liver through the use of alcohol, and in the brain through LSD use.

Normally the astral body and the ego depart from the ether body at night, and cosmic astrality (the planet world) then takes their place and readjusts what during the day has been disrupted.

But narcotic drugs are poisons that drive out the astral body, leaving the ether body 'unattended'. And an unattended ether body attracts elemental beings; one takes one's chances on what comes in then. One gains the impression that for opium these are luciferic beings, while for LSD and the Mexican poisons they are distinctly ahrimanic beings. What these beings do in the ether body one finds out upon return of the spirit-soul being, in the hangover. And this hangover is then the reason for a new intoxication.

Cocaine is a distinctly ahrimanic substance and quickly causes severe damage, as do the wekamines (pep-pills).

Not only substances can have an addictive effect, but there are also addictive *actions*. Smoking cigarettes, for instance, is at least as important for the *act* of smoking as for the intake of nicotine. An addictive activity such as visits to discotheques provides excarnation by means of flashing lights, 'thumping' rhythms, and wild motion. Investigations have determined that strobe lights as well as thumping rhythms can cause changes in the brain rhythms, which can be made visible in the EEG. The brain rhythms are a reflection in the cental nervous system of the activity of the ether body. With slight brain damage, epileptic attacks can occur. One does not need much imagination when viewing the ecstatic excarnation and the gyrations of the body to conclude that in such situations the higher ego has no access to the human being.

When we speak of youth addiction, a clear distinction has to be made betwen real, or *primary* addiction, and *secondary* addiction, brought on artficially from the outside by criminal activities.

The real tendency towards addiction, as a part of individual destiny, starts as a rule when towards age 18 the higher ego cannot gain access to the soul life of the adolescent. Life then becomes prospectless, empty, and cold. All joy in life disappears, and it is only the same old person who 'idles' onward. Disgust with oneself and with society, in which one has to live, lead to the uncontrollable urge to escape into intoxication or in a world of illusion.

As said before, true primary addiction can also arise sooner in the case of youngsters for whom the impulse of the higher ego was weak already at birth. What often happens is that a child at primary-school age does not belong in a group (class), and the ego experience at age 10 is disrupted.[3] Then they go through puberty with a more than average degree of insecurity and joylessness.

These children are often defenceless victims of all the desires that come up out of the astral body, and it only depends which of these are the strongest. Very early sexual experiences can then occur on the children's own initiative, besides theft and drug use.

The young addicts being discussed here are to be distinguised from the aggressive, precocious youngsters described earlier. They are, rather, a friendly lot, passive, and without the tendency towards any kind of deliberate activity. They can look you in the face in a most kindly manner, and in response to questions about the future tell you that is a totally meaningless subject. The only thing left for them to do is to sit up half the night 'smoking', preferably in the company of others, whereby everyone is enclosed in a world of his own. 'And when the money has run out, well, I'll probably die. So what? It's no big deal . . . '.

With heroin, however, because of the addiction, the necessity arises to become active in order to be able to afford the next 'fix'. Any moral consideration is put aside for this.

Since the heroin trade is big business, and the market has to be constantly expanded, young people even under 18 are *criminally lured* into addiction. This has nothing to do with pathological primary addiction. After all, one can make an addict even out of an infant by giving it certain substances! In the case of this provoked addiction, destruction of the physical-etheric organization occurs as well, particularly if the addiction starts as early as puberty.

A new form of addiction is that involving psycho-pharmaceuticals. This new addiction illness is the doing of modern medicine. It as a reaction to the inner symptoms of the unconscious threshold crossing (see the description of this in Part I). We are dealing here with a vicious circle, caused by the generally occuring depressions and fears, the finding and marketing of one new, ever more effective chemical compound after another, and the helplessness of the medical world in making truly meaningful therapy realizable.

The tendency to addiction, whether it be smoking, sleeping pills, pain killers or psycho-pharmaceuticals, or sex, and even fanatically chasing a career, is always a measure of the degree to which the higher ego has control of the incarnation. Should the higher ego slip away from the earthly incarnation, then the void has to be filled by 'workaholism' or chemical 'remedies'.

The starting point for therapy is based on the sentence from the verse cited earlier: 'Arouse good will for the spirit'. Without a will directed at the higher human being no drying-out cure works for longer than the supervised phase; a relapse is almost certain.

In view of the fact that there is always damage of the physical-etheric organization, medical and generally hygienic therapy are always necessary. Furthermore, there has to be stimulation of the interest, at the level and within the horizon of the person concerned. This is where the psychotherapist has to use his imagination to find ways and means together with the client.

Karma is never a question of one person by himself. Karma is always an inter-human process, and is the fruit of interaction with others. This also goes for future-oriented karma, which expresses itself in our leitmotiv. Only in co-operation with other people, preferably people that are familiar with your own kind of problems, can a stable future be built. This is the secret of Alcoholics Anonymous (A.A.), the club of ex-alcoholics who help each other. This is also the strength of a working community of ex-drug addicts, who run a store or a restaurant together.

The various existing centres for the reception of drug addicts use a wide variety of approaches, from rigorous behavioural therapy, or, rather, behavioural indoctrination, to alternative mutual aid. The anthroposophical centres can draw on anthroposophical medicine and the beneficial effects of eurythmy and art.

It is clear that everything depends on the question whether or not one ultimately succeeds in kindling 'goodwill for the spirit'. If it does succeed, a permanent cure is possible. It will succeed only, however, if the patients are part of a community that leads the way in this goodwill for the spirit and includes others in this.

The work with addicts is among the most difficult psychotherapeutic work there is. Etheric damage has undermined the will of the patient. The uncertain incarnation of the higher ego has the consequence that again and again one is dealing with the astral body, with the animalistic part of the human being, which in gaining its objectives is infinitely more clever that the ego-being.

Etheric damage can also lead to extreme criminal behaviour, in which any restraint from the ego falls away. 'Treatment' of this condition is still an unsolved problem, since in this case the necessity of protecting others against this criminal behaviour interferes with the therapeutic activity.

Anyhow, disappointment, relapses, and deceit are all in a day's work for the therapist in this area. Those who can stand this, who can persevere, have taken a big step in their own development, and it is only because of this that they can show the way to those among their fellow human beings who are in peril. As in every kind of therapeutic work in groups, whether that be in curative pedagogy or addiction therapy, one has constantly to ask oneself: for whom is the work important – only for the patients, or perhaps just as much for the helpers.

Chapter Eighteen
THE TRAINING OF THE THERAPIST

It is taken for granted today that psychotherapists undergo a long course of study in which they learn to master the capacities necessary to accompany the therapeutic process. Psychoanalytical training takes many years, and other specialties also have their specific training courses. The anthroposophical psychotherapist (psychiatrist or clinical psychologist), as well as the social worker who wants to work from this background, will similarly have to undergo a specific learning phase. This consists of developing the kind of inner experience that is necessary to be able to understand and share the experiences of the client, and to be able to accompany the patient to the point at which he can integrate his experiences into a socially and personally acceptable way of life. In other words, the therapeutic helper will have to know the path outward and the path inward from his *own experience*, at least in their first stages. This means a path of inner training of a meditative nature, and mutual contact and exchange of experiences among those who are training for therapy and counseling.

Only a general impression of this path of development can be given here. In reality it is an individual process depending on personal contacts in various training situations.

To begin with, exercises for the path *outward* will be discussed.

In the first place it is necessary that the student frees himself for some time each day for all cares, thoughts, duties, and concerns that ordinarily occupy his consciousness. In this condition of openness, the inner gaze is directed at each of a series of processes within the human being.

First the attention is directed at the *physical bodily nature*, in its solid condition and form. Our consciousness is focussed on the earth element within us.

We experience intensely the force of gravity working in us, in the weight of our limbs when we move them against this force. Perhaps we can recall after an illness when we were allowed to take the first few steps again. Or we may recall how we dragged our heavy body home in a final effort after a long hike through the mountains. The idea is to re-experience situations in which our weight, our relation to gravity, is felt intensively.

Next we direct attention at the forms in which the crystalized, solid parts of our physical body are in evidence. The hard skeletal forms, particularly in the head, are evident to the touch. What we then try to experience is the process of hardening, from the cartilaginous skull of the embryo to the crystallized skull of the adult. This process of hardening and crystallization is experienced as painful and sharp on the one hand, and as crystalline and clear on the other.

What we attempt to call up consciously here as *controlled experiences* takes the form of overpowering, sometimes threatening, and sometimes paralyzing experiences for those who have crossed the threshold involuntarily or as a result of chemicals. When for instance a patient tells you that at certain unexpected moments the world seems suddenly made of glass, that voices sound as if from far away, and suddenly he walks on a fragile glass world, while at the same time the irresistible urge overcomes him to drink enormous amounts of alcohol to rid himself of this 'glass world', the therapist will have to be able to fully acknowledge this patient in his humanity, and to help him find the way to a therapy. The patient tells you that this condition, which can arise a few times a year, usually lasts a few weeks, and then stops as suddenly as it started, with a 'snap'. In between occurrences the patient has no need at all for alcohol and can do his work normally. The problem is that because of the recurring periods of illness and subsequent weeks of recovery he is afraid of losing his job.

That experience, which the therapist has called up at *this* side of the threshold, the patient undergoes involuntarily because of the crossing of the threshold and falling prey to the elemental forces of the crystallizing, or life, ether. In the 'healthy' periods of the patient the therapist will, together with him, deliberately call up the experiences that at other times occur involuntarily, and get a grip on them, so that with the next involuntary threshold crossing ego-consciousness and ego control are more and more maintained and the patient can bring about the return across the threshold on his own. He learns to be no longer afraid, firstly because he understands what happens, and secondly because be can get back by himself.

In the next step the therapist directs his inner attention at his own *fluid organization*. He realizes that inside him there is a constant whirling flow of fluids. The therapist now has to start discovering differentiations in the flows.

The bloodstream is experienced inwardly as a mighty, seething wave, gushing forth from the heart in a powerful surge, and then slowing down in numerous channels branching out into the 'morass' of the capillaries, where it comes to a complete stop. This can be experienced in the tips of the fingers. From there it collects again in slow streams, which, with greater and greater speed, approach the heart and finally disappear in a whirlpool in the right chamber of the heart. It is important to experience the seething initial surge, as well as the standstill in the vortex when re-entering the heart. All of these experiences the therapist will meet in a form a thousand times more intense in his patients who have crossed the threshold leading into the elemental world.

But many other qualities can be experienced in the fluid being. In the stomach and the small intestine large quantities of body fluid are secreted, to be re-absorbed in the large intestine. It is an in- and outflow like the tide on the beach.

Slowly making its way, the lymph flows past and around the body cells and collects in small rivulets, which quietly merge into the bloodstream.

Crystal-clear as a spring high in the mountains, the cerebral fluid bubbles up in the cerebral cavity, bathing the brain and the spinal cord, and then re-absorbed again down in the spinal column.

More and more fluid qualities can be experienced, and finally they are assembled as an imagination of the fluid being within us. This fluid being is the carrier of numerous cycles of secretion and re-absorption, of numerous tempos and rhythms, numerous pressure drops and pressure equalizations.

One now understands not only Olav Åsteson when he hears the waters surge in the 'elemental world below the moon', but also all kinds of curious experiences of patients who have, fully or partly, crossed the threshold, and who project apparently absurd phenomena as experiences in their body.

Thirdly one directs the attention to the *air being* of man within oneself. Like a whistling wind, air enters the lung, dividing in thousands of air sacs, where the movement of air comes to rest. Then the oxygen is carried by the blood throughout the body, offering 'refreshment' and new life everywhere. One can experience this oxygen flow as a life-giving flow. One then understands something of the image of Adam having the 'breath of life' administered to him, and consciousness with it.

Then one directs the attention to the out-breathing, carrying carbon-oxide as a death force, collected from all over the body. This carbon-oxide is returned to the air, and is processed by the plant into sugars, starch, and finally wood fibre, releasing oxygen to the air again. In imagination one can then experience the cycle that connects man with the plant world. What in the plant becomes fibrous must not go that far in man, but has to be exhaled. Only a small portion is allowed to crystallize in the form of calcium carbonate in the skeleton.

Take note that it is not breath *control* that is the objective, as in hatha-yoga, but an inner experience of the flow of the breath throughout the body. One can then also understand the experience of breathing disturbances that occur in the form of hyperventilation and asthma. Both illnesses have a psychical origin, as is now widely accepted. In hyperventilation an uncontrolled release of carbon-oxide occurs besides excessive oxygen intake. This occurs at the onset of a threshold crossing into the elemental light, or air, ether. For consciousness on earth a certain degree of death force is required. In hyperventilation we find a tendency to escape from difficulties 'down below' by an escape across the threshold. Forced breathing also causes lightheadedness and dizziness. The hyperventilation patient escapes from his problems in this way. These will have to be brought to full consciousness and 'aired' during the therapy. Even the language knows the expression of 'airing' in the sense of bringing relief from a stress situation.

Problems of the air being are always at the same time consciousness problems – also with asthma. With a severe asthma attack, the patient can choke with his lungs full because of the inability to breath out. The asthma patient is 'asthmatic' in his entire attitude in life. He prepares endlessly, forever studying, but then he gets nowhere with it in a social situation. An over-protective mother who 'hovers' over her children sometimes prevents them from breathing out sufficiently, and can thus create the conditions for asthma, particularly for children that have trouble in expressing themselves anyway.

While the air being has to do with consciousness, the *warmth being* of man is the carrier of the ego. Again we direct the attention inward, and look for the finer warmth differentiations. The highest temperatures are found in the digestive organs. The coolest part is the skin of the limbs. We continuously radiate warmth produced by ourselves, and do not normally absorb warmth from outside. Wherever external heat affects us we respond. The blood vessels dilate, and our own warmth opposes the foreign warmth. Only if the latter becomes too strong are we overcome; even five or ten degress can be fatal. The same goes for low temperatures.

We do not have to know the very details of the miracle of constant warmth housekeeping to stand in awe of the subtle, narrow limits within which we can live as a spirit being in a body on earth. All those who go over the threshold and experience the flaming fire world of 'Muspelheim' know the horror, but also the blessing, of the fire element.

We try to experience how spiritual enthusiasm and warm feelings are converted into measurable body heat; how enthusiasm speeds up the breath, accelerates and intensifies the heart beat, sets the fluid being in motion, and overcomes gravity. Through enthusiasm, heaviness becomes lightness, and fatigue is overcome. There is nothing like enthusiasm as a therapy for neurosis; not the fake enthusiasm of the fanatic, which is in essence cold, and also not the false enthusiasm of the extrovert or one who gives in to uninhibited emotions, but true enthusiasm for one's *own* task in *this* incarnation.

When the therapist has thus learned to find his way in the elemental world, he will have to get to know the experiences of those who have passed right through this elemental world and have experiences of the cosmic world behind it. This is the world of 'world harmonies'. It is the world of the planetary qualities in their relation to the images of the twelve-fold zodiac.

What is experienced here is that one's soul structure harmonizes to a greater or lesser degree with that which sounds there as the 'harmony of the spheres'. It is an inspirational experience of one's own dissonance or consonance. This is experienced with such intensity that it leads to either the feeling on being totally rejected, or to an experience of utter joy. Most of the time it is a rejection of one's existence, and a shattering denunciation. Those who go through anything like it have a 'bad trip', which can make them psychotic for a long time. the therapist, however, will have to have at least an inkling of this experience. This results in a kind of existential modesty. From hearing, experiencing, and being touched by the judgement of yourself the promise can be born to continue for the rest of your life to work on the harmonization of your own thinking, feeling, and willing. Therapeutic strength comes not from what you can do already, but from that which you yourself as a therapist are struggling. Only then you meet the patient on a basis of equality as people striving together.

Thus the therapist has to be at home himself in the imaginative experiences of the elemental world and in the inspirational experiences of the cosmic soul world in order to help his patients on the path outward.

On the path *inward*, the therapist must similarly know the experiential world of the client in order to be able to help and accompany him.

We have stated that the way inward is the way *back in time*. The therapist will have to tread this path within himself.

First of all he will have to relive his life's path until the present. What this means is to do a retrospect in images without emotions. 'How was I five or ten years ago? What did I look like? What kind of work did I do then? Which people were around me?' And so on, back to childhood: 'How was I at age 8, 5, 3? What is my first memory?' All this should be 'objective' as if one is looking at someone else.

Only then is the attention directed at the inner being: What was it that occupied me 10 years ago? And so on. In this phase one should still refrain from re-experiencing inner conflict situations. These try to force themselves on you, but should still be held back.

Only in the next phase one can take counsel with oneself and determine whether there are certain conflict situations or failures that have kept returning. This way one already gets to know something about one's leitmotiv! 'Apparently there are certain things and situations I can not handle; this is where my primary learning task lies in life'. One can then ask the question: 'Has the way in which I handled these situations changed in the course of time? *Have* I learned something, and am I learning *now* by looking at it?

Next, one can turn to the question: 'Who was it who enabled me to meet people who have had a positive influence on my life, and when did this occur? What have these people changed in my life, what do I owe to them?' This makes my life visible to myself in its karmic relationships. A sense of deep gratitude can permeate the soul as a result, and this feeling will in the therapeutic situation work for the patient. Then one can bring to mind the highlights (the best experiences) of one's life so far. From these highlights, too, one develops a feel for one's own karma, in which all speculation and temptation to premature conclusions are to be avoided.

When one has carefully followed this path inward, one gains more and more insight during an anamnesis interview, and one develops a feel for distinguishing between those problems that have a deep karmic root and can only be overcome after a long time, or not at all, and those that have to do with more superficial reactions. This is of importance in the selection of a strategy for treatment.

The exercises mentioned are the *preparation* for steps on the path inward. These steps themselves are of a very intimate and personal nature, and are therefore difficult to describe in general terms. In a training situation they would have to be discussed in an atmosphere of trust and confidence. In general it can be said that in the preparatory exercises a judgement (and most of the time a negative judgement) of one's own deeds already appears.

An initial condition on the way into the depths of one's own being is that one now learns to 'look this judgement in the face' and to bear it. The judgement soon acquires an unpleasant physiognomical character. One discovers that the 'lesser guardian' appears from behind his veils. To look him in the face then amounts to saying to oneself: 'Yes, my friend, there you are, and that is what you are like; you have a lot to do to change that image.'

Through this conscious introspection one gets to know one's unconscious astral body, and one gets to know it much better than by dream analysis.

Going down further into the organic forces of one's ether body is always a hazardous proposition. Jung went through such an experience, but afterwards had to withdraw to his tower by the lake for years to recover.

For the sake of one's patients, however, one will have to get to know this world too. Most of the time one goes this path already partly during treatments, *together* with the patient, primarily in *his* compulsions, fears and depressions, but consequently also in one's own! In the encounter one constantly meets things one recognizes, which later, in a quiet moment, can be made the subject of further contemplation. Because one goes this path not for one's own benefit, but for someone else's, one is protected against the demons and ghosts that could otherwise take hold in one's own soul.

In the Egyptian mysteries one was protected by the help of a priest, as described in Chapter 2. This help is no longer ours to receive, and should not be. But the unselfish helper who does not withdraw into the aloofness of the 'psychiatrist providing treatment', but who has the courage to suffer through objectively with the patient, also in the case of deeper psychoses, and thus to be fully 50 per cent of the inter-human situation, will find that this selfless compassion, this openness, offers true protection. This is especially the case when there can also be a real sharing of joy with the patient when there is progress.

In summary we can say that on one's path outward one arrives in an objective spiritual world, and on the path inward in a quite subjective, but equally spiritual, world. The preparation for dealing with problems in both worlds must be the content of the training of an anthroposophical therapist. This is at least as intensive as a psychoanalytical training.

A second area of the training is concerned with the practice of treatment. In anthroposophical psychotherapy there are no 'learnable' techniques in this regard. This kind of therapy always comes about as a consequence of a true meeting of people. Accordingly, the second phase will also be quite personal, and possible only in a mutual relation of trust.

With this we close these considerations. They are intended as an indication of the way to a *biographic therapy*; 'biographic' because the therapy is seen as part of the totality of the path of development of those who seek help, from the world midnight hour, through life on earth, to the next world midnight hour, which is the finish of one, but at the same time the starting point for the next path of incarnation.

The small portion of this long path we are permitted to accompany here on earth can provide the opportunity for a 'push' through which the process of development is set in motion again and can be continued. Every success and every failure, however, has to be seen in the context of the great span between one world midnight hour and the next.

The titles of English translations have been cited throughout where available. Titles in other languages have also been included wherever they provide a reference. In some cases, where books are listed as possible further reading material, different English titles covering the same subject have been substituted for Dutch or German titles.

PART ONE

A personal foreword

1. The third, revised edition of this book appeared under the title, *Maat, ritme, melodie. De therapeutische werking van muzikale elementen*, Zest 1983 (no English translation available).
2. *Phases*, London 1979

Chapter 1 *Man on the threshold*

1. The concept 'realism' is used here in a different sense from what it is commonly understood to mean. In four lectures in 1914 (*Human and Cosmic Thought*), Rudolf Steiner describes twelve ways of looking at the world. The four main viewpoints are: *spiritualism, idealism, materialism*, and *realism*. Spiritualism means: the spirit is primary; in idealism, spirit becomes 'idea'; materialism holds matter to be primary; only in realism spirit *and* matter are seen as real. Rudolf Steiner's life's work has the objective of gaining knowledge about interaction between spirit and matter, and of making this knowledge bear fruit in cultural life.
2. The drawing is a simplified representation of a sketch Rudolf Steiner made during the second lecture (18 August 1918) of the cycle *Occult Psychology*.
3. Matthew 25:14. In Chapter 5 we return to this parable.
4. E. Neumann, *Depth Psychology and a New Ethic*, Harper, New York 1973.

Chapter 2 *The path inward: the Egyptian mysteries*

1. Rudolf Steiner, *Macrocosm and Microcosm*, a cycle of 12 lectures held in Vienna in 1910.
2. About these 'elemental beings' (*Elementarwesen*) Steiner has given many indications. A few titles: *The Influence of Spiritual Beings on Man*, (1908); *Spiritual Beings in the Heavenly Bodies*; Man as Symphony of the Creative Word, London 1970.
   Elemental beings are described as supersensible beings in the sphere of the four elements, water, earth, air and fire; they are at the lowest stage of the spiritual world. In fairy-tales they appear as gnomes, elves, etc.

3. The concept 'sentient soul'signifies a certain aspect of the human soul. In Chapter 10 we shall return to the subject of sould development.
Readers who are as yet unfamiliar with Rudolf Steiner's anthroposophy are referred to his basic works *Theosophy*, and *Occult Science – an Outline. Theosophy* in particular gives a good picture of man as a being of the body, soul, and spirit. In *Occult Science* there is a detailed description of the way in which the human being has developed through many phases and metamorphoses to his present condition.
4. See note 3.
5. Todt is the ancient Eghptian, Hermes the ancient Greek, and Mercury the Roman name. Since most of what we know about the Egyptian mysteries is from Greek descriptions, we know them as the 'Hermetic' mysteries. The word 'hermetic' has in language retained the meaning of 'closed, inaccessible'.

Chapter 3 *The path outward: the northern mysteries*
1. For more information about the northern mystery stream, see my booklet *Mystery Streams in Europe and the New Mysteries*, New York 1982.
2. Rudolf Steiner has renewed and deepened Christian teaching on the hierarchies, and made possible an entirely new kind of insight about the beings that work from the spiritual world. A summary of available literature: *The Spiritual Guidance of Mankind* (1911); *Occult Science – an Outline*, particularly the chapter 'Man and the Evolution of the World', in which the role of the hierarchies in the process of the creation of the earth is described; *Spiritual Hierarchies*, (ten lectures held in Düsseldorf in 1909)
3. About the 'Externsteine' an interesting book has been written by Hans Gsänger: *Die Externsteine. Mysterienstätte der Menschheit*, Schaffhausen 1978.
4. Anthroposophy does not speak abstractly about 'evil', but deals with various beings who wish to prevent or divert human development. 'Lucifer' and 'Ahriman' are two such beings. They work in individual man as well as in cultural life as counter-forces, but consequently also as forces of 'resistance' against human development, to be overcome.
In the literature mentioned under note 2, they are described in more detail, as well as in: *The Inner Aspect of the Social Question*, 'Luciferic past, ahrimanic future', Rudolf Steiner (1919).
5. The provisional German translation by Rudolf Steiner can be found in the lecture cycle *Kalevala* (1912), retranslated to English.

6. This translation has not been previously published, except privately in manuscript form by the translator.
7. The origin of this version is in Norwegian, presented and tranlsated into German by Erich Trummler (Orient-Occident Verlag, Stuttgart/Den Haag/London 1927). This has been translated by Benedict Wood into English, with the express purpose of using it as song.

Chapter 4 *Day-man and night-man*

1. F. Schiller, *On the Aesthetic Education of Man*, New York 1965.
2. Cf. Gordon W. Allport, *Becoming*, Yale University Press, New Haven 1955.
3. Cf. V.E. Frankl, *Homo Patiens*, Vienna 1950.
4. Desmond Morris, *The Naked Ape*, Jonathan Cage 1967.
5. Cf. H.S. Verbrugh, *Paradigma's en begripsontwikkeling in de ziekteleer*, Haarlem 1978.
6. The (original) text of the *Hymns* provides a few problems for philologists. The version printed in 1800 ('Athenäum-Fassung') deviates considerably from the original manuscript. The reason has not become clear. The translation included here, by Mabel Cotterell (*Hymns To The Night*, London 1948) follows the original text. Besides several editions of the *Hymns* in German, among English translations see also the translation by Charles E. Passage, Indianapolis 1968.

Chapter 5 *Second man in us*

1. See page 99 and onward.
2. An extensive, imaginative description of this incarnation process and of the building-up of the physical body by the human spirit-soul being can be found in the book by Fritz Wilmar, *Vorgeburtliche Menschwerdung*, Stuttgart 1979.
3. Matthew 25:14
4. See note 3, Chapter 2.
5. A clear explanation of concept 'moon node' can be found in many astronomy texts.
6. The 'preparatory year' of the Vrije Hogeschool in Holland is designed to assist young people in this important phase of life (see also Lievegoed biography).
7. A closer characterization of the phases of life mentioned here briefly can be found in the author's *Phases*, London 1979.
8. See note 4, Chapter 3.

Chapter 6 *Paths of development in the past and now*

1. See Rudolf Steiner, *At the Gates of Spiritual Science* (1906)
2. Rudolf Steiner describes certain periods in the development of earth and man that can not be verified by exoteric historical research. This has to do with the fact that the physical earth was preceded by non-physical forms of existence. There have been three such forms of existence; Rudolf Steiner calls them 'Old Saturn', 'Old Sun', and, 'Old Moon'. The subsequent earth phase begins with a repetition of the three previous conditions before the actual earth development could unfold. These repetitive phases are called 'Hyperborea', 'Lemuria', and 'Atlantis'. The Atlantic era ends with the Great Flood, well known from many old documents (such as the Old Testament). We live in the post-Atlantic era, which can be subdivided into seven so-called cultural periods: ancient Indian, ancient Persian, ancient Egyptian-Chaldean, Greek-Latin, our 'fifth' (since +1500), and two future culture periods. This development can only be indicated here in brief, which of necessity gives a somewhat schematic impression. In Rudolf Steiner's *Occult Science – An Outline* and *Cosmic Memory*, New York 1961, these developments are described in lively images.
3. In the book of D.J. van Bemmelen, *Yoga en Anthroposofie*, Zeist 1976, the yoga path of Patanjali is described.
4. The statements of Swami Mactanandra are cited from an article in the German monthly magazine *Die Drei*, May 1981.
5. Cf. note 4, Chapter 3.
6. See note 1, Chapter 3. Of the book by W.J. Stein a third printing has appeared under the title *Weltgeschichte im Lichte des Heiligen Gral. Das neunte Jahrundert*, (Stuttgart 1977).
7. See Rudolf Steiner, *Karmic Relationships* Vol. 6.
8. The well-known Parcival stories originated in the twelfth century. In the book mentioned in note 6, W.J. Stein indicates, however, that the historical sources for this grail story have to be sought in the ninth century.
9. About the connection between the French Revolution and the Rosicrucian stream see, for instance, Irene Tetzlaff, *Der Graf von St. Germain*, Stuttgart 1980.
10. See the lectures of 27-28 September 1911 in the cycle *The Christ Impulse in Historical Evolution* by Rudolf Steiner.
11. *Christmas Foundation*: A conference at Christmas 1923/24, during which Rudolf Steiner gave the Anthroposophical Society an entirely new form, including the founding of the General Anthroposophical Society, of which Steiner himself became president. As a

'foundation' for the new society, Steiner laid the 'Foundation Stone' (a meditative verse) in the hearts of those present.
Literature: Rudolf Grosse, *The Christmas Foundation; Beginning of a New Cosmic Age*, Vancouver 1984; F.W. Zeylmans van Emmichoven, *The Foundation Stone*, London 1963; Rudolf Steiner, *The Foundation Stone*, London 1957; B.C.J. Lievegoed, *Mystery Streams in Europe and the New Mysteries*, New York 1982.

Chapter 7 *The path of anthroposophy*

1. Genesis 30:24
2. *Knowledge of Higher Worlds and How to Attain it* by Rudolf Steiner originally appeared in installments in the magazine *Lucifer-Gnosis*. A follow-up series was later published under the title *The Stages of Higher Knowledge*, New York 1967; this booklet contains a description of the three stages, Imagination, Inspiration, and Intuition. Another description of the path of development is contained in *Occult Science – An Outline* in the chapter entitled 'The path to knowledge of the higher worlds'. Also to be mentioned in this connection is a book by Paul Eugen Schiller: *Rudolf Steiner and Initiation*, Spring Valley, N.Y. 1981.
3. Cf. for instance J.W. von Goethe, *The Metamorphosis of Plants*, Journal of Botany 1863; the book *Goethe's Conception of the World*, by Rudolf Steiner contains an instructive chapter about the manner in which Goethe found his way step by step to observation of the 'archetypal plant'.
4. Based on a note of Count Polzer-Hoditz about his last conversation with Rudolf Steiner.
5. See B.C.J. Lievegoed, *Der geistige Strom der heilpädagogische Bewegung* (manuscript publication), Rheineck (Switzerland) 1972.
6. See Rudolf Steiner, *Calendar of the Soul*, meditations for the weeks of the year. Cf. also Rudolf Steiner, *The Cycle of the Year as Breathing Process of the Earth* (1923).

Chapter 8 *About the human 'doubles'*

1. A splendid example is *The Picture of Dorian Gray* by Oscar Wilde.
2. In 1914 appeared *La forme humaine* by A. Sigaud. In 1947, an important continuation of Sigaud's work by Corman was: *La Diagnostic du Temperament par la Morphologie.*
3. Literature about the temperaments: Rudolf Steiner, *The Four Temperaments*, New York 1944; C. von Heydebrand, *Childhood, A Study of the growing Soul*, London 1942; A.C. Harwood, *The Way of a Child*, London 1940

4. 'Nervous system' and 'rhythmic system', in this context, are concepts related to the threefold nature of the human being. Based on the idea of polarity, we distinguish an 'upper pole' (the nerve-sense system, with the head as its centre), a 'lower pole' (the metabolic-limb system), and in between an independent middle sphere (the rhythmic system, with the heart as its centre). Rudolf Steiner wrote about this threefoldness for the first time in the book *Riddles of the Soul.* An introduction to the threefold concepts is the booklet by Walther Bühler, *Living with your Body,* London 1979.
5. Compare, for instance, the chapter 'Sleep and Death' in Rudolf Steiner's *Occult Science – An Outline.*
6. Cf. Rudolf Steiner, *Spiritual Hierarchies (1909).*
7. See note 6, Chapter 7.
8. The title of the lecture is: 'The mystery of the double. Geographic Medicine', in *Wrong and Right Use of Esoteric Knowledge..*
9. See note 2, Chapter 2.
10. Rudolf Steiner describes how because of the experiences of a male incarnation the necessity arises in the soul to incarnate as a woman in the next incarnation, and vice-versa. In this sense, therefore, there is a 'law', but exceptions to this law are quite possible. (Cf. Rudolf Steiner, *Manifestations of Karma,* London 1979, ninth lecture.)
11. Cf. *Occult Science – An Outline,* by Rudolf Steiner.
12. The citations in this chapter from *Knowledge of Higher Worlds and How to Attain It* are quoted from the English translation, except for the use of the modern form of the second person; italics are those of the author.
13. *A Road to Self Knowledge,* London 1956.
14. Rudolf Steiner wrote four 'mystery dramas', which are performed regularly at the Goetheanum in Dornach, Switzerland, and elsewhere. Cf. Rudolf Steiner, *Mystery Dramas.*

Chapter 9 *Planetary processes in the cosmos and in man*

1. Cf. B.C.J. Lievegoed, *The Working of the Planets and the Life Processes in Man and Earth,* Stourbridge 1951.
2. See note 4, Chapter 8.
3. G. Wachsmuth, *Erde und Mensch – ihre Bildekräfte, Rhythmen und Lebensprozesse,* Kreuzlingen 1945.
4. A good description of this function of the astral body is contained in the chapter 'Sleep and Death' in *Occult Sciences – An Outline,* by Rudolf Steiner.

5. Cf. *Supersensible Man*, seven lectures held by Rudolf Steiner in The Hague in 1923.
6. The following description of the planetary processes draws on the results of the research by L. Kolisko e.a., into the connection between planets and metals. See L. Kolisko, *Working of the Stars in Earthly Substances*, Stuttgart 1928.
7. Cf. J.W. von Goethe, *The Fairy-Tale of the Green Snake and the Beautiful Lily*, Edinburgh 1979; the fairy-tale also appears in: Rudolf Steiner, *The Portal of Initiation*, Englewood, N.J. 1961; and Rudolf Steiner, *Goethe's Standard of the Soul*, London 1925.
8. See note 1, Chapter 1.

Chapter 10 *The development of the sentient soul, intellectual soul and consciousness soul*

1. See Rudolf Steiner, *Macrocosm and Microcosm*, third lecture.
2. See note 2, Chapter 6.
3. See note 1, Chapter 4.
4. Cf. Rudolf Steiner and Ita Wegman, *Grundlegendes für eine Erweiterung der Heilkunst nach Geisteswissenschaftlichen Erkentnissen* (GA 27).
5. In 1919 Rudolf Steiner launched the idea of the 'threefold social order'. Cf. *The Threefold Social Order.*

Chapter 11 *The shadow on the path inwards*

1. *Kalijuga*: In the ancient Indian period it was known already that in the evolution of the earth and of humanity a 'dark age' would occur. This would last 5000 years and (according to our calendar) come to an end in 1899.
   Archangel Michael: The leadership in earthly culture rests with seven archangels, who take turns as the 'time spirit', each for about 350 years. In 1879, Michael took over the leadership from Gabriel. Cf. Rudolf Steiner, *The Mission of Michael*, and *karmic Relationships* Vol. III.
2. See note 14, Chapter 8.

Chapter 12 *The shadow on the path outwards*

1. Cf. Flo Conway, Jim Siegelman, *Snapping*, 1978.
2. Cf. *Die Himmlischen Verführer. Sekten in Deutschland*, Hamburg 1979.

PART TWO

Chapter 13 *therapeutic thinking in anthroposophical psychotherapy*

1. For the concept of karma in anthroposophy, see Rudolf Steiner's fundamental books (see note 3, Chapter 2) and the lecture series

Manifestations of Karma and *Re-incarnation and Karma.*

2. See any of the many good books about Jung.
3. Cf. Rudolf Steiner, *Curative Education* (12 lectures 1924). This course provides the basis for anthroposophical curative education.
4. A few titles of many about Waldorf education: Rudolf Steiner, *The Education of the Child in the Light of Anthroposophy*, London 1975; A.C. Harwood, *The Recovery of Man in Childhood*, London 1958; Ekkehard Piening and Nick Lyons, *Educating as an Art*, New York 1979; Mary Caroline Richards, *Toward Wholeness: Rudolf Steiner in America*, Middletown, Conn. 1980.
5. Cf. Rudolf Steiner. *The Younger Generation*, 1922.

Chapter 14 *Viewpoints for diagnosis and therapy*

1. A brief introduction to anthroposophical medicine, especially with respect to medicinal treatment, is given in a booklet by Otto Wolff *The Anthroposophical Approach to Illness and Medicines.*
2. A good understanding of the essence of an anthroposophical approach to artistic therapy (with an emphasis on painting) is the book by Margarethe Hauschka. *Zur kunstelerischen Therapie*, 1978.
3. A good introduction, although not an easy one, to Goethian observation is J. Bockemühl, *In Partnership with Nature*, Wyoming, R.I. 1981; a fine book in this field, although from a different background, is Paul A. Weiss, *The Science of Life*, New York 1973.

Chapter 15 *Therapeutic treatment for disturbances in soul development*

1. Cf. *Occult Science – An Outline.*

Chapter 16 *The hysteric constitution*

1. In investigations of sleep by means of the EEG, so-called REM (rapid eye movement) sleep has been interpreted as a form of light sleep; here, it is described as a form of sleep in which the deeply unconscious function of movement in man becomes active.
2. See note 2, chapter 13.
3. Comp. note 4, Chapter 10 and note 1, Chapter 14.
4. Bath therapy or hydro-therapy as well as rhythmical massage has been developed by the physician Margarethe Hauschka on the basis of indications by Dr. Ita Wegman. See M. Hauschka, *Rhythmical Message*, London 1979.
5. See note 3, Chapter 13.
6. Spirit-self, life-spirit, and spirit-man are the three highest members of the human being. See literature mentioned in note 3, Chapter 2.

Chapter 17 *Escape routes*

1. Comp. note 5, Chapter 9.
2. See Rudolf Steiner, *The Spiritual Individualities of the Planets*, 1923. In German the verse is as follows:

   Ich schaue in die Finsternis:
   In ihr ersteht Licht.
   Lebendes Licht.
   Wer ist dies Licht in der Finsternis?
   Ich bin es selbst in meiner Wirklichkeit.
   Diese Wirklichkeit des Ich
   Tritt nicht ein in mein Erdendasein.
   Ich bin nur bild davon.
   Ich werde es aber wieder finden
   Wenn ich,
   Guten Willens für den Geist,
   Durch des Todes Pforte gegangen.
3. About the ego experience of age 10: See B.C.J. Lievegoed, *Ontwikkelingsfasen van het kind* (Development phases of childhood – English translation in preparation).

SOCIAL ECOLOGY

Exploring Post Industrial Society–Martin Large

Social Breakdown or Breakthrough?

As the existing 'social household' or 'social ecology' break down - the challenges of personal growth, group work, organisational development and taking social intiatives emerge.

Social Ecology: Contents

Social Ecology describes an integral approach to individual, group, organisational and societal development. These originated with the N.P.I. – a Dutch consulting, training and research institute – through work in industry, education and government over the last 25 years.

The book includes sections on:–

* Working with the Process of Development
* Human Life Phases
* Group Work
* Organisational Development
* Societal Development
* Taking Social Initiatives
* Individual and Social Growth
* The Trebor Case

Who is 'Social Ecology' written for?

It will be of use to those in management, counselling, group work, adult education, training, social development, as well as students studying people in organisations and those interested in social questions.

Practical Optimism-

"The main strength of the book lies in the combination of a consistent and deeply founded concept of development with experienced-based practical approaches to creating social balances in the various spheres of life: for once we see ideas about individual, group, organisational and social development brought together in an organic way . . . "

Personnel Executive October 1981 **'Recognising Social Ecology'**

Social Ecology ' . . . is well written in a readily accessible and lively style, with plenty of references to other contemporary thinkers. Newcomers to this area will find no trouble in getting into this book, and those more familiar with social questions, will find it stimulating and provocative. My guess is that (readers) will find some new insights that directly relate to their own experience.'

Daniel Jones, reviewing in **The Anthroposophical Review** Autumn 1981

The Developmental Perspective

'It throws up much that is likely to be of real interest to readers with a wide range of concerns, including: new horizons in management and organisation; the present state of anthroposophical thought, and, above all, the social initiatives which will open the way for a post-industrial society whose goal is human development.

James Robertson, Resurgence Nov/Dec 1981.

ISBN 09507062 21 162pp

£4.95 post free from Hawthorn Press in U.K; U.S.A. $8.95 CANADA $10.95. Post free. Dollar cheques accepted.

LIFEWAYS
Working with Family Questions -
A Parents' Anthology
Gudrun Davy and Bons Voors
Illustrated by Gertraud Hofmann

Lifeways is about children, about family life and about being a parent. But most of all it is about freedom - and how the tension between personal fulfillment and family life may be resolved.

Rapid change and the pressures for economic survival, have set many families afloat. Although the integration of motherhood and identity, family and work is our own search - we do not have to seek this alone. For others are also looking for new 'life-ways'!

Lifeways originated amongst groups of women - and some men - who were seeking a renewing spirit for family life. They sought to create a new vision of the tasks of mothers and fathers, a new 'eye' for the meaning of 'home' as a place which supports all those involved, children and adults, in their 'life-ways'.

Lifeways is a resource book for parents, those involved in kindergartens and playgroups and for women's support groups.

"These essays affirm that creating a family, even if you are a father on your own, or a working mother, can be a joyful, positive and spiritual work. The first essay is one of the wisest and balanced discussions of women's rôles I have read."
Fiona Handley, Church of England Newspaper

ISBN 0950 7062 4 8 316pp
U.K./EUROPE £4.95 plus £1.00 p. & p.
U.S.A./CANADA $9.95 plus $1.50 p. & p.

FESTIVALS, FAMILY & FOOD

Diana Carey & Judy Large

"Packed full of ideas on things to do, food to make, songs to sing and games to play, it's an invaluable resources book designed to help you and your family celebrate the various feast days scattered round the year."

The Observer 27 March 1983

"A lovely book, Festivals recalled for me many of the delights I remembered from childhood . . . The book, which I feel every young couple should read – gives a round-the-year evocation of all the traditional feasts and customs which used to play such a large part in filling the home with pleasure and fun and . . . "

The Daily Mail 10 March 1983

"'We always remember before we go to bed to put out a drink and mince pie for Father Christmas and a carrot or two for the Reindeer, and possibly some hay for the fireplace. In the morning the food and drink are gone, only the tops of the carrots are left.' This charming disappearing act comes from Festivals, Family and Food."

Guardian Women 22 December 1982

A REAL FEAST

"This is the book I have been looking for . . . Festivals is a big book, beautifullly illustrated and produced . . . I don't think I have ever seen a book which deals with its subject so comprehensively."

Church of England Newspaper 11 March 1983

"An attractive book which will have year round usefulness."

Stroud News & Journal 16 December 1982

Festivals This a resource book for exploring the festivals – those 'feast days' scattered round the year which children love celebrating. It was written in response to children and busy parents asking, 'What can we do at Easter and Christmas? What games can we play? What can we make? How can we prepare for the festivals as centres of stability in our family life?'

Festivals, Family & Food is written with families, and especially children, very much in mind – for the children can remind us of the wonders we might otherwise forget. The underlying theme is a simple but bold suggestion: that if celebrating festivals was formerly the focus of community life, then rediscovered in the modern context, such seasonal activities may enrich family life.

Even though Christmas comes but once a year, there are at least eighteen other festivals to celebrate! Each festival, such as Candlemas, Whitsun or Midsummer, has its own chapter. There are songs to sing, games for fun, food to make, stories, poems and things to do with over 200 illustrations. The festivals are grouped into the four main seasons. There are also sections on Birthdays, Hungry Teatimes, Rainy Days. Convalescence, Extra Touches, a Birthday Calendar – and space for your own ideas. You will discover that once tried out, these festive suggestions will soon enter the family repertoire of activities. It is hoped **Festivals, Family & Food** will encourage a close relationship with the natural rhythms of the seasons – and will be enjoyed.

ISBN 0950 7062 3X 216pp 8in by 10in full colour cover paperback
£5.95 plus £1.00 p. & p. U.S.A. $12.95 plus $1.50 p. & p. Sterling or dollar cheques made payable to *Hawthorn Press*

MAN ON THE THRESHOLD

U.K./EUROPE £7.95 plus £1.00 p. & p.
U.S.A./CANADA $14.95 plus $1.50 p. & p.
Sterling or dollar cheques made payable to *Hawthorn Press*
1, Berkeley Villas, Lower Street, Stroud GL5 2HU, U.K.
An order of two books *sent to the same address* is post free, but orders for single books to *different addresses*, must include postage and packing.
Airmail orders: add 40% of the order's value.

TAKING INITIATIVES

Publication: Autumn 1985 – *Social Ecology Series*
Taking and nurturing initiatives in business, in education and in community projects is the theme of this book. The authors Tijno Voors and Christopher Schaefer, have a wide experience of fostering new ventures. The book includes sections on: the characteristics of initiatives; starting and nurturing initiatives; finding initiatives; working together; participation, wages and owndership; cummunity building as a path of inner development; case examples of initiatives.
The book will be of practical interest to anyone involved in an initiative, to those considering this as a next step, and to people concerned with social and community development.